PROBLEMS IN THE LITERARY BIOGRAPHY OF MIKHAIL SHOLOKHOV

ALSO BY ROY A. MEDVEDEV

LET HISTORY JUDGE
Macmillan, London, and Knopf, New York, 1971

A QUESTION OF MADNESS (WITH ZHORES A. MEDVEDEV)
Macmillan, London, and Knopf, New York, 1971

ON SOCIALIST DEMOCRACY
Macmillan, London, and Knopf, New York, 1975

POLITICAL DIARY (EDITOR)
A. Herzen Foundation, Amsterdam, Vol. 1 1972; Vol. 2 1975

PROBLEMS IN THE LITERARY BIOGRAPHY OF MIKHAIL SHOLOKHOV

ROY A. MEDVEDEV

TRANSLATED FROM THE RUSSIAN BY
A. D. P. BRIGGS

CAMBRIDGE UNIVERSITY PRESS

CAMBRIDGE

LONDON · NEW YORK · MELBOURNE

Published by the Syndics of the Cambridge University Press
The Pitt Building, Trumpington Street, Cambridge CB2 1RP
Bentley House, 200 Euston Road, London NW1 2DB
32 East 57th Street, New York, NY 10022, USA
296 Beaconsfield Parade, Middle Park, Melbourne 3206, Australia

First published 1977

Printed in Great Britain at the
University Press, Cambridge

Library of Congress cataloguing in publication data
Medvedev, Roï Aleksandrovich.
Problems in the literary biography of Mikhail
Sholokhov.
Includes bibliographical references and index.
1. Sholokhov, Mikhail Aleksandrovich, 1905– –
Tikhiĭ Don. 2. Sholokhov, Mikhail Aleksandrovich,
1905– – Authorship. I. Title.
PG3476.S52T5928   1977   891.7′3′42   76-14032
ISBN 0 521 21333 9

CONTENTS

PREFACE TO THE ENGLISH EDITION

The first version of this book was written between October 1974 and March 1975, a period when triumphant celebrations were being prepared in the Soviet Union for Mikhail Sholokhov on the occasion of his forthcoming seventieth birthday. In June 1975 it was published in French under a different title, *Qui a écrit le Don Paisible?*

The manuscript of the book has also been widely circulated inside the Soviet Union in *samizdat*, and unofficially reviewed by Soviet writers and critics. Generally speaking, the work was well received both by French critical opinion and by my Soviet colleagues and readers whose views have been communicated to me in various forms. The lively discussion of the book in literary and critical circles close to me and the great quantity of letters and reviews which I received, many of them containing much important new material and evidence – all this made it possible for me to begin work on a revised version in May 1975. A key incentive was the appearance in the Soviet press (and also to some extent abroad) of a large number of articles on Sholokhov's work and biography timed to coincide with the writer's anniversary on 24 May 1975. The 'Anniversary' material contributed very little towards solving the many problems of Sholokhov's literary biography, but in some of the articles it was possible to discern a hidden polemic with this present work – then available only in manuscript – and with the book written by the literary critic 'D' which was published in Paris in the autumn of 1974 under the title *The Mainstream of 'The Quiet Don'*. Many of the 'Anniversary' articles have thus facilitated new interpretations of certain problems discussed in the first version.

Virtually every chapter of the book has been revised and augmented for this edition. An extra 'post-Anniversary' chapter has also been added for the discussion of new material. Much new information has been adduced concerning the possible co-author of *The Quiet Don*, the Don Cossack writer Fyodor Kryukov. While we must refrain as yet from any definitive solutions and conclusions the mass of new information seems to us to speak in favour of the now familiar theory of the double authorship of *The Quiet Don*.

ROY A. MEDVEDEV
Moscow

I

THE NOVEL 'THE QUIET DON'

In the secondary school which I left during the war years, Mikhail Sholokhov's *Virgin Soil Upturned* was compulsory reading. *The Quiet Don* was mentioned in our manual of literature, of course, and described as Sholokhov's most important work, but somehow we final-year pupils never got round to reading this very long novel. It was several years later, when catching up on my literary education, that I first read *The Quiet Don*, in the 1947 edition if memory serves me correctly. By then I had already heard a fair number of enthusiastic accounts of the book. Even so, when I read it the grandeur of this epic exceeded all my expectations. Once I had started to read it, I could not put the book down until I had turned the last page. I was deeply impressed by the extraordinary power of the novel; I was carried away by the rich panorama of characters which unfolded unexpectedly before me and by thrilling events of which I had had only the vaguest conception until then. This single reading of Sholokhov's novel taught me a great deal about the harsh but colourful life of the Don Cossacks, whose dramatic fate during the years of war and revolution constituted the main theme of the book. The language of the novel with its amazing wealth of nuances also impressed me profoundly.

About ten years later I reread *The Quiet Don*. A second reading brought to light a number of faults in the novel; the shallowness of the politics, the aridity of certain chapters, the lack of colour and schematic nature of some of the character-drawing. My general impression of the book remained the same, however, except that I discovered in it many virtues which had escaped my attention before. *The Quiet Don* is normally compared with *Road to Calvary* and *The Life of Klim Samgin*. Yet compared with Sholokhov's epic, Alexey Tolstoy's trilogy, which this brilliant and experienced writer worked at for twenty-two years, seemed to me lacking in depth, less colourful in its language and its character-drawing. As for Gorky's epic, alongside Sholokhov's novel it even seemed rather boring. Though I was well aware of the great significance of this indisputably distinguished work of Gorky's, I still found it hard going to read right through. There is no doubt that of all the epic works of Soviet literature *The Quiet Don* is the most popular one in the USSR. I have come across quite a number of people in the teaching fraternity to which I belong who have never read, let us say, *The Life of Klim Samgin*. But I have never met a single intellectual who has not read *The Quiet Don*. Other incomplete epics such as A. Malyshkin's *Out-of-the-way People*, Artem Vesyoly's *Russia Washed in Blood* or A. Fadeyev's *Last of the Udegs* simply do not compare with Sholokhov's novel. D. Petrov-Biryuk's trilogy *Legend of the Cossacks*, which has gone through many editions and which S. Budyonny and K. Voroshilov once described as a 'stronger' book than Sholokhov's novel, is inferior in every way to *The Quiet Don*.

In his article, 'The universal significance of Sholokhov', the well-known Soviet literary scholar P. V. Paliyevsky exclaims:

According to the rule-book Sholokhov ought not to exist. How did he manage to spring out of nowhere immediately after the soaring achievements of Russian literature in the nineteenth and early twentieth centuries, especially after Tolstoy, Chekhov, Gorky? Such a concentration of genius is a rare phenomenon; it serves to cast a light forwards, showing the way to others. After them one might have expected some development of their material..., but a new and epoch-making turning point, achieved now, with the previous one scarcely assimilated – this could hardly have been expected...But time passes, the specialists get used to the idea, we read on, and we see that a turning point has indeed been passed, a new step taken, a new attitude to life has emerged, a new point of view...This book has aroused amazement and doubt amongst the experts. How could this have come about? Where did a young man – the first volume was written when he was only twenty-three – find such maturity? Those with a special interest in the form and technique of literature, whose approach is so popular nowadays, carefully avoid this issue. When you ask they say 'Oh yes, of course, but it comes from the nineteenth century.' You also hear things like 'Yes, there is *The Quiet Don*, but there's nothing else. Where's the rest?'[1]

Another Soviet literary scholar notes with surprise,

Shólokhov, when he 'got cracking' on *The Quiet Don*, was only twenty. He had behind him no more than two years' literary work, and even that slender booklet with a preface by A. Serafimovich, which contained a collection of his first stories, had yet to be published. Just imagine him all alone in a remote god-forsaken village on the Don, cut off from the centres of literature and from the friendly, reassuring support of those who might have been able to offer it by virtue of their own authority and experience.[2]

Probably the finest book in western literature on the First World War remains to this day E. M. Remarque's *All Quiet on the Western Front*. But so far as Russian literature is concerned many scholars consider that *The*

Quiet Don is the most truthful and powerful work ever to deal with that war. It is not surprising that one celebrated Sholokhov expert writes:

Sometimes readers of the first volume of the epic are surprised that Sholokhov, who was under age in 1914–18 and never visited the front line in the Imperialist war, should have described battle incidents of that time with such verisimilitude, detail and exactness. People wonder, 'Can someone who did not see that war with his own eyes really be capable of creating such pictures? How could Sholokhov, who was not an eye-witness, have re-created with such truth-to-life the experiences of the people in that front line, their moods, the rout of the army and all the rest?'[3]

I must confess that during my first readings of *The Quiet Don* questions like these never occurred to me. Although it was evident from the preface to *The Quiet Don* that the young Sholokhov had worked for just over a year on the first book of the novel, and actually for less than a year on the second, I was not surprised by this remarkable speed. It did not even seem strange that Sholokhov had created the remarkable third book of his novel in the space of a single year. We do come across examples of startling superhuman genius in various fields of human activity. Pushkin himself wrote his celebrated *Poltava* in under ten days, and the narrative poem *Count Nulin* in less than two!

At the time I was not surprised that a young man of twenty-one or twenty-two had managed to create in the first book of *The Quiet Don* a brilliant gallery of female characters, including those of Aksinya and Natalya, on a par with the finest achievements in world literature. Everyone knows that female characters present particular difficulties for many writers. Mikhail Sholokhov, however, penetrates the very depths of the female heart with extraordinary facility, showing us the subtlest shades of womanly love, and he does it in his portrayal of the simplest Cossack girls. With equal skill the author of *The Quiet Don* portrays the debauchery of Darya or Yelizaveta Mokhova and the strength of feeling of Aksinya or Natalya, which is appropriate to the age of shock and upheaval in which they live. These two female characters, along with Grigori Melekhov, comprise the real originality of Sholokhov. And only in the character of the young girl revolutionary from Rostov, Anna Pogudko, did the author of *The Quiet Don* meet relative failure.

I knew from the preface to the novel that Sholokhov's childhood and youth had been spent deep in the provinces, that he had only just managed to struggle through the fourth form at a boys' high school, and that at the early age of thirteen he had had to stop all systematic schooling. But I never considered it strange that the author of *The Quiet Don* should display a profound knowledge of the most disparate fields of human activity, or that he should have not just a gift for literature

3

but thorough-going literary erudition. As the literary scholar V. Pertsov rightly claimed, 'this book presents such knowledge of the real world as only several years of a man's life could provide'.[4] Well, what of that? After all, genius often does achieve with ease results which your mediocre hack will never attain after decades of hard work.

It was something else that surprised me when I read *The Quiet Don*. In its general content and in its overall literary tone *The Quiet Don* is a *tragedy*; that is how it is perceived by the greater part of its readers. Attempts by some critics to descry in Sholokhov's epic 'a triumphant victory, optimism, bravery in the overcoming of difficulties'[5] are quite without substance and are soon refuted when one considers the content of the novel and the general emotional impression of it which the reader retains in his heart. And yet *The Quiet Don* is certainly not 'the tragedy of a dying class' as was claimed by Alexey Tolstoy,[6] nor is it 'the tragedy of the doomed counter-revolutionary cause', as A. Fadeyev wrote.[7] It is not even the tragedy of a man who goes it alone, someone cut off from the people, as the author of the preface to my own edition of *The Quiet Don*, L. Yakimenko, attempted to show,[8] his words being echoed by the majority of present-day students of Sholokhov.[9]

No, in *The Quiet Don* we see the tragedy of *a fundamental section* of Cossack society which includes most of the working-class Cossacks.

This novel gives us an astoundingly truthful picture of the tragic fate of the Cossacks during the years of revolution. More than that, the author of the novel shows clearly and unambiguously that the terrible tragedy of the Great Don Cossack Military Region is explicable not just as the failure of the Cossacks for the most part to understand the October Revolution but also by the fact that this revolution and the Bolsheviks in charge of it *failed to understand the Cossacks* and were unable to find a common language with the kind of working-class Cossacks who are represented in the novel by the figure of Grigori Melekhov.

In the first book of the novel the author paints a broad picture of the life, the ways and the military service of the Don Cossacks in the immediate pre-war years and the first months after the beginning of the First World War. We see clearly the tensions inherent in the society of the Cossack people, for all their outward appearance of unity. Tensions between rank-and-file Cossacks and landowning officers, between poor and rich Cossack families, between Cossack peasant farmers and Rostov traders who had settled in Cossack villages and communities. Later, we learn also of the tensions between the more prosperous Cossacks of the Lower villages and the Cossacks of the Upper Region. From various incidents in the novel we learn of the friction between Cossacks and 'outsiders' and also between the Cossacks and the peasants who had always lived on the territory of the Don province. We see clearly, however, that the social contradictions in that province have yet to reach the acute stage felt in other areas of the Russian Empire. We learn from *The Quiet Don* that the 'outsiders' – workers and tradesmen – in Cossack villages and settlements were few in number. Equally few were the dissatisfied Cossacks. This is why Shtokman, the Bolshevik, when he comes to Tatarsk, a large settlement of 300 homesteads, can only muster a very small group of sympathisers (the mill-workers, Valet and Davydka, the Cossack engineer, Ivan Alekseyevich, the young Cossacks from impoverished families, Mikhail Koshevoy and Khristonya, and Filka, the cobbler). So far as the peasants, mostly Ukrainians, were concerned, their villages were outside the Cossack *yurts* (lands held by the Don Cossack Army) and they had little effect on events within the province. In the terms of contemporary Marxism, Don Cossack society consisted basically of solid middle-Cossack holdings, large patriarchal families like that of the Melekhovs, whose fate was deliberately singled out for attention by the author.

The war which had burst upon the peaceful lives of the Cossacks did not evoke much enthusiasm on the Don. Yet we can see clearly from the second book of the novel that dissatisfaction and war-weariness failed to grow here on the Don and in the front-line Cossack regiments to the same extent as in the other provinces of Russia and in other military units. After all, the Cossacks were a nation of warriors and every one of them was prepared for war from an early age. Though in central Russia and in the capital an explosive revolutionary situation had arisen by early 1917, that was certainly not true of the Cossack provinces. No kind of revolutionary movement was apparent here, and in the Cossack villages and settlements no revolutionary party, least of all the Bolsheviks, had any influential organisations or groups. The demoralisation which spread quickly through the Russian army in 1917 scarcely touched the Cossack companies. There was virtually no desertion from Cossack units, which kept themselves organised and disciplined in the highest degree, and this was why the counter-revolutionary movement placed its greatest hopes in Cossack forces after the February Revolution. It is true that by 1917 even the Cossacks had become weary of the war, which dragged on, badly conducted. So the anti-war stance of the Bolsheviks found sympathy in a considerable number of front-line Cossack soldiers. The Cossacks were also attracted by the concept of 'Soviets', which fitted the concept of Cossack self-government. Other Bolshevik slogans held little appeal for the Cossacks, and the programme for land reform evoked an attitude of extreme caution or hostility. In the novel even Podtelkov comes out against providing the muzhiks with land at the expense of the Cossacks. It is significant that, after rising against the officers in charge of Cossack divisions in the revolutionary-minded St Petersburg of 1917, the Cossack company led by the pro-Bolshevik Ivan Alekseyevich marches in formation not home to the Don but back to the front line, an inconceivable decision for the other sections of the demoralised Russian army to have taken.

Unfortunately, the peculiar nature of this general Cossack attitude was beyond the comprehension of the Bolsheviks, as depicted in the novel in the characters of Shtokman, Bunchuk, Abramson and one or two others. Either they exaggerated the dissatisfaction of the Cossacks with their position or, on the other hand, they exaggerated Cossack conservatism and 'inertness', looking on them as merely a potential punitive force or Tsarist bodyguards. Apart from that, the Bolshevik party had no considered programme of revolutionary reforms applicable to the Cossack regions. This single fact was one of the main reasons behind the many tragic occurrences of 1918–21.

Revolution always brings with it both destructive and creative principles. Of course revolution proposes to do away with everything that has outlived its use and now prevents society's further progress; of course it means to create new relationships opening up vast new potential for the country's development. Unfortunately it does not work out like that always and everywhere. The Cossack regions of Russia were those where, since the social contradictions had not reached full maturity because of the peculiar position of the Cossack people in the country, and since the Bolsheviks knew so little about the special characteristics of Cossack regions and problems, what showed up most starkly was the destructive side of revolution. As it was, the fearful brunt was borne not only by the outmoded or decrepit institutions but by the Cossack people as a whole. For this very reason the tragic theme of *The Quiet Don* is incomparably stronger than all the others. And, engrossed in this fearful tragedy, I gave no thought whatsoever to the problem of how a twenty- to twenty-three-year-old youth who did not even belong to the Cossack people could have found the power, the knowledge and the talent needed to create this majestic epic. *The Quiet Don* was so essentially different from all the books on the Revolution which I had read that it seemed to me odd that this book had not only been printed and given official support but that it had been admitted into the golden treasury of so-called Socialist Realism. For *The Quiet Don*, as A. Fadeyev rightly indicated in one of his speeches, lacks both 'revolutionary optimism' and 'revolutionary development'.

We see in *The Quiet Don* that the Cossacks entered into armed conflict with the Bolsheviks several times. The first such involvement is associated with the name of General Kaledin. But this was essentially a revolt of upper-class Cossacks unsupported by the war-weary rank and file. So the Kaledin revolt was easily quelled by front-line Cossacks united around the Provincial Military-Revolutionary Committee. Cossack regiments and batteries returning to the Don certainly did not want a new war, least of all a war with revolutionary Russia; many of the front-line Cossacks sympathised with the Bolsheviks and hoped to find a common language with them. The author of *The Quiet Don* gives an impressive, historically accurate, description of this early and comparatively short period of civil war on the Don. But unlike many other Soviet writers Sholokhov depicts both the brutality of Kaledin's men and also the brutality of the chairman of the Don Revolutionary Committee, Fyodor Podtelkov.[10]

Before the publication of the second book of *The Quiet Don* a number of historical works and memoirs had included descriptions of the first clashes between Kaledin's officer corps and the Cossack units siding with the Revolutionary Committee. Even so, the imprisonment and death of Chernetsov as described in them bear no resemblance to their portrayal in *The Quiet Don*. For example in Dan Delart's book *Fire on the Don* (Rostov-on-Don, 1927) we read that the captured Chernetsov, when he was brought before Podtelkov, suddenly drew a hidden revolver and made as if to shoot the chairman of the Revolutionary Committee. The latter killed Chernetsov in self-defence. Delart makes no mention at all of the dozens of other captured officers. This same version of the murder of Chernetsov is to be found in the first volume of V. Antonov-Ovseyenko's *Civil War Notes* (Moscow, 1924), and in A. Frenkel's book *Eagles of Revolution* (Rostov, 1922). Even in the Revolutionary Committee reports filed in the Rostov archives it is stated that Chernetsov was killed in an attempt on the life of F. Podtelkov. Mikhail Sholokhov, as we shall see, had certainly read Delart's and Frankel's books. Nevertheless, in describing the death of Chernetsov, Sholokhov gives his own account of the execution of unarmed prisoners, something which, in all probability, no other Soviet author would have been prepared to do, especially since we are dealing here with real, historical personalities and not fictional heroes.

We learn from the novel that a large group of officers has been taken prisoner and disarmed by a detachment under the command of Golubov. Grigori Melekhov, who has gone over to the Reds, has taken part in the battle and been wounded. The 'dense crowd of captured officers' is taken away under reinforced escort to be dealt with by the Revolutionary Committee. Golubov warns the escort, 'Listen to me!...You are responsible for the safety of these prisoners under the strict discipline imposed during military revolution.' Golubov also asks for Chernetsov to be placed in his custody and he sends Podtelkov a note to that effect, also telling Grigori about his decision. But Podtelkov refuses to hand Chernetsov over.

'I'm not giving him up!...I tell you I'm not! That's final! He's going to be tried before a revolutionary tribunal and without delay...'

'No need to yell!' said Grigori, also raising his voice. Inside he was all of a tremble as if he had been infected with Podtelkov's fury. 'You've got too many judges here! Go back there!' He pointed behind, his nostrils quivering. 'Too many of you sorting out prisoners!'

'I've been there! Don't start thinking I've grabbed a cart and saved my own skin. That's enough from you Melekhov! All right? Who do you think you're talking to? Just you forget that fancy officer stuff! The committee does the judging, not any old woman who...'

And then, before the eyes of Grigori Melekhov, who has not been physically held even though Krivoshlykov and Minayev had rushed at him, he fells Chernetsov, killing him, slashing at him with his sword as he lies on the ground in a pool of blood, and gives the order: 'Kill the bastards!! All of them! No prisoners taken...Let's see them bleed...go for the heart!'

The escorting soldiers hack and shoot down the unarmed prisoners, including a cadet who is still only a lad, and this whole ghastly scene is set out in great detail in *The Quiet Don*.[11] This vicious execution without trial which contravenes every concept of military honour, evokes not only Grigori Melekhov's condemnation but also that of most readers. Whenever I have recalled *The Quiet Don* it has always been that incident which has arisen in my memory.

Another unforgettable scene is that page of *The Quiet Don* where Bunchuk, recently made commandant of the revolutionary tribunal of the Don Revolutionary Committee, says to his girl-friend Anna Pogudko:

'Only yesterday we had to shoot three Cossacks in a group of nine... working-men...I started untying one of them...touched his hand... it was like leather...all rough...horny with callouses...His palm was black...cracked and chapped...all cuts and bumps...Oh well, I'm off.' He broke off suddenly and, unseen by Anna, he rubbed his throat which was tensed up in a violent spasm, tight as a wire noose.[12]

This kind of rule could not endure for long in Don Cossack territory and we see from the novel that the Cossacks who had scattered in January–March 1918, returning to their settlements and villages, turn away from the Don Council of People's Commissars situated somewhere in Rostov and then actually rise against the new ruling power. What is more, Sholokhov does not hide from the readers the reason behind the revolt of the Cossack villages, which is the excesses of the Red Guards of the Second Socialist Army who during their retreat before the Germans through the Don province robbed the Cossacks, slaughtered their cattle and raped their women. We read in the novel,

That night the [Red Army] guards got drunk. (Every cart in the convoy carried spirits.) Meanwhile three mounted Cossacks dispatched from the village were now raising the alarm in the surrounding villages. In the dark night Cossacks were saddling horses, taking up arms, hurriedly drawing up detachments from anyone available, front-line soldiers and old men. Commanded by officers and even sergeant-majors who lived there in the villages they were joining forces near Setrakov, surrounding the Red Guards and building up their numbers in the gullies and behind the hillocks. From Migulinsk, Kolodezny and Bogomilov half-formed companies were moving forward in the night. Men had risen from all the nearby villages.[13]

In his later description of the collapse of Soviet power in the villages and settlements and the election of atamans the author of *The Quiet Don* never condemns the Cossacks who rose in defence of their homes and their wives, neither in the general tone of his narrative nor in the facts which he chooses to present. Even when Grigori deserts to support the Cossacks in revolt against the Bolsheviks, this is not presented as something which deserves condemnation. For we see that not only Grigori but all the front-line Cossacks of Tatarsk have risen against the Red Guards. Only one person, Mikhail Koshevoy, dreams of going over to the Reds.

The attempt made by General Krasnov to set up an independent state on the Don, the alliance with the Germans, the battles between the Don Cossack Army and the Red Guards in the spring, summer and autumn of 1918 – all of these are virtually ignored in *The Quiet Don*. In the tenth chapter of Book 3 we learn that the Cossack regiments, unable to resist Red Army pressure, are now retreating southwards and Grigori Melekhov leaves his company to go home. A week later comes the revolt of the 28th Cossack Regiment and the collapse of the front line has begun. One by one the Cossack regiments leave their positions, and the Cossacks, mainly from villages on the Upper Don, stream back home in their thousands. Into the resulting breach march the Red Army divisions.

However, the northern Cossacks did not stay at home for very long. In March 1919 a general Cossack revolt flared up, which came to be known historically as the 'Veshensk Uprising'. The dramatic events connected with their revolt, in which Grigori Melekhov takes an active part, and which was to result in the rout of the southern front of the Red Army, form the main content of the third book of *The Quiet Don* and the first twenty chapters of the fourth book.

We know now that the main reason behind the Veshensk Uprising was the directive on 'Decossacking' received from the Moscow Organisational Office of the Central Committee of the Russian Communist Party (Bolsheviks) at the end of January 1919. This directive has never been published in full in the Soviet press. Only extracts from it, and by no means the most important ones, were published in the 1970 editions of *Essays on the History of Party Organisations on the Don* (Rostov) and in the third of the many volumes which make up *The History of the CPSU*. The author of *The Quiet Don* also omits the text of this directive, though he certainly knows of it and of its practical implementation. It is therefore useful to cite here the full text of this fateful directive:

To all responsible workers in Cossack regions. Recent events on several different fronts in Cossack regions including our deep thrusts into Cossack areas...make it necessary for us to issue instructions to party workers concerning the nature of their work in the said regions. In view of our experience of the Civil War against the Cossacks it is essential to recognise that the only correct policy is to pursue an utterly ruthless campaign against Cossacks of the Upper Class using techniques of mass extermination. You are therefore ordered,

(1) To pursue massive terrorism against rich Cossacks aimed at mass extermination. To pursue massive terrorism without mercy against all Cossacks taking any part, directly or indirectly, in conflict with Soviet power. It is essential to take any measures against Middle Cossacks which shall guarantee no further attempts on their part at new attacks on Soviet power.

(2) To confiscate grain and arrange for all surpluses to be poured into storage places as indicated, this applying not only to grain but to all agricultural produce.

(3) To take all steps to assist the resettlement of the incoming poor peasants, organising such resettlement wherever possible.

(4) To bring the incoming non-Cossack peasantry up to the same level as the Cossacks in respect of land and in every other way.

(5) To carry out total disarmament and to shoot anyone found in possession of arms after the amnesty period. To issue arms only to reliable elements of the non-Cossack population...

The Central Committee resolves to carry out through the appropriate Soviet institutions the obligation of the People's Land Commissar to work out as a matter of urgency practical measures for the mass resettlement of poor peasants on Cossack land.

January 29 1919. Ya. M. Sverdlov[14]

This directive was annulled six weeks later, on 16 March 1919, as misguided and harmful. However, the Cossack uprising in the Upper Don region where the directive, once received, had been implemented with particular zeal, was already under way and from the very text of *The Quiet Don* we see clearly that the excesses perpetrated by the numerous tribunals and Revolutionary Committees, guided by the directive on 'Decossacking', were what led to the Cossack uprising.

In *The Quiet Don* we are told openly about the general rebellion of the Cossacks inspired by the recent shooting of innocent people, not only officers or the rich 'Upper Class' Cossacks (most of whom had moved south with the retreating Don Cossack Army) but mainly ordinary, rank-and-file Cossacks, poor and middle-class people who had only recently left the front *voluntarily* or surrendered to the Red Army.

At a village assembly the one-armed Alyoshka Shamil says to Shtokman and Koshevoy:

I see it like this. If it's wrong what I say, it's wrong. Give it me straight. I'll tell you once and for all what all of us Cossacks are thinking and what we hold against the communists...You told us, mate, that you weren't against working-class Cossacks as long as they weren't your enemies. You're against the rich and for the poor, like. Well, haven't you shot people from our village, eh? I'm not talking about Korshunov – he was one of the bosses, he rode about all his life on other people's backs. But what about Bigmouth Avdeich? What about Matvey Kashulin? Bogatyryov? Maydannikov? What about Korolyov? They were just like us, they didn't know nothing. They were ordinary lads, they weren't involved. They'd been learned to use ploughs, not books. Some of them couldn't read and write. If men like that said something wrong was that enough to have them put up against a wall? Them as you've shot, they'd have drove their last bull off the farm for you if you'd let them live. You didn't even ask them for nothing. You just took them and wrung their necks.[15]

Sholokhov later shows the village assembly to be quite unimpressed by Shtokman's explanation: Bigmouth Avdeich was shot because he was 'putting about propaganda saying that Soviet rule must be overthrown'. Kashulin was doing the same thing, Maydannikov 'put on epaulettes and walked down the street shouting out against Soviet rule' and old Bogatyryov 'spoke out against Soviet rule in the guardroom'.

In another chapter an elderly Cossack Old Believer says to Shtokman:

You've squashed us Cossacks, you've mucked us about. If you hadn't you'd have been all right. There's a lot of fools amongst your lot, that's what caused the uprising...You've shot a lot of people. Somebody gets shot today, somebody else gets shot tomorrow...Who's going to sit there and wait for his turn to come round? You take a bull out to be slaughtered and he'll shake his head. Just take Bukanovsky village, for instance...Commissar there with some soldiers. Name of Malkin. Well, did he treat everybody right? I'll tell you, listen. He gets together some of the old men from the villages, takes them out into the woods, sends their souls up to heaven, strips their bodies and won't let the family bury them...It was Malkin that spotted another old man called Mitrofan walking down the street. 'Hey,' he says, 'you've grown a beard like a fox's tail.' He says, 'People like you, fat pigs, we'll make soap out of you! Third category, this one!' This old lad, for his sins, did really have a beard like a long grass broom. And he got shot because he'd grown a big beard and Malkin happened to come across him at a bad time. Isn't that coming it over the people?[16]

Shtokman refuses to believe this story but when he arrives in the village of Ust-Khopersk he asks the regimental Commissar about Malkin and this man answers 'wearily':

'He did once go a bit too far there. He's a good chap but he doesn't known much about politics. Still, you can't make an omelette without breaking eggs. Now he's busy evacuating all the male population of the villages, sending them off into the middle of Russia...Drop in on the manager, he'll put your name down,' said the Commissar, wincing painfully.[17]

We can see from the third book of the novel that the Veshensk Uprising was a general one in which even women, old men and youths took part. The author of *The Quiet Don* does not conceal the bitterness of the two opposed sides. He depicts not only frightful scenes showing the murder of Red Army prisoners but equally frightful scenes showing the murder of Cossack prisoners by Red Army soldiers and Mikhail Koshevoy. Although the logic of battle leads to a union between the divisions in revolt and the White armies which went over to the attack in the summer of 1919, nevertheless the Veshensk Uprising is depicted not as a counter-revolutionary plot but as a popular revolt, as a tragedy for the people. Two forces became intertwined on the quiet Don, the Bolshevik 'Reds' and the 'Whites', generals and officers like Fitzkhalaurov and Georgidze. Neither of these understands, nor has any desire to understand, the nature and the peculiarities of the Cossack people, their mentality, their way of life. Such, at least, is the clear-enough conception of the author, about which we shall have more to say later.

The union between the White armies and the insurgents, their combined attack on Moscow and then their retreat southwards are all decribed in the fourth and final book of *The Quiet Don*. The Cossack regiments are forced back into the Kuban, tens of thousands of Cossack families flee southward, and typhus claims the lives of Cossack men and their fathers, wives and children. The Red Army marches back into the deserted villages large and small, but it no longer pursues a 'Decossacking' policy, no longer takes vengeance on the Cossacks, no longer burns down the villages. Many of yesterday's 'White Cossacks' are given a chance to join the Red Army. Grigori Melekhov reaches Novorossiysk with his friends but does not manage to get himself evacuated to the Crimea. Along with many other Cossacks he takes the decision to join the First Cavalry and fights bravely on the Polish front. As a reward for his courage and service Melekhov rises to become adjutant to the regiment commander, but when the war is over he applies for demobilisation and returns to his home which now stands deserted. Pyotr, his brother, has been killed, Darya has drowned in the Don and Natalya is dead. Earlier, during the retreat, Grigori has buried his father Panteley Prokofyevich. Grigori's mother, Ilinichna, is also dead.

Although Soviet power has been established on the Don for a year or so now, peace has not yet come to the area. The Don Cossacks rise in revolt for the fourth time. This time the Red Cossacks, until recently members of the Red Army and the Red Cavalry, are the insurgents. Although Sholokhov calls the rebels 'bandits' and their units 'gangs', although he writes that these uprisings are 'a response by prosperous Cossacks and kulaks to the establishment of grain-requisitioning units, to the strengthening of measures taken by the Soviet government to ensure proper food distribution',[18] we can see nonetheless that this is far from being so. The commanders of most of the insurgent groups were until quite recently honoured commanders of the Red Army, their units having rebelled virtually *en masse*. The main reason for the widespread discontent was the series of 'extreme measures' taken to promote food-distribution for which the reader is also unable to find justification and which Lenin was later to describe as giving a *lawful* reason for peasant discontent. Grigori Melekhov flees from his home village and joins Fomin's group only after learning from Dunyasha, who is now married to Koshevoy, that her husband has ordered four cavalrymen to ride to the village and arrest Grigori, which in those times meant certain execution.

Cossack and Red Army blood is spilt again in new clashes. Fomin's group alternates between being thinned down to a few men and reinforced with new young Cossacks. Grigori, however, has no more strength left for fighting. He abandons his unit and returns home in secret in order to pick up Aksinya and leave with her for the Kuban or even further away. But Grigori does not get far. Aksinya is killed by a bullet from one of the grain-requisitioning soldiers and Grigori, after spending the winter with other deserters in their dug-out, comes once more in the spring of 1922 to the gate of his home. The novel ends with Grigori meeting his little son Misha. We close *The Quiet Don* unable to forget the events and the personal destinies which have been recounted, and with a deep sense that this is a great book which could have been written only by a great writer.

2

IF 'THE QUIET DON' HAD APPEARED ANONYMOUSLY...THE AUTHOR'S DISTINGUISHING FEATURES

In conversations about *The Quiet Don* in Moscow and Leningrad I have often heard different people ask the question, 'Do you think Sholokhov really did write that novel?' I have also had to listen to endless variations of the legend that tells how Sholokhov apparently found the manuscript of an unfinished novel in the map-case of a Cossack officer who had died or been killed.

The history of literature records a wide range of hoaxes; disputes concerning the authorship of this or that classical work are not uncommon in literary criticism.[1] For instance, classical scholars have long debated the authorship of *The Iliad* and *The Odyssey* and whether a poet called Homer ever existed in Ancient Greece. Renaissance scholars have frequently argued about the authorship of individual tragedies and comedies of Shakespeare or even whether such an English dramatist ever existed at all. Many Shakespearean tragedies have been attributed, for example, to the playwright Christopher Marlowe, to the philosopher Francis Bacon, to the Earls of Oxford, Derby and Rutland, as well as to several other authors. Literary activity in the Middle Ages rarely brought material or any other benefits; more frequently it was the cause of persecution and abuse of every kind. For this reason many distinguished works appeared anonymously or else under pseudonyms which have still not been identified. There are plenty of instances of an unknown author signing his work with the name of a dead classic writer. Under the names of Plato, Aristotle, Cicero, Cervantes and many fathers of the Christian Church, books have appeared which were written by quite different authors who had real abilities but who nevertheless sought neither glory nor honour. There are examples of this 'antiplagiarism' also in Russian literature.

Direct plagiarism, however, is also well represented in literary history. In the fifteenth century the Venetian Alziono published amongst his works a treatise 'On Fame' which was really by Cicero, having first taken the precaution of destroying the manuscript of the treatise which he had discovered. In the eighteenth century the Chancellor of the University of Paris, Barre, published a long historical work which included about 200 pages from a work by Voltaire, *The History of Charles XII*. Alexandre Dumas *père* and Alexandre Dumas *fils* both had a proclivity for plagiarism. The latter, for instance, once published under his own name in a French journal a translation of Alexander Pushkin's *The Shot*, one of the *Tales of Belkin*. In Russia the year 1837 saw the publication of a book entitled *Russia in Historical, Geographical, Statistical and Literary Terms* under the name of Faddey Bulgarin. This work created quite a stir, whereupon it emerged that the real author was the historian N. A. Ivanov, later to become a professor in the universities of Kazan and Dorpat. He had lacked the means to publish his book and Bulgarin had offered him material support, insisting, however, that the book must bear his (Bulgarin's) name. It is also known that in the early years of his literary career the Russian playwright Alexander Ostrovsky had occasion to defend his authorship against the claims of one of the actors with whom he had written several scenes of a comedy which had received public approval, *The Bankrupt*.

But one may ask whether any writer has been so persistently beset by rumours and accusations of plagiarism as Mikhail Sholokhov. Talk of Sholokhov not being the real author of *The Quiet Don* began in literary circles immediately after publication of Book 1 of the novel in the journal *Oktyabr'*. These accusations first arose within the Russian Proletarian Writers' Association (RAPP), which Sholokhov had joined after the publication of his *Tales of the Don*. Many RAPP leaders considered *The Quiet Don* a betrayal of 'proletarian' literature. They accused Sholokhov of 'siding with the kulaks' and simultaneously began spreading doubts about the authorship of the novel, which had proved an immediate success with the reading public. In 1929 Sholokhov wrote to A. Serafimovich:

What am I to do, Alexander Serafimovich? I'm fed up to the back teeth with being a 'thief'. I've had so much mud slung at me...Things are pretty hot just now, I'm finishing Book Three, and these conditions don't make it easy to work. My hand's dropping off and I feel like death. What evil have I done that my brother writers should gang up on me for the third time? For it all starts in literary circles.[2]

'During the years when the question of Sholokhov's authorship was first raised', one of the oldest of our literary critics writes to me:

I worked in the State Publishing House with which Sholokhov was associated; he was then a very retiring young man. Naturally we editors listened to all the arguments about *The Quiet Don*. Many literary men considered the novel to have been plagiarised. At the very beginning of 1929 a special commission was set up to examine the accusations brought against Sholokhov. This commission, it was said, was comparing handwriting, and wanted to see Sholokhov's rough drafts which he was unable to produce. No-one had ever seen or read, for instance, the manuscript of the novel *Life on the Don* which had been completed in draft, according to Sholokhov, as early as 1925 and from which only a couple of printer's sheets had been subsequently included in *The Quiet Don*. (The overall size of *Life on the Don*, according to statements made on various occasions by Sholokhov, came to between six and twelve printer's sheets.) It must be allowed, of course, that not all writers, especially tiros, hang on to their drafts and rough copies.[3]

It is reasonable to assume that some pressure was put on the commission. Stalin had just read *The Quiet Don* and everyone knew that he had liked it.[4] The issue might also have been affected by the fact that the chairman of the commission was A. Serafimovich, who was a protector of Sholokhov. It must not be forgotten that Serafimovich was then considered a most upright and incorruptible judge in literary matters. At all events the commission rejected as unfounded the accusations of plagiarism levelled against Sholokhov. On 29 March 1929 a letter to the editor was published in *Pravda*, signed by A. Serafimovich, L. Averbakh, V. Kirshon, A. Fadeyev and V. Stavsky. The letter said that rumours to the effect that the novel had been copied from someone else's manuscript were being put about by 'the enemies of proleterian literature'. 'In order to teach the slanderers and gossip-mongers', the authors of the letter continued, 'we call upon Soviet literary and public opinion to assist us in exposing individual ill-wishers so that they may be brought to justice.'

This letter to the editor contained no convincing arguments in favour of Sholokhov's authorship, and so, despite the threats, the rumours of plagiarism continued to spread. According to one writer, D.B., his close friend, Boris Gorbatov, voiced doubts about Sholokhov's authorship on more than one occasion. Similar doubts were expressed by the writers D. Petrov-Biryuk, A. Bibik and even the old-established author Novikov-Priboy. A meeting between Sholokhov and Maxim Gorky arranged by I. S. Shkapa was not too successful. Shkapa tells us that Gorky was taken aback not only by the youthfulness of Sholokhov but by his obvious narrow-mindedness and timidity. Talking to Gorky, Sholokhov was shy and embarrassed, answering Gorky's questions in a few monosyllabic, unexpressive phrases. 'It's all very strange', Gorky said pensively to Shkapa, then his assistant, after the interview.[5]

The talk and the rumours of those days certainly did not include references to the name of Fyodor Kryukov. The Revolution had been such a decisive turning point in the life of our country that many well-known writers of as little as ten years before had been entirely forgotten. There was general mention of a White Cossack officer whose diary or unfinished novel had been found in a map-case after his death by the young Sholokhov. People also spoke of the Don Cossack ataman P. Krasnov, the author of several novels about the Don Cossacks, some of which he had already had published as an émigré.

The name of Kryukov as the author of the original version of *The Quiet Don* began to appear only in 1937–8. At that time, according to D. Petrov-Biryuk, the editors of the newspaper *Molot* and the Rostov Regional Party Committee started receiving letters from individual Cossacks accusing Sholokhov of plagiarism. Sholokhov's acquisition of the manuscripts and other materials of Kryukov's was linked in several letters with the name of P. Gromyslavsky, a Cossack regimental clerk who had been at Kryukov's side when he had died. Three years later, Gromyslavsky's daughter, Mariya Petrovna, became the wife of the young writer Sholokhov upon his return from an unsuccessful visit to Moscow. However, no-one placed any credence in all these letters; at that time it was often very difficult to distinguish between a genuine letter and a malicious denunciation or a piece of libel and most letters of this type were handed over to the NKVD.* Arrests were made, not only of those who had sent these letters but even of one man who had been receiving them, the writer Petrov-Biryuk, who spent more than two years in a Rostov prison and was rehabilitated only in 1939.

We shall give detailed consideration to Fyodor Kryukov in Chapter 4. For the moment it is enough to say that, in the first eighteen years of the twentieth century, he was a fairly well-known writer of the populist persuasion, a public figure and publicist, one of the editors of the liberal journal *Russkoye Bogatstvo* headed by Vladimir Korolenko. The main theme of Kryukov's work was the life of the Don Cossacks to whom he belonged by extraction. After making his literary début in the 1890s, Kryukov published many stories and novellas in different editions, entitled *Cossack Themes* (1907) and *Stories* (1914). A convinced populist and socialist, Kryukov was secretary of the Don Cossack Military Assembly in 1917–18 and he took part in the Civil War on the Don as an officer in the Cossack Army. During the retreat of this army into the Kuban Kryukov, like thousands of other Cossacks, died from typhus. An obituary article on Kryukov published in the journal *Vestnik Literatury* included the following tribute:

A sensitive and attentive observer, an affectionate and humorous portrayer of the spirit and the life of the ordinary people, F. D. Kryukov is one of those second-rank but nevertheless genuine creators of the written word of whom Russian literature is justly proud. The individual figures of his work do not impress themselves upon the reader's mind

* These initials were used from 1934 to 1943 to denote the Secret Police of the Soviet State, which has been known at other times by different acronyms: OGPU (1922–34), NKGB (1943–6), MGB (1946–53) and KGB since 1953. (*Translator's note.*)

as eternal generalisations of human destiny and character, but from out of the total mass of his stories of the life of the people one all-embracing image arises, immutable – the image of that people, anxious, searching, feverishly coming to terms with the confusion which has shaken their life and their spirit during the last quarter of a century. Kryukov has depicted the disturbed spirit of this people both in the peaceful course of their everyday life and in their violent clashes with innovation, he has depicted it thoughtfully, attentively and with that strict simplicity and spiritual honesty which flowed naturally from his forthright, uncomplicated nature. This creative honesty found particularly distinct expression in his excellent use of language, in the rich, true-to-life regional speech of his heroes which even when put to the inevitable exaggeration entailed by caricature manages not to recoil in theoretical word-fabrication or contrivance...A gentle humour, amusing and often touching, pervaded the atmosphere with which he liked to inform his stories.[6]

The gossip and the doubts about Sholokhov's authorship were renewed in the mid-1960s especially after the publication by the Rostov newspaper *Molot* of an article by V. Molozhavenko, 'Concerning an Undeservedly Forgotten Name', dedicated to the memory of Fyodor Kryukov. After a brief résumé of the life and literary career of Kryukov, 'whom we may justly consider one of the greatest Don Cossack literary figures of the pre-revolutionary period', Molozhavenko asserted that to this very day Kryukov is still remembered in every last Cossack village. According to Molozhavenko, Kryukov started writing a long novel based on Cossack life before the war began. The fate of this writer, who left the Don in the winter of 1920 along with the retreating White Cossack units, is compared by the author of the article in *Molot* with the fate of Grigori Melekhov. Of the last days of Kryukov Molozhavenko says,

Feverish and delirious from typhus, when he [Kryukov] could pull himself together for a moment or two, he would look round reproachfully at the villagers who had lured him down this hard, unnecessary road, he would snatch convulsively at a metal box containing his manuscripts and beg them to look after it. He had no Tsarist coins, no treasure at all, except those cherished papers. He seemed to sense disaster and, it seems, not without justification...the villagers retreating before the Red Army had no time to bother with papers. The manuscripts disappeared without trace. Talk of Kryukov the turncoat assisted in no small degree the process whereby literary critics lost him from memory over several long years and his books were not published.[7]

I was told in literary circles that the edition of the newspaper *Molot* containing the articles by Molozhavenko was kept away from Sholokhov for a long time. He learned of the article from a visitor of his only many months afterwards. Sholokhov was furious and demanded a refutation.

Finding no support in the regional organisations he turned to his friends in Moscow. As a result of this, on 14 August 1966, that is a year later, an article by A. Podolsky, 'Concerning an Undeservedly Revived Name', was published in the newspaper *Sovetskaya Rossiya*. After producing a number of quotations from speeches made by Kryukov in 1918–19 which criticised the Bolsheviks and their policy on the Don, Podolsky calls Kryukov 'an inveterate counter-revolutionary', 'herald of the White Guards', 'a dyed-in-the-wool White Guard' and 'an ideological inspirer of Kaledinism'. Podolsky cites a statement made by two old Bolsheviks to the effect that 'the whole working population of the Don hates that butcher'. Then the author of the article continues:

Painting a vivid and tearful picture of the writer's 'tragic end' on the banks of the Yegorlyk, Molozhavenko grieves over the fact that his manuscripts disappeared without trace at the same time. What manuscripts were these? Between the lines you can discern the hint that at least another *Quiet Don* has sunk into oblivion with the metal box. This notion arises in the reader's mind especially since later on we are told how the young Cossack of Glazunov village, while still a student, began writing short stories imitative of Chekhov and then became 'the Gleb Uspensky* of the Don Cossacks'.

The article in *Sovetskaya Rossiya* ends with this significant assertion:

A year has passed since the publication of V. Molozhavenko's article in *Molot*. More than long enough, one might suggest, for the Regional Party Committee and its newspaper, as well as the Don area organisations of writers and journalists, literary critics and historians to have worked out a clearly defined attitude towards Kryukov's work. It is particularly important that this should be done because the restoration of this literary name entails a political amnesty for one of those who stood on the other side of the barricades during the Revolution... The whole of our country is preparing for the fiftieth anniversary of Soviet power. Its heroic pages must be restored carefully, with a real sense of responsibility. Under no pretext should enemies of the Revolution, hatred of whom will never be forgotten by the Soviet people, find their way into these pages. Only clean and pure names which have somehow been unjustly forgotten should be restored.[8]

We can see that Podolsky's arguments entirely follow the logic of the obscurantism and intransigence of the Stalinist era. All the world is aware that quite a few of the greatest Russian writers of the early twentieth century found themselves 'on the other side of the barricades': Bunin, Kuprin, Alexey Tolstoy, Gumilyov, Tsvetayeva, I. Surguchev, Leonid Andreyev and others. The distinguished Russian writer Vladimir

---

* Gleb Uspensky (1843–1902) was a writer in the Russian nineteenth-century realist tradition celebrated for his sympathetic and minutely documented portrayals of peasant life. (*Translator's note.*)

Korolenko, a friend of Kryukov's, also made pronouncements highly critical of the Bolsheviks. Even Maxim Gorky came out at first against the October Revolution and the dictatorship of the proletariat. None of this prevented the subsequent restoration of the literary names of these writers or the publication of their works, though all of this, it goes without saying, certainly does not amount to a political amnesty. Yet Kryukov's works, despite their considerable artistic and social value, have never once been republished in Soviet times, which fact alone is very strange.

One cannot help noting that the position of Mikhail Sholokhov himself encourages all sorts of rumours about plagiarism. In historical novels, especially in the writing of large-scale epic works, the use of all sorts of memoirs, diaries and private archive material of various kinds is more than simply usual; it is imperative. Today researchers concerned with the work of Leo Tolstoy can determine with some accuracy which memoirs were used by the great writer in the creation of his epic novel *War and Peace* as well as a number of other works (*Hadji Murat* etc.). Yet Sholokhov for some reason stubbornly refuses to name the basic sources and memoir materials which he used when writing *The Quiet Don*. Thus the many researchers dealing with his work more often than not are forced to evade this issue.

Doubts of various kinds concerning Sholokhov's authorship have also been voiced abroad. Thus, for example, in the U.S. journal *Harper's Magazine* in September 1969 the American playwright Arthur Miller wrote that Sholokhov was certainly not the man who had created *The Quiet Don* but that he had in some mysterious way become the author of the work.

During recent months discussions and doubts about the authorship of *The Quiet Don* have again begun to arise in literary circles mainly because of the publication in Paris of the book by the literary critic known as 'D', *The Mainstream of 'The Quiet Don'*. The initiative behind the publication belongs to Alexander Solzhenitsyn, winner of the Nobel Prize for Literature, who wrote the preface to 'D's' book. Both the critic 'D' and Solzhenitsyn consider Kryukov to be the main author of *The Quiet Don*, or, more precisely, the most probable author of the epic. Sholokhov they consider to be a co-author who spoiled the novel.

I am no literary critic, but I have decided to set down some considerations which seem to me to have real substance relating to this problem which has been evoking all manner of controversy for the last forty-five years. I have decided to do this not just because *The Quiet Don* remains to this day one of my favourite works but also because I have in recent times made a close and detailed study of the history of the Don Cossacks in the period 1917–21.

Every great literary work is distinguished by a series of special features, distinct characteristics which are as it were a copy taken from the mould of the author's personality at the time when the masterpiece was written. Of course, the author's personality may undergo radical changes at a later date and the process allows not only of improvement but also of decline. However, at the time of writing the configuration is pretty well exact. One commentator, in a letter to me, comes to the proper conclusion that,

The author's personality may 'equal' the work or may 'exceed' it (the iceberg principle: you see less than is hidden under water). The copy can never exceed the author's personality just as the ice that shows can never exceed what is under the water. In subtle shades and details we can re-establish the personality of the anonymous author of *The Lay of Igor's Campaign*. Had *War and Peace* appeared anonymously we should have explained without too much trouble, even proved, that it could not have been written by Nekrasov or Turgenev or any other of the titans of literature at work in the sixties and seventies of the nineteenth century. The process of elimination would probably indicate a man who had taken part in a recent war, a landowner, and so on, in other words, the man from Yasnaya Polyana.

Another correspondent, G. N. Fein, writes as follows:

It is not just the theme, the assembling of artistic resources, the uniqueness of language and style and the political ideas which constitute the inimitable individuality of the artist but *first and foremost* his conception of the world and his conception of man, which may be exposed by an analysis of his artistic method. Tolstoy could write about the peasants (*The Power of Darkness*), turn satirist (*The Fruits of Enlightenment*), come out in favour of the idea of patriotism (*Sevastopol Sketches*) and against it, he could use both the instrument of painstaking analysis to study the minute changes in a human spirit (*The Death of Ivan Ilyich*) or the hand of the builder on a monumental scale..., the only thing he could not do was stop being Leo Tolstoy, in other words start viewing and treating the world like Boborykin or Mordovtsev.

May we not also approach an analysis of *The Quiet Don* from that same standpoint? May we not also imagine for a while that this, the greatest of all twentieth-century epic novels, appeared anonymously and then, by analysing the main distinctive features of its author, seek him out among the writers of the first quarter of the twentieth century?

Some of our opponents consider that this sort of method, the determining of the author of an anonymous work through the analysis of the various peculiarities of this work, is unacceptable in literary criticism. One letter we received asked,

What if a play like *Woe from Wit* had appeared as an anonymous work? Or *The Golden Calf* and *The Twelve Chairs*? Or *In the Land of the*

Unvanquished (that is, after *Brusky*)? And so on and so forth. It is clear that all of these, compared with the picturesque quality and the grandeur of *The Quiet Don*, are works of smaller significance and scale. However, I should like to stress the impropriety of putting the question like that at all. It gives unlimited freedom for speculation and fabrication. Are there not plenty of writers of only one book in literary history? Writers who created only a *single* outstanding piece of work after a number of very mediocre books and who also never managed subsequently to produce anything of significance or appreciable quality?

There is, of course, substance in these objections. Like all other methods, the method of determining an unidentified author through the text, content and style of his work can be considered neither the only one possible nor exhaustive. If, for example, the novel *Far from Moscow* had appeared in 1948 not under the name of a hitherto unknown far-eastern writer Vasiliy Azhayev but anonymously, it is scarcely possible that any specialist literary critic could have identified him as the author, a modest employee on the journal *Far East* who had so far published nothing more than two quite unremarkable collections of stories. In addition to this, the original text of *Far from Moscow* received by *Novy Mir* was then subjected to considerable polishing and editorial improvement in which prominent writers like F. Vigdorova and K. Simonov took part.[9]

Nevertheless, even when we are dealing with an average work, or perhaps a mediocre one, published anonymously, the method of determining the author through the various peculiarities of his text is a perfectly legitimate and scholarly one widely used in literary criticism as well as in a number of academic and non-academic institutions quite remote from literature. The determining of authorship *via* a given text (anonymous or pseudonymous) has become in recent years one of the most important methods of so-called content-analysis in which computer technology has come to be employed.[10] How much more proper it is to use a similar method when studying the texts of distinguished literary works! It is well known that a lot of interesting and original research has been done into the question of the authorship of *The Lay of Igor's Campaign*. We might just mention one of the latest and finest pieces of research on this great Russian twelfth-century epic, a book by academician B. Rybakov, *Russian Chroniclers and the Author of 'The Lay of Igor's Campaign'*.

Rybakov is clearly aware of the difficulties of the task he has set himself. Great writers often possess the ability not only to work in different literary genres but also to vary their use of language. Both *Poltava* and *The History of Peter the Great* were written by Pushkin. Rybakov properly points out that, 'if either of those works were anony-

mous it would be immensely difficult to show that both belonged to one
author, the former an inspired narrative poem containing wide-ranging
historical generalisations, the latter consisting of an arid, almost annali-
stic compilation of facts'.[11] Nevertheless Rybakov does not consider his
problem insoluble. After all, nowadays we have knowledge of virtually
every Russian chronicler of any significance and of their different ways
of writing, their allegiance to a particular court or church, their political
sympathies and antipathies. Furthermore, Rybakov shows that

The Lay of Igor's Campaign is brimful of its author's personality; every
judgement, every appeal, every hint, everything in it is coloured by the
author's attitude to people and events. The author's 'sub-text' blends
so well with the speech of his heroes that some researchers would like
to attribute the famous Golden Lay of Svyatoslav Vsevolodovich to the
author himself. The author of The Lay of Igor's Campaign tells us
nothing about himself directly but he still manages to give a fairly
complete description of himself through his living language, his passionate attitudes to his contemporaries, to current events and to people
of the distant past, as well as through his knowledge of so many
different aspects of life.[12]

Rybakov, not being a specialist in stylistics, defines his research techniques in advance:

Search principle. A poet rising eagle-like above feudal frontiers and
warring princes, overlooking in his mind's eye the whole of Russia, half
of Europe and the endless Polovtsian Steppe, a poet who dared to pass
judgement on princes and their ancestors – this is the man whom we
must seek among the strong ones of the earth. The author's indifference
to church affairs, his bold use of secular archaisms, his anticipation of
Renaissance ideas, the complete absence of Christian Providentialism,
all this, together with his splendid knowledge of warfare, cause us to
exclude the Church from our search and look for the great poet in the
ranks of the boyars and princes. On the other hand, the profound
historical erudition of the author of The Lay of Igor's Campaign, his
historical cast of thought, his constant desire to draw comparisons
between different ages of history and his searching the past for the
sources of contemporary Russian misfortunes lead us in another direction, towards the pléiade of Russian chroniclers in the second half of
the twelfth century. In the Middle Ages poets and historians shared the
same task, the celebration or description of heroic military
achievements.[13]

Rybakov then proceeds to the enormous task of comparing the Russian
chronicles with The Lay. He analyses the author's political sympathies
and his historical views, remarks upon the anonymous writer's extensive
knowledge of warfare and the pastimes of twelfth-century aristocrats,
draws comparisons between many other theories and research
works, such as those of A. A. Shakhmatov, M. D. Priselkov and D. S.

Likhachov, and then comes to the conclusion that the most probable author of *The Lay of Igor's Campaign* was the 'one and only Russian chronicler from Kiev working in the second half of the twelfth century who was not a churchman, who knew a lot about warfare, had a broad view of the whole of Russia, was concerned to defend her from the Polovtsians and who quite daringly passed judgement on the princes while taking a patriotic stance'. The one such prominent and singular figure in Russian twelfth-century chronicling who seems to coincide at every fundamental point with the author of *The Lay of Igor's Campaign* was the Kievan chronicler Pyotr Borislavovich. He is the man whom Rybakov considers to be the creator of this great Russian epic, though he naturally admits that there can be no question of coming to a definitive decision. This is no more than a hypothesis; it is impossible to judge with absolute certainty whether Pyotr Borislavovich was the author of *The Lay* or whether it was a contemporary double of his.

Let us therefore proceed to an analysis of *The Quiet Don* from the same standpoint. What, we may ask, are the main discernible distinguishing features of the creator of this great epic?

Love for the Cossacks, whose tragedy the author not only comprehended but interpreted as his own

Maxim Gorky noted this peculiarity of the author's attitude towards the Cossacks when he pointed out in an article that the author of *The Quiet Don* 'writes like a Cossack in love with the Don, the Cossack way of life and character'.[14] The well-known Soviet critic S. Dinamov wrote in 1931,

The artistic construction of *The Quiet Don* is fragile and uneven, its beginnings and endings are different, though they are tied with the same knots. Yet there is a certain unity in its seething diversity. This is the author's attitude to the free-and-easy, full-blooded Cossack way of life before it was shattered by war and revolution. He pours out his love for this exuberant life in more than full measure. Everything here seems to him significant: trivialities grow into something large and worthy of attention, small details take on a special importance.[15]

It is a curious fact that in western countries, where the first parts of *The Quiet Don* proved very successful, almost every critic, lacking most of the information about the author's origins and biography, assumed that he was a Don Cossack. 'The author of *The Quiet Don* is a Cossack tied with the tightest bonds to his native land.' 'The author blends perfectly with his heroes in the Melekhov family, Cossack folk and farmers.' 'Writing as a Cossack from the Don region the author has drawn a monumentally broad picture of Cossack life during the war, times of peace, revolution and civil war.' These are but a few extracts from the western press in the early 1930s.[16]

24

It is well known that the Cossacks formed a special military and farming caste in Tsarist Russia. The Cossack people traces its origins back to the fourteenth and fifteenth centuries, mainly to runaway peasants, serfs and townsmen fleeing from feudal servitude and oppression to free steppe-lands in the south-west and south-east. The chief occupations of the Cossacks were hunting, fishing and wild-honey farming; they subsequently took to agriculture and cattle-breeding. Armed Cossack units made frequent sallies into Turkish and Tatar lands and attacked caravans of merchandise. Their peculiar position in the borderlands, the need to defend themselves against the claims of the Moscow Tsar and other states meant that the Cossacks had to create a specifically military organisation which infiltrated the whole way of life of their people. As the Russian Empire expanded and grew stronger, the Russian Tsars became more determined in their attempts to subjugate the Cossack regions. This conflict immediately became a sanguinary business which could have only one end, the victory of the centralised Russian state. However, even when they had subjugated the Cossacks the Russian Tsars held back from committing them to serfdom and the surrender of their lands to the Russian nobility. The Tsarist government saw the importance of maintaining special military Cossack communities on the borders of the Russian Empire. Thus, as the borders of the Empire expanded, new Cossack regions came into being and new Cossack villages and settlements sprang up. By the beginning of the twentieth century there were twelve Cossack regions and military forces, the largest of which was the Great Don Cossack Military Region. About a hundred Don Cossack regiments served at the front in the First World War, to say nothing of all the other smaller-scale units (single batteries, individual companies of Cossack infantrymen, etc.). The Cossack military regions possessed their own lands, capital, industrial enterprises, stud farms and also their own administration. All Cossacks did military service and were available for conscription between the ages of eighteen and thirty-eight. In addition a Cossack had to provide himself with a service horse and necessary personal arms, all at his own expense. On the other hand, the average allotment of land for a Cossack was substantially greater than that of the average Russian peasant. The Cossacks retained many other privileges which maintained them as a special caste. Despite the differences in property and social status within this caste, it still preserved a particular kind of *self-awareness* not far removed from *national* self-awareness. ('We are not Russians, not muzhiks, not serfs.') Cossacks were jealous of their title not merely because of the privileges it entailed but out of pride in the long and, as they saw it, glorious history of the Don Cossack people.

The author of *The Quiet Don* does not hide the dark side of the majority of the Don Cossacks, the many uncivilised ways and practices which survived in their way of life. He shows us vicious marauding Cossacks, cruel in their aggressiveness. But he also shows us many attractive features of Cossack life and traditions. '*The Quiet Don* is by no means an idyll', writes F. Biryukov,

The antediluvian, old-fashioned system, the worst kind of patriarchal rule, barbaric superstitions, the out-of-date way of living which is sometimes horribly repulsive, all find their way into the novel. However, the immeasurable preponderance of bright, positive qualities like the conserving of strength, the titanic invincibility, the underlying health, all of this, on which *The Quiet Don* is founded, causes it to stand out from the ranks of gloomy tales and novels with a superabundance of horror and out-and-out absurdity, with a tendency to be obsessively biological, to ramble on in tedious descriptiveness and scenery-painting.[17]

It is indeed true that the author of *The Quiet Don* frequently emphasises the great love of the Cossacks for the land, labour, prowess in war, virility and physical strength. He emphasises also their feeling of superiority, a quality well developed in many Cossacks, their mettle and their broad-mindedness, their sociability, their readiness to support each other at work and in war. In many places in his book the author seems to admire the Cossacks, this peculiar tribe of men, this distinct and sturdy breed of Russians. We read, for example:

He [the English colonel] looked with typically English hauteur on the dark faces, each with its own character, of these warlike sons of the steppe, surprised at the racial mixture which is always so striking when you look at a crowd of Cossacks. Alongside a blond Slav Cossack stood a typical Mongol; his neighbour was a young Cossack as dark as a crow's wing, with his hand on his dirty shoulder-strap, and he was speaking in hushed tones to a grey-haired Biblical patriarch – and you could stake your life on the fact that in the veins of that patriarch leaning on his staff, dressed in an old-fashioned Cossack jacket, there flowed the blood of the Caucasian mountain folk.[18]

Lieutenant Atarshchikov, for whom the author clearly has great sympathy, since he sets him against Listnitsky in a number of incidents, says,

You know, Yevgeny...I'm damned fond of the Don, all this old Cossack way of life that's grown up over the centuries. I love my Cossacks, the Cossack women – I love every one of them! The scent of wormwood on the steppe brings tears to my eyes...And when the sunflowers are in bloom and you can go down by the Don and smell the grapes fresh after the rain...I love all of it so deeply that it hurts.[19]

The author of *The Quiet Don* also has a great love for Cossack men and women. For example, Grigori Melekhov, returning home from the war, looks at Natalya and Darya and thinks, 'You can always tell a

Cossack girl. She dresses to show all she's got. "Look if you want to; don't if you don't!" Peasant women, you can't tell their back from their front. Their clothes look like sacks.'[20]
Cossack women in *The Quiet Don* are almost always beautiful.

Down the steps came the mistress, a tall, beautiful Cossack woman as sturdy as a boyar's wife. The sleeves of her pink blouse, tucked into her skirt, were rolled up exposing the dark skin and fine lines of her arms. She was carrying an iron bucket. She glided freely along, walking in that slightly swaggering way that Cossack women have, as she made her way to the cowshed.[21]

There stood a young Cossack girl, not tall but with a good figure, shapely as a partridge; she had a dark face and black, finely moulded eyebrows; she stood there with her back to the stove knitting a stocking.[22]

Galloping towards him was a woman on a superb dark bay horse...She sat him with an easy confidence and held the correctly deployed reins firmly in a strong, dark-skinned hand...Prokhor, admiring the lovely round face of the Cossack girl, drinking in the gentle timbre of her deep contralto voice, croaked out his words.[23]

Hostility towards 'outsiders'

Just as the author's love for the Cossacks is made obvious in *The Quiet Don*, so is his hostility towards all groups and levels of 'outsiders'; that is, the section of the Don Cossack population which did not belong to the Cossack people. The question of the relations between Cossacks and 'outsiders' as seen by the author of *The Quiet Don* is considered in detail and in a convincing manner in the book written by 'D' which we have already mentioned, *The Mainstream of 'The Quiet Don'*. Perhaps one ought to add that this is the only issue which is solidly and thoroughly examined in the book.[24] 'D' writes as follows:

The Upper Don village of Tatarsk with all its creeks and woods occupies the foreground [of *The Quiet Don*] and retains most of the reader's attention but this limited little world, washed by the waters of the Don tributaries, seems like a vast area simply because it has projected onto it crucial events connected with all of Russia. The foreground of the novel is the Don Cossack region represented by the most varied assortment of ordinary personalities, the people themselves; their real uniqueness, which holds great significance for Russia, is revealed not through their remoteness but through their organic and age-old connection with Russian life as a whole, although this connexion entails conflict between the cossacks and all 'outsiders'.
    'Outsiders' are presented in *The Quiet Don* through the eyes of the Cossacks, with their peculiarly harsh, even merciless outlook and this accounts for the distorted view of everything proceeding from Moscow

...It is inevitably through the eyes of the Tatarsk villagers that the reader sees the wealthy Mokhov and his promiscuous daughter Yelizaveta Sergeyevna...It is Grigori Melekhov, and then Aksinya Astakhova who present to the reader the nobleman's son from St Petersburg (also, however, a lieutenant in a Cossack regiment) Yevgeny Listnitsky. Yevgeny's father, a retired Russian general, is viewed by the reader through the medium of Grigori and his ill-starred service under him, and seen as a keen hunter and horseman and a typical Russian noble who has settled cosily in the Don region lowlands. The reader encounters Osip Davidovich Shtokman through Fedot Bodovsky who screws up his Kalmuck eyes into the kind of penetrating stare normally reserved for a wild duck on the wing...Balanda, the teacher who works for Mokhov, living out his revolutionary ideology, has become a member of the family and never associates with the villagers; he is characterised not so much by his ardent post-revolutionary words addressed to the people in the Tatarsk market-place as by the reactions of the Cossacks who are there listening to him...General Fitzkhalaurov, a typical representative of those White Guards who, despite zealous service, brought about the ruin of the Volunteer Army, is seen by the reader solely through the eyes of an infuriated Grigori Melekhov.

The main hero of *The Quiet Don*, Grigori Melekhov, almost always expresses the judgement of the author concerning the 'outsiders'. This is merciless where the absurdly reactionary upholders of the old régime are concerned. It is contemptuous (though not unrestrained) towards the Russian nobility and the riotous officers of golden Russian youth. However, Grigori cannot but admire real courage and genuine patriotism even when it involves allegiance elsewhere. Hence his vigorous protest against the execution of Chernetsov and the officers in his squad. From the same source comes his admiration of the courage of the communist Likhachov who is so barbarously disposed of by the Cossacks and the hysterical reaction of Grigori to the desperate encounter with the brave sailors.

Even though he creates an image of the 'outsider' as a man from another region who cannot understand Cossack village life and who is preventing the self-determination of the 'Quiet Don', the author nevertheless strives always towards objective truth, historical objectivity.[25]

In this context it is interesting to compare *The Quiet Don*, with D. Petrov-Biryuk's trilogy *Legend of the Cossacks*.[26] Although the author of this trilogy is writing for the most part about the Cossacks of Khopersk, the main hero of his epic, Pyotr Ilyin, is an 'outsider'. The village ataman Belikov is most displeased when his daugher Paranya falls in love with Ilyin. A Bolshevik sympathiser, Ilyin is an active member of the small Social Democrat group set up in the village, and he certainly never expresses a wish to become a Cossack, which is what his father-in-law does achieve. Only when advised to do so by the Bolshevik Gerasim Lukich, a future divisional commander in the Red Army, does Pyotr

Ilyin agree to undertake the quite complex and difficult process of gaining official acceptance as a Cossack.

'Stop being awkward,' says Gerasim Lukich to Pyotr, 'let your father-in-law make you a Cossack...Our Cossack girls don't trust outsiders, they look down on them. Once you're a Cossack it'll be different. They'll respect you like one of their own. Don't be awkward. No, ask him to get things moving. Damn good thing.'[27]

Then Pyotr Ilyin, carrying out his 'party assignment' not only agrees to become a Cossack but, while still an 'outsider' and in civilian clothing, he deliberately takes part in a *jigitovka* and performs tricks on horseback the like of which no Cossack dared to execute in front of the high command. Scenes like this are unimaginable in *The Quiet Don*, where the rivalry at the races between the young Cossack Korshunov and the Russian nobleman Listnitsky ends, to use the words of 'D',

in victory for the good Don Cossack mount over the prize-winning St Petersburg mare, which fills the winner with pride and his whole village too. The same Mit'ka Korshunov is 'after' a fashionable young lady, the daughter of a wealthy Russian, Mokhov, (an 'outsider' by birth) who lives locally. The adroit Cossack and his venerable grandfather (Grishaka) are quite convinced that the girl's father 'must consider it an honour' that his daughter is being courted by a Cossack.[28]

Briefly speaking, although the 'outsiders' in *The Quiet Don* live cheek-by-jowl with the Cossacks they are none the less separated from them by a seemingly unbridgeable abyss. Not only are they unable to do anything to bring a better sort of life to the Don, they are in fact more likely to ruin the Don Cossack way of life which is so dear to the author. (It is to these 'outsiders' that the author of the epic refers when speaking of the 'evil of tall weeds and hooves' which is encroaching from all sides and undoing, choking, the Cossack people.)

The Cossack peasant at work: joy and celebration

Most Russian writers early in the twentieth century depicted peasant work as hard labour, wearisome servitude, a cruel necessity of their existence. In *The Quiet Don*, or at least in its first parts, we see something quite different. Almost any work performed by the Cossack peasant is shown as a celebration, a great joy. The author has his own peculiar cult of labour and the land. In the earliest chapters of the novel we read,

After Whitsuntide the haymaking began. From early morning the meadow blossomed with the women's skirts, brightly embroidered aprons and coloured scarves. The whole village went out together to mow. Reapers and rakers alike dressed up as if it were an annual holiday. This was how it had been done from ancient times.[29]

Between battles in the First World War and during the Civil War the Cossacks' first thoughts are for their homes and their work.

Sometimes he [Grigori] imagined himself getting ready for the spring, preparing the harrows and the carts, weaving mangers out of willow and then, with the earth uncovered and dried out, driving out on to the steppe. His hands were aching for some hard work and how they would grip the plough! He would follow behind, feeling its life, its beating and bumping about. He imagined himself drinking in the sweet scent of the new grass and the black earth newly turned by the blade . . . how his heart warmed![30]

The author's encyclopaedic knowledge of the Don Cossacks and their region

One is struck by the author's encyclopaedic and precise knowledge about everything concerned with the Don Cossacks. He knows all there is to know about every last stratum of Cossack society and gives us an exact description of all Cossacks, young and old, officers and other ranks. He presents a splendid picture of village intellectuals meeting together at the home of the merchant S. P. Mokhov, in the course of which he sketches in the very layout and furniture of the house. He depicts with equal accuracy the furniture and the layout of the home of the Listnitskys, a Cossack landowning family; he gives evidence of a sophisticated knowledge in his description of the landowners going out hunting, visiting and so on. He knows perfectly all the subtle details of the demanding military training undertaken by the Cossacks, and their active service, their military assemblies in the summer and that special atmosphere within Cossack companies which did not exist in other, non-Cossack, formations. With a profound technical knowledge the author describes the movement by rail of Cossack companies and their movement on horseback, the whole set-up and way of life in Cossack regimental headquarters, the inspection of horses on unloading, the process of mobilisation, and so on.

The author is closely familiar with the topography of various cities (Moscow, Petrograd, Novocherkassk, Rostov) and also with the geography of the whole Don Cossack region, its settlements, villages and stations.

The novel includes a marvellous description of all kinds of farm work, from sowing-time to harvest and the care of cattle, with particular regard to Cossack farming which differs in many respects from that of peasants on the Don and in other Russian regions. The author of *The Quiet Don* knows the weather signs and all the scents associated with Cossack work and domesticity. He shows himself an expert both on Don Cossack steppe-land herbs and their therapeutic properties, especially in the treatment of horses. He has a strikingly good knowledge of all cavalry matters and anything else to do with horses, which are, of course, the great love of the Cossacks. The folklorist I. Kravchenko tells us that,

In *The Quiet Don* the reader encounters an artistic, yet at the same time ethnologically accurate account of various ceremonies, sending a Cossack away for military service, funerals and weddings, taking leave of the Don, and descriptions of Don Cossack clothing, accoutrements, embroidery, dances, song tunes, accordion-playing, the carved decorations on huts and gates, embossed patterns on weaponry, etc.[31]

The author of *The Quiet Don* has a first-rate knowledge of the history of the Cossacks and especially of the period at the end of the nineteenth and the beginning of the twentieth centuries. He tells us about the part played by Cossacks in battles on the Russo-German front and at the same time demonstrates his sound understanding of overall strategy and the course of military operations at various specific points along the front. As for the history of the Civil War on the Don and particularly the history and the course of the Veshensk Uprising, here the author displays a knowledge beyond historians in the 1920s. We must also add that in *The Quiet Don* the war is depicted from several standpoints. For instance, military activity on the Russo-German front is seen through the interpretation made by Grigori Melekhov and his brother Pyotr and also as interpreted by Lieutenant Listnitsky. There is a description of the war as seen through the eyes of a student volunteer and recorded in his letter-cum-diary before he is killed in the first months of the action. It goes without saying that the author also possesses an intimate knowledge of the Don Cossack popular dialect, which he uses in the speech of his heroes, and also, to extremely good artistic effect, in his authorial speech.

After all this, one cannot but agree with one western literary critic who, referring to the encyclopaedic knowledge possessed by the author of *The Quiet Don*, as well as his vast experience of life and mature mind, gave him the title 'Doctor of Social Sciences'.

Craftsmanship of power and originality

In *The Quiet Don* there are quite a lot of badly written pages, even whole chapters, and there are certain feebly drawn and unexpressive characters. Most readers, however, simply do not notice these badly written sections, so great is the effect of the narrative power upon their attention, their mind and imagination. It is hard to decide where the talent (or, we can say without exaggeration, genius) of the author shows most strongly: in the skilful plot-construction, in the psychological depth and 'visual' impact of the leading heroes and episodic characters alike, in the rich style of the dialogues, in the epic power of the battle scenes, in the love scenes with their obvious passion and yet propriety, in the pictures of nature, or in the unobtrusive humour.

A master of detail, the author of *The Quiet Don* achieves maximum expressiveness while using a minimum of words. The language of *The Quiet Don* is, of course, unique. The author has a first-rate knowledge of the Don Cossack dialect and he uses it with remarkable skill in the speeches of his heroes and when he is speaking as an author. However, he also has a knowledgeable command of all other aspects of Russian vocabulary and style. He renders with great accuracy the speech of many different people, simple Cossacks and the nobility (the Listnitskys), old Russian generals and Bolshevik agitators, the rural intelligentsia, speech strongly laced with Ukrainian, and so on.

In both its speech and its characters *The Quiet Don* shows the clear and profound influence of Tolstoy (the obvious parallels between Anna Karenina and Aksinya, between the doubts of Grigori Melekhov killing for the first time in battle and similar states experienced by Nikolay Rostov, etc.), Turgenev (especially in the landscapes), Chekhov and Bunin. The author also knows his Blok and Merezhkovsky. Nevertheless he possesses many distinctive features which allow us to single out this great and original prose writer from among his compatriot authors.

First and foremost we have, of course, that Don Cossack dialect so skilfully used by author and heroes alike. We must agree with L. Yakimenko that the language of *The Quiet Don* is 'one of the amazing phenomena of Russian literature, even world literature in the twentieth century', that the author of this novel was 'the first since Pushkin to draw with such power on the inexhaustible treasure-house of the colloquial language spoken by ordinary people, so rich in poetry and folklore'.[32]

The descriptions of nature in *The Quiet Don* are not only bright and expressive, they are not only linked to events occurring in the lives of the Don Cossacks and especially the heroes of the novel. The greatest single peculiarity of *The Quiet Don* in this respect is the author's ability to see nature actually through the eyes of a peasant farmer or a Cossack warrior. For example, this is how he describes rain at various stages in the novel.

The wind scattered tiny raindrops sparingly, as if strewing alms upon the black palms of the land.

Burdened by the vernal warmth the land was being sown by the first seeds of rain.

The sieve-scattered rain drummed drowsily on the canvas roof of the booth.

The sky, bright and stiff, had been washed clean by the rain.

Here are pictures of storms on the Don:

Storm clouds began to build up thickly across the Don. Despite the dry crack and rolling boom of thunder no rain fell upon the blazing, burning-hot ground. Free-wheeling lightning split the sky into angular blue slices.

Lightning ploughed an oblique line through the black earth on the dark hill of storm-clouds, the silence gathered and gathered, and somewhere far away the thunder gave a warning rumble. A sharp scattering of rain began to flatten the grass.

Here we have a spring morning in March 1914:

The ginger sun brought a gentle warmth as it clung to the thawing hill, the ground swelled up on the chalky headlands that flowed down through bare patches to the water, and the early grass shone malachite green.

Dawn is described like this:

On the blue-grey curtain of the sky red-tailed dawn was pecking up the starry millet.

One of the most important properties of *The Quiet Don* is what V. Litvinov and L. Yakimenko term 'the realisation of feeling through action'.[33] This property was noticed by the very first critics of the novel. For instance, A. Selivanovsky wrote, 'In *The Quiet Don* the characters of the main heroes are revealed without detailed description of their psychological experiences. Sholokhov provides the clue to the psychological states of his heroes through their actions, their facial expressions, the tension in their bodies.'[34] The author places his heroes in the most dramatic situations, there are clashes between people of strong passions, sharp conflict occurs between different social groups, the reader follows the events described far from dispassionately, he endures the fate of the heroes in this epic. Yet the author himself, conducting his tense narrative with amazing adeptness, tells us virtually nothing of the sufferings of his heroes, while they themselves speak of them only rarely and laconically. We ourselves *see*, as it were, these powerful feelings which seize people; everything occurs as it does in the theatre where it is not so much the words of the heroes which tell us about their feelings, but the gestures, the mimicry, the poses, the intonation, and we forget that this is the theatre and not real life. This explains one of the secrets of the constraining economy of the novel; with a few phrases more can be said than in a dozen pages in other novels. The suicide of General Kaledin is illustrative of this.

Yanov, taking his greatcoat as it was offered to him, heard a noise on the staircase and looked round. Moldavsky, Kaledin's adjutant, was leaping down the stairs. 'Quick. Get a doctor.' Hurling his coat aside, Yanov sprang towards him. The duty adjutant and the orderly, who filled the small entrance hall, were standing round Moldavsky who had run on down.

'What's wrong?' Yanov cried, going pale.

'Alexey Maximovich has shot himself!' sobbed Moldavsky, collapsing with his chest on the banister rail.

Bogayevsky ran out, his lips trembling as if they were terribly cold. He stammered out, 'What?... What?'

They all shot upstairs, everyone trying to get there first. Their feet rapped and drummed on the stairs. Bogayevsky, gulping, open-mouthed, wheezed as he went. He was the first to bang open the door and race through the ante-room into the study. The door leading from there into a little room was wide open. From inside crept a winding cloud of acrid blue-grey smoke and the smell of burnt gunpowder.

'O-o-oh!... A-a-a-gh! My l... love!' came the unrecognisably ghastly and distraught voice of Kaledin's wife.

Bogayevsky rushed in, tearing his shirt open at the neck as if he was choking. By the window, hanging on to a faded gilt handle stood Karev, all hunched up. His shoulder blades heaved up and down in great spasms under his coat; he gave an occasional massive shudder. A dull, moaning animal-like sob from his burly figure all but knocked Bogayevsky off his feet.

There on his officer's camp-bed lay Kaledin, stretched out on his back, with his arms crossed over his chest. His head was turned slightly to one side, towards the wall. His damp, bluish forehead and cheek pressed into the pillowcase stood out against its whiteness. The eyes were half-closed as if he was drowsy, the corners of that severe mouth were twisted in pain. His wife had dropped to her knees and was writhing about at his feet. Her searing, frenzied voice cut sharper than a knife. A revolver lay on the bed. A thin dark stream of blood wound happily past it, flowing down his shirt. A service jacket was hung neatly over a chair by the bed; a wristwatch stood on the bedside table.

Bogayevsky reeled and fell to his knees, pressing his ear to the soft, warm chest. The stench of male sweat was as sharp as vinegar. Kaledin's heart had stopped beating. Bogayevsky, whose whole life at that moment was concentrated in his hearing, listened and listened with incredible eagerness, but all he heard was the even ticking of the watch on the bedside table, the hoarse, choking voice of the now dead ataman's wife, and outside the window the loud, coarse, doom-laden cawing of a crow.[35]

A further example may be seen in Book 3 of the novel: the scene where the Tatarsk Cossacks are arrested before being sent (as we now know) to Veshensk where they are to be executed by the tribunal of the 15th Inzensky Division. The arrested men fear the worst, but the author says hardly a word about what they are going through. They themselves also remain silent but we can *see* nevertheless what is happening to them inside.

A few hours later the arrested Cossacks were sitting around on the felled oak-tree benches in Mokhov's big yard, guarded by militiamen, waiting for relatives to bring them something to eat and a cart for their belongings. Miron Grigoryevich had all new clothes on as if he was going to his death, a tanned sheepskin coat, new shoes and clean white stockings neatly turned down, and he sat at the end next to old Bogatyryov and Matvey Kashulin. Bigmouth Avdeich was fussing about in the yard, looking aimlessly down the well, picking up the odd splinter of wood, wandering back from the gate to the steps, wiping his sleeve across his sweaty face which was as round and full as an apple. The rest sat there in silence with their heads bowed, drawing in the snow with their sticks. Then the women ran up into the yard all out of breath, handed bundles and bags to the arrested men and spoke in whispers. Lukinichna's eyes were full of tears as she buttoned up her old man's coat and tied his collar with a white woman's handkerchief. She looked into the eyes; the light in them had gone out like a fire covered with ashes. She begged him, 'Now listen, Grigori, you're not to worry! Perhaps everything will turn out all right. Why are you looking so down? For goodness sake!' Her mouth was stretching out in a wide, grimacing sob, but she pursed her lips with a great effort of will and whispered, 'I'll come and visit you...I'll bring Gripka too. You're very fond of her, aren't you?'

The militiaman called out from the gate: 'The cart's here! Put your things on it, move! You women, get over there. No good drowning the place with your blubbering!' For the first time in her life Lukinichna kissed Miron's hairy hand. Then she tore herself away. The bullock-sledge crawled slowly across the square in the direction of the Don.

Seven men under arrest and two militiamen brought up the rear. Avdeich dropped back to tie up his shoelace then ran like a lad to catch them up. Matvey Kashulin walked along beside his son. Maydannikov and Korolyov were lighting up as they walked. Miron Grigoryevich held on to the back of the sledge. Last of all came old Bogatyryov striding out majestically. The wind blew at him, fluffing out the ends of his white patriarchal beard and making the frayed ends of the scarf flung over his shoulder flutter in the air as if they were waving goodbye.[36]

Here is another scene. Stepan Astakhov, returning home after being captured by the Germans, arrives at Yagodnoye and goes to see his ex-wife Aksinya at the Listnitskys.

Once they were in Aksinya's room they sat down across the little table from each other. Aksinya licked her lips which had gone dry, and asked him, 'Where have you come from?'

Stepan was unnaturally cheerful and he waved vaguely as drunken men do. His lips still formed the same bitter-sweet smile.

'Been a prisoner...I've come to you, Aksinya.'

He then jumped up and made an absurd fuss pulling a little parcel out of his pocket, wrenching the cloth off it with his fingers trembling uncontrollably and extracting a woman's silver wristwatch and a ring with a cheap-looking blue stone in it. He thrust all this towards her on his sweaty palm, but Aksinya could not take her eyes off this alien face twisting itself into a humble smile.

'Take it. I've kept it for you. We did used to live together...'

'Why me? Wait a minute...' Aksinya formed the words with numbed lips.

'Take it...Don't insult me...We've got to stop all this nonsense...'

Aksinya put up her hand, rose and walked over to the stove.

'They told me you'd had it...'

'You'd have been glad?'

Without replying she looked at her husband, taking in the whole man from head to foot and she needlessly straightened the folds of her neatly ironed skirt. Then, putting her hands behind her back, she said, 'You sent Anikushka's old woman to see me, didn't you?...She said you wanted me back...to live...'

'Will you come?' Stepan broke in.

'No'. Aksinya's voice had a dry ring. 'I'm not coming back.'

'Why not?'

'I've got used to living without you...Besides it's just too late now.'

'But I want to get down to some farming again. On the way back from Germany – and while I was there – I never stopped thinking about it ...What are you going to do, Aksinya? Grigori's left you...Maybe you've got somebody else? I did hear something about you and the Listnitsky lad...is it true?'

The blood rushed to Aksinya's burning cheeks, her eyes drooped with shame and tears squeezed out from under her eyelids.

'Yes, it's true. I do live with him now.'

'I'm not blaming you,' Stepan said, suddenly alarmed. 'I only said it because I thought perhaps you hadn't decided how you were going to go on living. He'll not want you for long. You're just a bit of fun. Your eyes have got wrinkles under them...He'll leave you. He'll get bored and send you away. Where will you go then? Aren't you fed up living like a serf? Look at this, I've brought some money back. When the war's over we'll have a good life. I thought we might get together again. I want to forget the past...'

'Why didn't you think of that before, Styopa my dear old friend?' Aksinya said, with merrily shining eyes and a trembling voice. She came away from the stove and leaned across the table. 'Why didn't you think of that before? When you trampled my life into the dust? It was you who made me go to Grishka...You dried me up inside. Can't you remember what you did?'

'I haven't come here to have a showdown. You...how do you know this hasn't made me ill? Don't you think I might have remembered it all while I lived another life?'

'Now you feel like settling down to a quiet life?' Aksinya asked, her nostrils flaring in fury. 'A bit of farming? You probably want a few kids and a wife to do your washing, and feed you, and give you a drink?' She gave him a nasty dark smile. 'For God's sake, no! I'm past it...You said I've got wrinkles...I can't remember about having children. I'm

somebody's mistress and mistresses don't have children. Is that the sort
of woman you want?'

'So you mean "no"?'

'No. I'm not coming. No.'

'All right. I hope you'll keep well.' Stepan got up, twirled the watch
round in a meaningless gesture and then put it down again on the table.
'You think it over and get in touch.' Aksinya went with him to the gate.
She stood there for some time watching as Stepan's broad shoulders
disappeared through the dust thrown up by the wheels. She fought down
painful tears. She sobbed once or twice, upset by the thought of what
might have been, and wept for her sad life, once again thrown to the
winds.

The next day Aksinya was given her wages. She got her things
together and as she said goodbye to Yevgeny she burst into tears. 'Don't
think badly of me, Yevgeny.'

'Don't be silly, my dear girl. Thank you for everything you've done.'
There was a forced cheerfulness in his voice as he covered up his
embarrassment.

Then she left. That evening she came to Tatarsk. Stepan met her at
the gate.

'You've come then?' he asked her with a smile. 'For good? I hope
you'll never go away again.'

'I shan't' was all Aksinya said. She felt a tightening about her heart
as she looked round the ruined hut and yard overgrown with all sorts
of weeds.[37]

Few writers would have made the brave decision to omit the description of the night spent by Aksinya in tearful reflection which made her
change her mind. In *The Quiet Don*, however, that description seems
superfluous. The actions of the characters are depicted in such a way
that they subsume the feelings.

Of all the many other special gifts of the author of *The Quiet Don* let
us conclude by considering his skilled *portraiture*. The portraits of most
of the heroes of *The Quiet Don* are unmistakably drawn by the hand of
a distinguished master. The author singles out skilfully the most characteristic and enduring features of his heroes and also a number of small
but appropriate details to complete the image. In his portraiture the
author almost invariably uses *colour* and, following in the footsteps of
Leo Tolstoy, he also usually indicates what kind of impression this or
that character has made or might have made on those around him. For
this reason the portraits in *The Quiet Don* are not cold descriptions. To
an ever greater extent than the descriptions of nature, the portraits in
The Quiet Don are imbued with *mood*. Thus the author's language simply
burgeons with dialect, since he is seeing his heroes through the eyes of
their neighbours, comrades-in-arms, friends and foes.

This skilled portraiture shows itself in the earliest pages of the novel
when the Melekhov family is described.

Under the burden of the passing years Panteley Prokofyevich had put on some weight. He had filled out and now he stooped a little, though he still cut a fine figure as an old man. He was dry of bone and lame, having broken his left leg in his youth during the races at an Imperial Review. In his left ear he wore a silver half-moon ear-ring, and his beard and hair were as jet black as ever. When he lost his temper he used to go berserk, which had helped to age his wife prematurely. She was a plump woman who had once been beautiful but was now a mass of wrinkles.

The elder of his sons, Pyotr, now married, took after his mother. He was a small, snub-nosed chap with a shock of flaxen hair and brown eyes. The younger son, Grigori, however, looked like his father. Although six years younger than Pyotr he was half a head taller. He had his father's prominent hooked nose. His eyes were like almonds dyed blue under slightly slanted slits. His ruddy brown skin was stretched tight over flat, angular cheek-bones. Grigori even shared his father's stoop, and they both had the same rather untamed look about them, even when they smiled.[38]

Or take the portrait of Mit'ka Korshunov:

Mit'ka was walking along fiddling with the end of his metal-studded belt. His mischievous round eyes gleamed yellow in their narrow slits. His cat-like irises gave him a shifty, evasive look.[39]

Or the portrait of General Kaledin in the morning on the day of his suicide:

Kaledin was the last to leave his quarters. He flopped down heavily at the table and reached for his papers. His cheeks had gone yellow towards the top from insomnia and dark blue shadows lay beneath the morose and faded eyes. His face had thinned and seemed as if it had begun to yellow from decay. Neatly flattening a pile of telegrams under his broad white palm and without raising his puffy blue-shadowed eyelids he spoke in a dull murmur.[40]

The female portraits of *The Quiet Don* usually include a detailed and meticulous description of the way the heroines are dressed.

Aksinya

A cap embroidered with coloured silk sat flaming on her heavy knot of hair. The pink blouse tucked into her skirt fitted tight and unwrinkled across her round back. She was leaning forward as she walked uphill and the long hollow down the middle of her back was clearly visible. Grigori could see brown rings under her armpits where the sweat had faded her blouse. He followed her every movement.[41]

Natalya

Her bold grey eyes shone out beneath her dusty black lace scarf. A little pink dimple danced on her elastic cheek from the effort of holding back a smile. Grigori turned his attention to her hands; they were large and work-scarred. Underneath the green blouse which enveloped her strong, healthy body, her girlish breasts thrust out firmly, heaving in pitiful innocence, their nipples protruding like little buttons.[42]

In this way the author of *The Quiet Don* always remembers to include details like Ilinichna's 'jacket with lace sleeves', Aksinya's 'green woollen skirt', Panteley Prokofyich's 'shirt embroidered with little crosses', Sergey Platonovich's 'large kidskin boots' and Grigori's 'blue satin shirt'.

In the portraits of the Cossacks (just as in the landscapes) there are many similes which could occur only to a Cossack farmer or warrior. For example:

Smoothing out the yellow hemp of his tangled beard.

His cheeks were sown with the black stubble of a long unshaved beard.

A light-blue scar ploughed across his cheek and buried itself in the tow of his hair.

He raised his broad black palm, as solid as a horse's hoof.

He looked up sharply like a war horse at the sound of the trumpet.

Your neck has gone slimmer like a bull's after ploughing.

Even when speaking of people who clearly are not among his favourite heroes the author of *The Quiet Don* invariably mentions good things about them. Neither does he hide his heroes' shortcomings. The German writer Willi Bredel puts it like this:

With genuine objectivity he movingly depicts in bright and tender colours both kinds of people, their aspirations, their aberrations, their indecision and hesitancy; he shows them in their human majesty and their human imperfection. He reveals the origins of their opinions by indicating their social and psychological background. He neither judges nor condemns. He just shows us how life is.[43]

Take, for instance, the case of Miron Grigoryevich Korshunov, a kulak for whom the author has no sympathy and who is hated for his greed by every Cossack in the village. The author still has a regard for this man's capability as a farmer and his capacity for hard work. Although the Civil War demolished his fortune and eroded his power he still feels inclined to work.

In Miron himself a bitter struggle was raging between two principles. His red blood was in revolt, driving him to work, making him go out sowing, making him build barns, mend his equipment, build up his fortune, but nowadays he was visited more and more frequently by depression which gave to everything the deathly hue of indifference. His great ugly hands no longer seized the hammer or hand-saw as once they did; now they lay idle in his lap twitching those dirty fingers monstrously deformed by so much work.[44]

Miron's son is a plunderer and pillager who takes delight in the war and, as he puts it, would be happy to go on fighting for another five years. The military tribunal court martials him more than once for rape. Yet here is the portrait, quite typical of the author's method, of this future Don Army thug and butcher:

With a smile on his face Mit'ka padded over the ground on his light wolf-like feet. He had a lot of that savage breed about him, his easy, measured gait, the sly look in his wide-open eyes, even the turn of his head – Mit'ka never turned his wounded neck; if he had to look round he turned his whole trunk. Made up entirely of tight muscles stretched over a broad skeleton he was an easy, economical mover, radiating the stinging scent of health and strength just as the black earth gives up a strong smell when turned in a gully by the blade of the plough. Life for Mit'ka was straightforward, stretching ahead like a long furrow along which he was walking with complete authority. His ideas had the same primitive simplicity. When you were hungry you could steal, even from friends. If your boots wore out it was the simplest thing in the world to help yourself to a similar pair from a German prisoner. If you were at fault you had to go out and make up for it and Mit'ka did just that; he went out reconnoitring and captured and brought back half-throttled German sentries, and he volunteered for the most dangerous missions ...And although he commanded less respect than anyone else the Cossacks loved his happy, smiling way, his bawdy songs, his comradeship and straightforwardness. The officers loved him for his roguish dare-devil spirit.[45]

Personal involvement

A combination of fantasy, imagination and theoretical knowledge is the first essential for the creation of any significant work of art. The author has to have a sufficiently wide experience of life, a good understanding of people and sound factual knowledge of a wide range of everyday practicalities. All of this, varying greatly, of course, in mixture and proportion, will be reflected in his stories, novellas and novels.

It follows that the problem of whether it is essential for an author to have participated himself in the events which he is describing, or at least to have seen them, cannot have one blanket solution. There are genres to which this problem simply does not apply, such as the historical novel, a tale of the fantastic, the biographical novel. Walter Scott did not have to consort with Richard the Lion Heart in order to write his novel, Mikhail Bulgakov could not have travelled through Ancient Judaea, Stanislav Lim has not taken part in intergalactic flights, nor did Stefan Zweig hold conversations with Joseph Fouché. It is possible to write about war without ever having served in the front line or ever holding a gun. Lion Feuchtwanger wrote about the wars of Ancient Rome using nothing more than classical source material and his own imagination.

There are, however, a number of works which could have been created only by people who took a direct part in the events described. The pages of these books radiate the feeling of direct contact and the obvious personal involvement of the author. E. M. Remarque's *All Quiet on the Western Front* could have been written only by a man who had seen action in the First World War. Viktor Nekrasov's *In the Trenches of Stalingrad* could have been created only by a man who saw action in the Second World War. Tvardovsky's *Vasiliy Tyorkin*, which recounts the exploits of a private in the Russian army, could have been written only by a poet who, if he did not take part directly in any battles, did at least work throughout the war for the military press. Only an ex-detainee could have produced a story like *One day in the Life of Ivan Denisovich*. *The Quiet Don* clearly belongs to this class of literature. The sensation that the author himself has seen the Don clear itself of ice many times over, has saddled a horse, built up stooks of hay, dug and sown the Don Cossack soil, that he knows every nook and cranny of a Cossack hut, merchant's house or landowner's country seat – this sensation never leaves the reader. Something else that never leaves him is the certainty that the author did visit the front lines during the First World War, 'knocked about' in those heated goods vans, trod the roads to the front, found himself under fire and took part in the civil strife on the Don in February and October. Pictures like those rising before the reader of *The Quiet Don* could not possibly have been created solely by consulting veteran Cossacks and supplementing their accounts with the aid of the imagination, or from documents, which were in any case far from plentiful in the Rostov and Novocherkassk archives in the mid-1920s. Most of the chapters on the war and the Veshensk Uprising could have been written only from notes taken on the spot at the time, only with the benefit of direct contact with real historical people, Kaledin, Kornilov, Bogayevsky, Alekseyev and others. We must allow of one further possibility, that the author made use of someone else's detailed memoirs and diaries. Even in this case, however, the author's personal military experience (though not in any particular campaign) must still have been very considerable. When writing *War and Peace* Leo Tolstoy used various (by mid-nineteenth-century standards, numerous) memoirs written by veterans of the 1805–13 campaigns. But we are at liberty to doubt whether even Tolstoy's genius could have enabled him to write such wonderful battle scenes, so rich in the very sounds, hues and scents of war, and such profound psychological descriptions of a *man* at war, if he had not had personal experience of the Crimean War of 1853–5. No doubt Alexander Solzhenitsyn used much memoir material written by veterans of the First World War when he was working on *August 1914*. However, Solzhenitsyn drew also to a great extent on his own impressions and experiences as a participant in the Second World War. Analysing *The Lay of Igor's Campaign*, Academician B. Rybakov rightly points out that the author of the *Lay* is

not simply an ordinary man of his times who happened to see many soldiers and to have the ability to describe them. He is himself a soldier of experience who has heard the cavalry thundering across the steppe and the wind whistling melodiously through the vertically strapped cavalry spears as the regiment rides downhill...The author sees not individual soldiers but thousands of riders galloping up hills and down valleys, drying up small streams, stirring up the silt in lakes. He knows how the ground rumbles and the steppe grass swishes when the Polovtsian waggons hurtle by, he knows the whole range of Russian weaponry and military armour.[46]

The same may be said of *The Quiet Don*. The ghastly scenes of the war in the autumn of 1916, the two-page description of the trail of corpses killed during the officers' offensive, the picture of the vanguard after being gassed by the Germans, all of this, together with many other detailed and expressive scenes could have been witnessed and described only by a participant in the war. The last day in the ataman palace, the day before Kaledin's suicide, the conference on 15 May 1918 between the Don Cossack Command and the Volunteer Army, these are detailed with too much precision for us to sense anything but the presence there of an eye-witness. Another passage which reads like an eye-witness account is the one in which Listnitsky recalls the last hours spent in Mogilev by the Tsar Nicholas II after his abdication:

His face drained of colour as he recalled with disturbing vividness that colourful February dawn, the Governor's house in Mogilev, the iron railings sweating with frost and the snow beyond them, spotted with dark red patches of light from behind the steaming frosty veil which covered the low sun. Above the steep slope of the Dnieper the sky was painted with azure, vermilion and rusty gilt; every last brushstroke on the skyline was so untouchably delicate that it was painful to look upon. By the gate stood a small crowd of Headquarters officials, civil and military personnel...A saloon car drove out. On the other side of the glass sat two men, almost certainly Frederiks and the Tsar, who was leaning back in his seat. His pinched face had a kind of purplish hue. Over the pale forehead the black half-circle of an Escort's fur-cap sat at an angle. Listnitsky all but ran past the astonished people who turned to look at him. His eyes took in the Tsar's hand descending from his cap in a salute, his ears rang with the noiseless movement of the car as it drove off amid the humiliating silence of the crowd bidding farewell to the last of the Emperors without a sound.[47]

This is the writing of a man of considerable imagination, a master of detail, but, first and foremost, a man who watched those events himself or else simply copied out the memoirs of an actual eye-witness.

The author's political sympathies

It is clear from the underlying logic of the story and the leading heroes of *The Quiet Don* that the author of this novel adopts an attitude of disdain, even contempt, for the collapsed Russian monarchy and for the Provisional Government which took over from the Tsarist rule. He shows himself to be decisively against what he considers the senseless imperialist war, he finds the ideals of the nobility, the generals and the officers controlling Russia quite unacceptable, and he paints a scornful picture of Krasnov, whom he sees as a man of empty rhetoric. On the other hand, he has no sympathy for the Bolsheviks either, especially those who were striving to overturn and transform the whole Don Cossack way of life which had been built up over centuries. The author's strongest attachment is to the ideals of the Cossack farming-class and the Cossack commune known as the *obshchina*. His political views align him most closely with the political platform of the Cossack version of working-class populism. It may be supposed that this author had greatest sympathy for the idea of re-establishing popular Cossack self-rule and partial autonomy for the Don region, but essentially within a united Russia.

The author of the epic is a bitter opponent of the exploitation of the Cossacks through commercial capitalism (as personified by Mokhov), and he relishes the troubles which come to Mokhov and the Listnitskys after the February Revolution. Yet he himself is no revolutionary; the elemental inundation caused by revolution produces anxiety in him and in the ordinary Cossacks whom he is depicting:

'Serve the bastards right!'
  'Does that mean us Cossacks have had it?'
  'Here we are getting up strikes and the Germans are getting nearer to St Petersburg all the time.'
  'Once they get talking about equality, all it means is that they want us cut down to the level of the peasants.'
  'Hey, do you think they'll take over our bits of land?'[48]

It is no accident that when a meeting is called in Tatarsk to discuss the downfall of the autocracy the main speaker is 'the skinny teacher Balanda consumed by colossal egoism and tuberculosis'.

The Cossacks listened to Balanda looking down in embarrassment, clearing their throats and hiding their smiles. Even then he was not allowed to get to the end of his speech. A sympathetic, deep bass voice sounded out from somewhere at the front, 'Yes it'll be a marvellous new life, but if you keep on like that you'll not last that long. Get yourself off home, there's a breeze getting up here...' Balanda broke off in mid-sentence, drooped visibly and left the crowd.[49]

This scene has a deeply symbolic meaning. So too does the conversation between Sergey Platonovich Mokhov and the Cossack villagers:

Sergey Platonovich gave a forced smile and looked round the anxious faces of the old men who were feeling darkly and horribly depressed. With a familiar gesture he separated his reddish-brown beard and began to hold forth, fulminating against no-one in particular. 'Now you old fellows, you see what Russia has come to. You are being brought down to the level of the peasants, you are losing all your privileges and they won't forget the old scores either. We're all in for a hard time... Everything depends on who comes to power now. It could mean the end of everything.'

'If we're still alive, we'll see!' said Bogatyryov with a shake of his head, looking warily at Sergey Platonovich from under his big bushy eyebrows.

'You'll look after yourself. What about us? Is this going to do us any good?'

'How can it do you any good?' Sergey Platonovich spat out.

'New government...it might stop the war. Mightn't it?'[50]

It turns out, of course that Mokhov's misgivings are well founded; before long he has to flee from the Don and follow his nose to freedom. But old Bogatyryov's hopes come to nothing. Within a year the Don becomes the setting for a most vicious civil war and Bogatyryov himself is shot by the incoming Bolsheviks, one name on a list drawn up by the Tatarsk revolutionary committee.

We shall speak further of the political views of the author of *The Quiet Don* in the following chapter. For the moment, however, it is important to note that these very political sympathies were what determined the choice of the main hero, Grigori Melekhov, a man from a working-class Cossack family, proud to be a Cossack, jealous of all Cossack habits and traditions. The character of Grigori and the ideas of the author also give a better understanding of other characters, such as the two Grishkin 'friends-and-foes' (an expression borrowed from 'D') and, later on, the brothers-in-law Mikhail Koshevoy and Mit'ka Korshunov. The histories and destinies of the three young Cossacks, Grigori, Mikhail and Mit'ka, form the vital pivot around which turns the whole grandiose epic under consideration. Setting aside all forms of political journalism, it is in the characterisation of these three personages that we can trace precisely both the personal and political sympathies of the author.

While they are still only youngsters who have not yet started military service proper, Grigori, Mikhail and Mit'ka are already quite different in outlook.

In Grigori the author emphasises not only his rather wild attractiveness but also his capacity for hard work, his attachment to the soil, horses and farming. Grigori is bold and independent, he has a height-

44

ened sense of fairness and complete self-confidence. He may be untamed and hot-tempered but he is capable also of deep and strong feeling. He goes to Aksinya scorning village gossip, and even Stepan Astakhov with his 'iron fists'. Yet even his love for Aksinya, which soon causes him to leave his own family, cannot exceed his love for the soil, his native Don Cossack steppe-land. 'I shall never move from the land', he tells Aksinya when she invites him to go off to the mines where her uncle will provide help. 'It's no good... Here there is the steppe, a man can breathe. What is there there? Engines roaring, coal burning and air thick with it. I just don't know how people can live there. I suppose they've got used to it ...I'll never leave the village. I'm not going anywhere.'[51]

We see before us, in other words, no 'vacillating middle peasant' but a nature which is healthy and whole, the best kind of Cossack farmer and future soldier. (He goes on to say to Aksinya, 'I've got to go and do military service again this year.')

It seems no accident that *The Quiet Don* begins with a description of the tragic fate of a Turkish woman, the mother of Panteley Prokofyevich, who introduced Turkish blood into the Melekhov line.

The Don Cossacks, as is well known, were clearly divided into two kinds, 'Upper' and 'Lower', a distinction which is mentioned briefly but inadequately at the beginning of Book 3 of *The Quiet Don*. In a pamphlet entitled *A Political Sketch–History of the Great Don Cossack Military Region*, issued by Don Cossack Army Headquarters in 1919, this subject is treated as follows:

From the very first the Cossacks divided themselves into two kinds, Upper and Lower, the former settling upriver along the Don, the latter downriver from the Donets. The Upper and Lower Cossacks immediately formed somewhat different life-styles. The Lower Cossacks intermingled with what was left of the indigenous steppe-peoples and created a special racial type, whilst living alongside Tatars and Circassians (in the Kuban) and being in perpetual conflict with them developed their particular character. Black-haired, of good physique, active, exceptionally warlike and reckless, the Lower Cossacks created a more complete and vivid type. The Upper Cossacks were of more homogenous Russian stock, actually related to the Russians who had fled from the region of Ryazan'. They dwelt at a distance from those long-standing enemies, the Tatars, Turks and Circassians, and therefore led a more secure and peace-loving life. They retained more of the Great Russian characteristics, light-coloured hair, beard and eyes, less active. They were also more domesticated than the Lower Cossacks.[52]

In this respect Grigori Melekhov appears to combine the best qualities of both the Lower and Upper Cossacks, the ardent personality, warlike nature and severe taciturnity of the former and the latter's attachment to the land and to hard work.

Mit'ka Korshunov is something quite different. He too is handsome and strong, but he has no attachment to the land, nor any restraining moral principles. He rapes the merchant Mokhov's daughter Yelizaveta, importunes his own sister-in-law Natalya when she comes back home after her break with Grigori, threatening to come to her during the night, and he mocks her grief. He is vicious and vindictive.

Mikhail Koshevoy is conceived and portrayed by the author as a grey, insignificant, undistinguished personality. He is by nature the reverse of cruel and brave. He comes from a poor Cossack family. His father was a barge-hauler for many years and when he died he left a wife and four children of whom Mikhail was the eldest. But Mikhail made no attempt to make a go of farming, his hut is unsightly and we never see him in the field following the plough. Here we have a clear glimpse of a secret thought of the author's, one that was widespread also amongst the prosperous Cossacks. Koshevoy, like several others among the poorer Cossacks, welcomes the Revolution because he hopes it will provide him gratis with what other people have earned by the sweat of their brow.[53]

Koshevoy cannot work up strong feelings even for a woman. Whereas Grigori continues to think of Aksinya all the time, even after what seems like a complete break between them, Koshevoy does not think of the Dunyasha he was courting before mobilisation.

'Life's funny, isn't it?' says Koshevoy to one of his friends as they sit in the trenches. 'When I think how many beautiful women there are in the world, my heart jumps! Just think I couldn't get through all of them in a lifetime. I could scream just thinking about it! I'd get on top of any of them, any woman at all – as long as she's a good looker... Otherwise, you know, they've got life pretty cleverly worked out. You get one palmed off on you "until death us do part"... and no good getting fed up with her once you've had it.'[54]

Once in the army, Grigori immediately rebuffs a cavalry sergeant-major who is renowned for his bullying of the lower ranks. He also rushes to stop the Cossacks raping the servant girl Franya and has to be dragged aside and tied up. War does not suit Grigori and he finds it hard to reconcile himself to the necessity of killing people. When Chubaty, instead of taking an arrested 'squealer' to headquarters, cuts him down in the nearest wood Grigori fires at him in fury and Chubaty is saved only by Mokhov's corporal who jogs Grigori's elbow. Nevertheless Grigori remains, in the author's words, a 'good Cossack', he fights with courage and 'worthily defends his Cossack honour'. Of course, war leaves its imprint even on him:

Grigori had defended his Cossack honour strongly, losing no opportunity to display selfless courage, taking risks, behaving recklessly, going in disguise behind the Austrian lines, taking sentries alive, riding his horse in true Cossack style and coming at last to feel that the worry about hunting people which had oppressed him early on in the war had now gone for good. His heart had turned hard and coarse like a salt marsh during a drought and just as the salt marsh absorbs no water so his heart refused to absorb compassion. With cold contempt he treated his own life and everyone else's as a game and thus became accepted as a brave man. He won four St George Crosses and four medals. On the infrequent parades he stood by the regimental standard redolent of the powder and smoke of many a battle. But he knew he could no longer laugh as he once had done.[55]

We have already seen how Mit'ka Korshunov revealed his character in the war. As for Koshevoy, he revealed nothing in the war and did not win a single distinction in his four years of service.

On his return from the front line Grigori goes over to Podtelkov's side. Wounded in a clash with Kaledin's troops he soon returns to his native village. He can neither forgive nor forget Podtelkov's execution of the officer prisoners without trial. But most of all he feels the pull of the land and peaceful labour.

He was broken with war-weariness. He felt like turning his back on all that seething enmity, that hostile and incomprehensible world. Back there everything was confused and contradictory. He found it hard to pick out the path. It was like walking down a boggy brushwood road with the soil shifting under his feet and the road dividing so that he could not tell which fork to take. He was drawn towards the Bolsheviks, he set off and others followed him, then he stopped and reflected and his heart hardened...He felt an urge to take out the cattle, to stack hay, to breathe in the scent of clover and couch-grass and the heady smell of manure. Peace and quiet was what he wanted.[56]

When the Cossacks rise in protest against the excesses perpetrated by the Red Guards pouring across the Don, Grigori and his brother, Pyotr, join their village company. With some reluctance Grigori stays on as a platoon-commander in the Don Cossack Army formed by General Krasnov. Mikhail Koshevoy serves in the same army but only after an unsuccessful escape attempt and a public flogging in the square. He hopes constantly for a chance to desert to the Reds. Mit'ka Korshunov serves willingly and with pleasure. Before this he has volunteered to take part in the execution of a Podtelkov detachment, for which he was made a senior NCO.

When the Upper Don Cossacks yield the front to the Red Army in 1919 Mit'ka Korshunov flees south to join the Whites. Grigori, who has already left the front line, waits on in his village. Mikhail Koshevoy not only goes over to the Bolsheviks but actually heads his village Revolutionary Committee along with Ivan Kotlaryov.

The new government set up in the villages of Veshensk and Tatarsk fails even before receiving the fateful directive concerning the liquidation of the Cossacks to win the sympathy of the majority of the Cossacks. We read in the novel:

A little group of men had gathered around the village Revolutionary Committee, David from the rolling-mill, Timofey, Mokhov's former coachman Yemelyan and Filka the pock-marked cobbler. Ivan Alekseyevich now depended on these men to get through his day-to-day duties for he sensed more sharply every day that a wall had grown up between him and the rest of the village. The Cossacks no longer turned up at meetings and when they did it was only after David and the others had run round the village half a dozen times calling at every house. They came then but they stood there in silence and agreed to everything that was said. The predominance of younger men was very obvious, but even they had no sympathisers in their midst. When Ivan Alekseyevich conducted a meeting in the square he would look out upon stony faces, alien, wary eyes and lowering stares. This made his heart go cold, a weariness came into his eyes and his voice faded into uncertainty. Pock-marked Filka once blurted out meaingfully, 'We've got cut off from the village, comrade Kotlaryov!'[57]

Grigori is another who does not take to the new government. He is tormented by one vital question: what is the new government going to give to the Cossack peasant farmer? With his typical no-nonsense frankness he goes one evening to the Revolutionary Committee to see his one-time friends Kotlaryov and Koshevoy and 'chew the fat'. Kotlaryov answers his question by saying that the new order will give the Cossacks 'freedom and rights'. Grigori finds his reply unsatisfactory. He interrupts them:

That's what they said in 1917. Do you have to think up something new now? Are they giving us land? Are they giving us freedom? Equality? We've got bags of land already. We don't need any more freedom or people will be murdering each other in the streets. We used to choose our own ataman, now he gets planted on us...this government won't bring us anything but trouble! Give power to the muzhiks, they need it. We don't even need generals. Communists, generals – they're just yokes round our necks...You talk about equality. The Bolsheviks have used that to fool the ignorant people...Where is this equality? What about the Red Army? They marched through our village. Commanders wearing chrome leather boots, your ordinary soldier in leg-rags. I saw a Commissar, he was all dressed in leather, trousers, coat, the lot, and the others don't have enough for a pair of shoes. We've had a year with them in power, they've got well dug in now – where's the equality gone?

Neither Kotlaryov nor Koshevoy can give Grigori an answer.

'What you are saying is counter-revolutionary talk!' said Ivan Alekseyevich icily but without looking up at him. 'You won't get me in your furrow. I won't break you either. I've not seen you for a good while. I won't hide my feelings – you're not the same man. You are an enemy of Soviet rule.'

'I never expected that of you...So, if I so much as think about this rule I'm a counter-revolutionary, am I? That makes me a Constitutional Democrat?'

Ivan Alekseyevich borrowed Olshanov's tobacco pouch, then said, more gently, 'How can I convince you? Some men get there using their brains. Some listen to their hearts. I haven't got the words to do it because I don't know enough; I've not had enough schooling. I'm having to grope about a bit myself...'

'Stop that!' Mishka barked out furiously.[58]

It is as a result of this conversation that the embittered Koshevoy puts down Grigori Melekhov's name on the list of men to be arrested, and also that of his father Panteley Prokofyevich who has still not recovered from typhus. Only Grigori's chance departure from the village with the carts saves him from death, and they simply never manage to execute Panteley Prokofyevich.

The sudden arrival of Shtokman does nothing to help the Revolutionary Committee in Tatarsk. When Kotlaryov finds out about the execution of the arrested Cossacks and rushes to see Shtokman, shaken by the news, to point out reasonably that his piece of barbarism will alienate the Cossacks from Soviet rule once and for all, this is what happens:

Shtokman had so far apparently remained unmoved. He had rubbed his chest, covered with greyish hair, with his palm. Now he exploded into activity, grabbing Ivan Alekseyevich by his shirt collar, and drawing him up close. He did not so much speak as wheeze at him, stifling a cough.

'They will not be alienated, not if we instil our truth about the class-struggle into them. The working-class Cossacks will see it is in their interests to come with us and not the Kulaks. You...The Kulaks live off them, off their hard work! They grow fat on it! You...you pansy! You're losing your grip. You've got a soft heart. I can see I'll have to take you in hand! Numskull! A working lad like you blathering like an intellectual...Just like some lousy Social Revolutionary. You keep your eyes on me, Ivan.'[59]

These words spoken by Shtokman, and his other words elsewhere on the subject of the working-class Cossacks contain, of course, nothing but demagoguery. He knows as well as Kotlaryov that they have executed not just the kulak Korshunov but many genuine working-class peasants as well. When he learns of the conversation between Kotlaryov and Grigori, Shtokman regrets that Grigori has avoided execution.

That Melekhov has slipped through our hands, though not for long. He's just the sort who mustn't be left out of things. He is more dangerous than all the rest put together. Never forget him. That conversation he had with you in the committee – that's the talk of tomorrow's enemy. What's happening to you here is nothing. In the front line the finest sons of the working class are dropping in thousands! They're the ones we should feel sorry for.[60]

It is perfectly obvious that here the author's sympathies are not on the side of Shtokman, Kotlaryov and Koshevoy. This is demonstrated merely by the emotional impact of these pages upon the reader. For Shtokman does not merely regret that Grigori has escaped arrest; he orders Koshevoy and a group of militiamen to search for Melekhov and arrest him. Once he learns that Grigori has gone into hiding, Shtokman cannot contain his anger and rides out himself with Koshevoy and four militiamen to arrest Grigori in Singin where rumour has it he has taken refuge with his aunt. Every single reader of *The Quiet Don* must breathe a sigh of relief when he reads that 'the exhaustive search made at Singin produced no results'. Another occasion when the reader can have no sympathy for the Revolutionary Committee is when old Panteley Proko-fyevich is arrested when he has just risen from his bed after being ill with typhus. We are told that

he had turned grey and was so emaciated that he looked like a horse's skeleton . . . The militiamen gave him ten minutes to get ready, then took him away. Before being sent to Veshensk Panteley was locked in Mok-hov's cellar where there was a strong smell of aniseed. Besides him there were another nine old men and a venerable judge imprisoned in it.[61]

Once again we breathe a sigh of relief when we learn that they did not manage to execute all of these old men.

The Veshensk Uprising sees Grigori made commander of an insur-gent division. He fights with vicious skill against the Red Army troops thrown forward to quell the uprising. The Cossacks rush to support the uprising against the Red Army but they themselves do not want a return to government by the Generals. Grigori takes part with eagerness and agony. At one moment he is sufficiently embittered to order the execu-tion of Red Guard prisoners, at another he allows a Red Cossack prisoner to go off home who was due to be shot. Learning that a Red unit including Kotlaryov and Koshevoy has been taken prisoner he dashes back to his own village to rescue the Tatarsk captives. He opens up the prison in Veshensk at gunpoint and then goes straight back to command his division in the defence of his home territory against the Red Army.

Koshevoy has also turned vicious and become embittered, though without any doubts or indecision. We do not see a lot of him in battle, but he does excel in executions and mindless vandalism, burning down half of every village taken by the punitive forces.

After Shtokman's murder and after Mishka had heard the rumour about the death of Ivan Alekseyevich and the Yelansk communists his heart boiled with a burning hatred of the Cossacks. Now when a Cossack insurgent came into his hands he did not think twice or listen to the murmuring voice of compassion. From now on he made not the slightest concession to any of them. He would turn his ice-blue eyes upon the villager and ask him, 'So, you have been fighting against the Soviet government, have you?' Then, without waiting for a reply and without glancing at the prisoner's ashen face he would hack him down. There on the spot in cold blood! He would then 'put the red cock' to the roofs of the abandoned huts, and when the frenzied, terror-stricken, roaring bulls and cows charged the fences of the burning yards and stampeded through the gaps he would pick them off at point-blank range with his rifle.[62]

Koshevoy burns down 150 farms in the village of Karginsk alone and is ready to go to his native Tatarsk and 'burn down half the village'. Arriving there he does, in fact, destroy dozens of farms, starting with Korshunov's house and outbuildings and he also finds time to use his carbine to kill old Grishaka, a centenarian. Here, naturally enough, he forfeits the sympathies of author and reader alike.

Even Mit'ka Korshunov, however, fails to command the author's sympathy. Mit'ka is in fact commissioned, but for his outstanding zeal as an executioner rather than for his exploits on the battlefield. He too ruthlessly kills off prisoners, deserters and anyone suspected of sympathising with the Cossacks or Ukrainians. Returning to Tatarsk following the defeat of the Red Army on the southern front Korshunov savagely slays Koshevoy's mother, brother and two sisters.

It is therefore difficult to accept as justified the charge of 'political objectivity' brought against the author of The Quiet Don by a number of Soviet critics. Even the regular editor of Sholokhov's works, Yu. Lukin, has reproached the author of The Quiet Don for 'objectivity' in the depiction of the White generals who are portrayed in the novel as patriots, misguided ones, certainly, but men who had the good of Russia at heart. Lukin asserts that, 'This is noticeable, for example, in the characterisation of General Kornilov because of his dilly-dallying which creates the impression of a certain "subjective integrity" in his motivation.'[63]

No, the author of The Quiet Don is not a dispassionate chronicler. He is a man of love and compassion, hatred and contempt. It is clear from the artistic fabric of the novel that the one character who does enjoy his sympathy is Grigori Melekhov, a man who is brave without being cruel, a Cossack farmer and a democrat to the last gasp, who stands opposed to both 'Red Commissars' and 'White Generals'. The fact that this hero who comes closest to the author in his politics turns out to be a loser, that he is brought to ruin and destruction by the end of the epic, is perceived by the reader not as an illustration of the 'incorrectness' of the middle Cossack line, not as the result of Grigori's searching unnecessarily for a 'third road', but as the author's affirmation of a tragic *historical truth*.

When, in the winter of 1919–20, the Red Army re-occupies the Don region after overrunning the thinned-out ranks of the Don Cossack and Volunteer Armies in the Kuban, Koshevoy returns to Tatarsk as chairman of the village Revolutionary Committee. The Red Army, passing through the villages and settlements, no longer burns down Cossack farms or executes Cossack people. Koshevoy, however, remains as embittered as ever. He goes so far as to tell Dunyasha, now his wife, who has reproached him for his cruelty, that her words are 'counter-revolutionary' and that they cannot go on living together unless she abandons this 'enemy' talk. When Grigori returns from service in the Red Army, passes a security check and goes off home dreaming only of getting back behind the plough, neither reader nor author can sympathise with Koshevoy, who persuades the village authorities to arrest him. Naturally the reader rejoices when Dunyasha manages to warn her brother of his impending arrest and he, in turn, manages to get away, although he now has only one course open, to join Fomin's unit against the Soviet Government. A year later Grigori, having lost Aksinya, again returns to his home. Great is our relief when we discover along with Grigori that Koshevoy has left the village and is serving in the Red Army, though most readers are already aware that returning home means certain death which is acceptable only on Don Cossack soil. For there is little hope that, despite all the previous ups and downs of his hard life, Grigori will finally be able to return to the peaceful working of this, his native soil washed so liberally with the blood of Cossacks, peasants and working men.

The author's general philosophy

The general philosophy of the author of *The Quiet Don* is a humanism which embraces all mankind. As we know, some Marxist theoreticians have made groundless attempts to prove that there is no such thing as this (which they call 'abstract humanism'); the only kinds acknowledged are class-conscious and proletarian humanism. The author of *The Quiet Don* distinctly disagrees. His belief is that humanism must embrace the whole of mankind and that so-called 'class-conscious humanism' is not humanism at all.[64]

Terrible tragedy descended upon the 'quiet' Don with the First World War and especially the Civil War. We see in the first two parts of the novel a village of more than 300 farms 'overweight' from the rich harvest, one which could mobilise when called upon two or three companies of healthy young Cossack soldiers; whereas in the concluding chapters of the epic we look upon a ruined, starving village to which only a few dozen Cossacks return from their innumerable battles. The wars have seen off many old men and infants, a fair number of Cossack men and women have died from typhus during the retreat, some Cossack families have been completely wiped out in murderous enmity and many Cossack dwellings have been destroyed, neglected or burnt to the ground.

The Quiet Don overflows with violence and constant bloodshed; we cannot number the Cossacks who have been killed or the Red Army soldiers and sailors whom they have killed themselves. It is an accepted truth that the opinions of the heroes in a given work cannot be considered the same as those of the author. The majority of the heroes in *The Quiet Don* have been brutalised by bloodthirsty battles and for them killing a man presents no moral problem. Some even raise it to the status of a virtue. Thus, for instance, the Cossack Chubaty, instructing the young Grigori, tells him:

'You are a Cossack and your job is to kill without questioning...Every time you kill a man God forgives you a sin, as if you'd killed a snake. Don't ever kill an animal without good reason – a heifer, say – but do kill men. They're a heathen lot. Filthy swine. They make the earth stink. They are like mushrooms.'[65]

Then again Bunchuk, whose ideological motivation is quite different, says to Anna, as he passes the village and sees two Red Guards executing a captured officer:

'That's very sensible. They must be killed, exterminated without mercy! They won't show us any mercy and we don't ask for it, so there's no reason to spare them. To hell with them. Filthy swine, they want shovelling away off the face of the earth. It's no good being all sentimental, not when the Revolution's at stake. They're right, they're doing a good job.'[66]

Nevertheless, *The Quiet Don*, through its underlying emotional tone, delivers a decisive protest against murder and violence from any quarter and whatever the ideological justification. The artistic methods employed by the author are such that we invariably find it painful to recall all the murders which we have encountered in the pages of the novel. There are ghastly pictures of front-line Russian officers and men dying during the First World War, but the deaths of the Austrian officers and men are equally appalling. Naturally the author condemns the excesses of the Red Guard units which marched through Don Cossack territory in the spring of 1918. But he does not seek to vindicate the Cossacks who murder their Red Guard prisoners and throw their bodies unceremoniously into a pit. The author's sympathy and compassion extends always to those who are suffering; he denounces and condemns those who murder and torture. The officer Kalmykov who threatens the enemies of Kornilov with execution and is virtually a butcher, and the Kalmykov who dies at the hands of Bunchuk are depicted by the author in two ways, each with its own intonation. The Podtelkov who kills Chernetsov evokes obvious revulsion in the author:

Podtelkov walked right up to him. His whole body trembled. His unblinking eyes swept slowly over the pitted snow, then rose, clashed with the fearless, contemptuous gaze of Chernetsov and demolished it with massive hatred. 'Got you, you swine!' said Podtelkov softly, seething with fury, and he took a step backwards. A twisted black smile slashed across his face like a sabre cut. 'You've betrayed the Cossacks! Scum! Traitor!' Chernetsov's voice rang out through clenched teeth. Podtelkov turned his head away as if to avoid a blow, his cheekbones stood out black, and he sucked air in through his wide-open mouth.[67]

But Podtelkov's own executioner, Spiridonov, also evokes the author's revulsion; we are given an enormously painful description of the distress of Podtelkov's men as they await their execution.

We suffer every time we encounter a page in the novel describing the murder of a Cossack from Tatarsk, but the reader undergoes the same torment over the fate of the Red sailors killed in the battle of Klimovka. His heart goes out to Lukinichna as she implores Pyotr Melekhov to bring back Miron Grigoryevich's body from Veshensk after he has been shot. But he is moved no less by the Cossacks' savage execution of the captured commander of the punitive force, Likhachov. We share the sorrow of the Melekhov family at the death of Pyotr, who has been killed by Koshevoy. But the reader is incensed to learn of the excruciating deaths suffered by the Tatarsk communist Kotlaryov and his friends.

Another important aspect of the philosophy of the author of *The Quiet Don* has been highlighted quite properly in an unpublished article by G. N. Fein, who refers to

the comparison between the grandeur, the exuberance, the inconsistency in people's lives and the limitations, the poverty and schematism of all social systems and cerebrally conceived constructions created by men. The tragedy of Grigori Melekhov consists mainly in the fact that the passage of time and party-minded people endeavour to force his extremely complicated inner being into a clearly defined pattern of behaviour. The artistic logic of the novel precludes the possibility of compromise. The author can see no harmony in the world, for it is too fragmented for there to be any solutions to its problems which are acceptable to all men. Thus Melekhov's tragedy has a profound philosophical basis reminiscent of Classical and Shakespearean tragedy. In *The*

Quiet Don both the communists and those who uphold other political credos (the Cossack separatists, monarchists, etc.) are depicted by the author as over-schematic, doctrinaire and academic minds who dull popular consciousness and prevent the people from living. The author does not look at the people through their eyes; on the contrary he evaluates them from the standpoint of the people as he understands them. Thus it is that he places in the centre of his epic narrative a character whose nature is above all original, one who evaluates life not according to a dogmatic ideology of any kind but directly, through his own feelings and his own unfettered reason.

It goes without saying that this philosophy of the author of *The Quiet Don*, this outlook on life, is open to criticism. We cannot but agree, however, that this is the philosophical attitude which the author seeks to establish with every artistic means at his disposal.

Such, it seems, are the distinguishing features of the personality which created *The Quiet Don*.

3

IF 'THE QUIET DON' HAD APPEARED ANONYMOUSLY... MIKHAIL SHOLOKHOV AS A POSSIBLE AUTHOR OF THE EPIC

In the preceding chapter we attempted to extrapolate from the text of *The Quiet Don* the main distinguishing features of the man, whoever he was, who created the novel. These are, above all, a love for the Cossack people and a feeling of inseparable attachment to them 'in sickness and in health', a hostility towards 'outsiders' rich and poor, an encyclopaedic knowledge of the Cossacks, remarkable artistry and an exceptionally good literary education, undoubted personal participation in the events described, a celebratory attitude to Cossack farm work, a sympathy for the political outlook of the Cossack farmer and for the idea of Cossack self-government, a humanism embracing all men and an awareness of the contrast between the true lives of real people and any form of dogmatic ideology.

Working on the basis of these distinguishing features let us now attempt to answer the question: if *The Quiet Don* had been published anonymously in 1928, which Soviet or Russian writer could best be said to correspond to the pattern of the author's personality as we have drawn it?

The first possibility to arise concerns, of course, the young Sholokhov. We are at liberty to assume that no researcher or literary critic would have been likely to include him among the possible authors.

Naturally we ought to begin our analysis with Sholokhov's *biography*. It is of vital importance for us to examine the environment in which he grew up, to draw a detailed picture of his parents, his hobbies and interests during childhood, his secondary education and so on. Here, however, we run into our first difficulties and misgivings. Although Mikhail Sholokhov has long been accepted as a leading Soviet classic writer, we have yet to see any biographies or research works relating to him. About the early period of his life, his parents, his family and so on, we remain particularly short of information.

To judge by what little we know from the brief autobiographical jottings and statements made by the man himself and one or two pieces of research done by Sholokhov experts, we know that he was born on

24 May 1905 in the Veshensk village of Kruzhilin. At various times Sholokhov has provided information about his mother A. D. Chernikova. In the brief autobiography now kept in the archives of the Institute of World Literature it is stated that A. D. Chernikova was a Ukrainian, the daughter of a serf who went at the age of twelve to work as a servant for an old widowed lady. According to different data, also provided by Sholokhov, his mother was half-Cossack, half-serf. In a speech at a Conference of Ukrainian Writers Sholokhov also once stated, 'My mother was Ukrainian'.[1] His mother subsequently married a Cossack, apparently not a young man, who died soon afterwards. Sholokhov tells us nothing about the date of the death of his mother's first husband, but it probably occurred after 1905, that is after the birth of Mikhail Sholokhov who at first considered himself the son of a Cossack and joint owner of some land which belonged to the family. Soon, however, Chernikova married again and her new husband, Aleksandr Mikhaylovich Sholokhov, who was actually the boy's father, adopted him formally and gave him his own name. Sholokhov's father was an 'outsider' and for this reason any claim that the family might have had to land was lost. Sholokhov's father was not well born, neither was he of poor stock. With a little money behind him and a good business head he went from profession to profession. He was a cattle-dealer, he bought land from the Cossacks and grew corn, he worked as a salesman in a village-wide commercial undertaking and in 1910 he went to Karginovsk to work for a merchant, Levochkin, as manager of a steam-mill. One way or another it is certain that by extraction and social position the Sholokhovs were 'outsiders' and also that the formation of the young Sholokhov's character occurred away from Cossack people and traditions.

In 1912 Sholokhov entered the second form of his village primary school. Soon, however, the father sent his son to Moscow to be educated in a private high school. Sholokhov informs us that he was educated in Moscow 'for two or three years' (??), though he does not say which high school he went to. (There were not many of them at that time.) A very recent article makes it clear that the nine- and ten-year-old Sholokhov was educated at the Shelaputin High School in Moscow.[2] However, none of the Sholokhov experts has published any information about those years, about his educational achievements, his appreciation of Russian literature, and so on. A Moscow education was expensive and his parents shortly transferred the boy to the Bogucharsk High School (Bogucharsk then being part of the province of Voronezh). At the start of the Civil War in 1918 Mikhail Sholokhov returned to the Don and spent a few months at the Veshensk High School. Then he broke off all systematic schooling. Sholokhov himself defines his education as 'fourth-form'. 'I did not get beyond the fourth form at high school', he once said in a conversation with V. V. Gura.[3] We know virtually nothing about what Sholokhov did from the summer of 1918 until the summer of 1920. According to the meagre details supplied by the experts the Sholokhov family kept out of the civil strife on the Don and the young Mikhail spent most of his time educating himself, especially reading the classics, Tolstoy, Chekhov, Gogol, and so on.

When Soviet rule was re-established on the Don the Sholokhovs moved to Karginsk where Sholokhov senior had obtained the post of management of the Procurement Office for the Don Grain-Requisitioning Committee and the fifteen-year-old Sholokhov became clerk to the village Revolutionary Committee. During those months Mikhail Sholokhov also worked as a teacher, showing a group of young Cossacks how to read and write. The young Sholokhov was also a keen member of the local dramatic society in which he served as performer and author, writing short verses and playlets which, however, have not survived. He also had to work as a docker. Like many others, Sholokhov took part in grain-requisitioning exercises. 'From 1920 onwards I worked and wandered about the Don region', he wrote in one of his brief autobiographies. 'I worked on grain-requisitioning for quite some time, chasing the gangs that ruled on the Don in 1922, and being chased by them. Everything went as one might expect. I got into a lot of scrapes.'[4]

However Sholokhov did not spend a long time requisitioning grain. In the spring of 1921 the NEP (New Economic Policy) period began and requisitioning was stopped, though in 1922 Sholokhov did transfer to Bukanovsk for a short while to work as a grain-allotment inspector.

At that time life on the Don was rich in the most vivid impressions. Nevertheless we must remind ourselves that at no time in his childhood, nor in the early years of his independent work, did the young Sholokhov ever work on the land, plough the soil, sow the seed, reap the corn, bring in the harvest, tend the cattle or horses. Even when he subsequently became a famous writer Sholokhov showed no interest at all in gardening or running an allotment. Many visitors and friends wrote later about his love of fishing and hunting, but no one ever saw him working in his garden or growing vegetables. Behind the high walls which surround his big house in Veshensk a large part of the ground is asphalted over.

In the second half of 1922 Sholokhov, then aged seventeen, went to Moscow with the aim of extending his education and starting a career in literature. However he was refused entry into a Workers' Faculty because he was not qualified by length of service. He was even less acceptable as a college student because of his lack of secondary education. He had to go down to the labour exchange. For some months Sholokhov was out of work and then finally he did get several jobs, as a labourer, bricklayer and accountant in housing.

In 1923 Sholokhov began to write short stories and satirical sketches. His first sketches, *The Test* and *Three*, were published in September and October 1923 in *Yunosheskaya Pravda*, and a few months later a satirical story called *The Inspector*. Sholokhov excluded these first stories from his collected works and they certainly do not make easy reading. The stories are crude and derivative. Not only is the title of *The Inspector* borrowed from Gogol; so is the plot. An insignificant Young Communist worker is mistaken in a regional centre for an inspector who is supposed to be coming. The plot of *The Test* repeats that of Chekhov's famous story *Oversalted*. Sholokhov now joined the Moscow literary circle called *The Young Guard* and attended a number of literary meetings. He did not, however, get to know any famous writers.

In December 1923 Sholokhov returned to the Don where, in January 1924, aged nineteen, he married a twenty-five-year-old Cossack girl by the name of Mariya Petrovna Gromoslavsky. This intimate personal detail from Sholokhov's life-story deserves greater attention than it has generally received from the experts. In no piece of research or article dedicated to Sholokhov can one discover any information about the Gromoslavsky family even though it would be a simple matter for local scholars to collect such material on the spot. According to my own information, Sholokhov's father-in-law was not only a Cossack but had once been a clerk in a Cossack regiment, and was also a literary man, rather mediocre but by no means a tiro. His Cossack status is unknown but we do know that he did what he could for the White Cossacks in 1918–19 and in Novocherkassk he worked on the paper *Donskiye Vedomosti* which was edited at the time by the well-known Russian and Don Cossack writer Fyodor Kryukov. Gromoslavsky's work also appeared in one or two other newspapers and journals of the Don region but he was not an established literary figure. His name does not appear in any pre-revolutionary lists or reference works pertaining to authors and journalists. I am informed that his eldest son (Sholokhov's brother-in-law) was keen on writing and had a degree in literature from Petrograd. It appears also that Gromoslavsky senior returned to his home village in 1923 and became an officer of the Church, though not for long. Other sources confirm that he and his son I. P. Gromoslavsky were arrested in 1930 and released in 1932 (or early in 1931 according to another version). Sholokhov did all he could to secure his relatives' release, even travelling to Siberia to see the local authorities there. Gromoslavsky was at one stage elected ataman of his village but his career was undistinguished. In the Central State Military and Historical Archives there is a file on 'Village Ataman Gromoslavsky' (Fund 330, schedule 83, box 5389, file 32, 1915) which contains material concerning his misdemeanours in office.

When the Red Army was nearing Novocherkassk in December 1919, all military installations began to be evacuated into the Kuban. Fyodor Kryukov and P. Gromoslavsky withdrew along with the Don Cossack Army. No reliable information exists concerning the retreat of these two men. There is evidence that Gromoslavsky gave Kryukov assistance after he had fallen ill, and after his death buried him with a group of Cossacks just outside the village of Novokorsunsk. It is therefore feasible that Gromoslavsky was the man who took over Kryukov's 'metal box' containing manuscripts which is mentioned by Molozhavenko in the newspaper *Molot*. Other versions of Kryukov's death also exist, however, and we shall consider them in the next chapter. In any event Gromoslavsky did not go on down south, but shortly returned to his family in Bukanovsk.

For a while after his marriage Sholokhov attempted to live on in Moscow. From February to April 1924 the newlyweds lived in a small room on Ogaryov Street. But life in Moscow did not go too well and in May 1924 Sholokhov and his young wife returned for good to the Don region, living first in Karginsk then in Bukanovsk. Next door to Sholokhov's father-in-law lived a blacksmith who let the young couple a small underground room. It was some time later, in January 1926, that all the Sholokhovs (including Gromoslavsky, it seems) moved to Veshensk which remains to this day the permanent home of the writer.

Following the uniting of the Sholokhov and Gromoslavsky families the literary activity of Mikhail Sholokhov became more intensive and more successful. His story *The Birthmark* was published in 1924 in the *Molodoy Leninets* and then a number of Moscow newspapers and journals printed further stories of his: *The Shepherd, The Foal, Alyosha's Heart, Woman with Two Husbands*, and others. In 1924–5 Mikhail Sholokhov wrote about twenty short stories and two novellas, *The Farm Labourers* and *The Way and the Road*. Many of these came out in 1926 as *Tales from the Don* and later in the collection entitled *The Azure Steppe*.

All these stories are now collected together in Vol. 1 of Sholokhov's *Complete Works*. These early tales do indeed reflect the civil strife that swept the Don region, they re-create the atmosphere of the Don and the vastness of the steppe, they include a good amount of typical Don Cossack speech, plenty of original metaphors and some impressive, well-written scenes.

The days stole by stealthily like thieves...Spring was followed by days burned by the sun, curly-headed and grey from the thick dust of the steppe. Then it began to pour. The teeming water washed every last house in the village. The wind then flooded the whole greenish-white Don region with the honeyed scents of blossoming poplars, the morning meadow shone like a pink lake covered with the fallen blossom of wild apple-trees. Lightning-flashes winked at each other like young girls across the night sky and the nights themselves were as short-lived as fiery lightning.

(from *Alien Blood*)

The night had dumped darkness down all over the streets, gardens and steppe.

(from *An Enemy Till Death*)

Here is an extract from the first of the *Tales from the Don, The Birthmark*, which shows a narrative style typical of the young Sholokhov:

Plantain the colour of little mice curls all over the tussocky summer meadow and in every rut, caressed by the breeze. Goosefoot and dande-lion are crawling about thickly everywhere, lop-eared and overgrown. The hay has been carted off to the barns cooling in the amber spray of the steppe and the long smooth road has tucked itself away round the hill by the telegraph poles. The poles run away into the murky whitish autumn distance, striding across the hollows and gullies, and down the gleaming high road the ataman leads his band of men past them, a half-company of Cossacks from the Don and the Kuban who are against the Soviet government. They have been on the run for three days, like a marauding wolf running from the flock, along the roads and over the trackless ground, pursued all the way by Nikolka Koshevoy's unit.

They are a hard lot, they've been around, seen some service, and yet the ataman is thoughtful. He stands up in his stirrups, gazes out over the whole steppe, counting the miles between him and the bluish edge of the woods all along the far bank of the Don.

On they go, wolf-like, Nikolka Koshevoy hard on their heels.

These are lovely days on the Don steppe. Under a rich, limpid sky the ears of corn sway with a silvery tinkle. It is just before mowing-time when the full, ripe wheat is blackening on the stalk like the cheeks of a seventeen-year-old lad and the corn strains upwards striving to grow taller than a man.[5]

In several stories Sholokhov manages to convey with succinct expres-siveness the tension of the continuing struggle and the heroes' strong feelings virtually without having recourse to detailed descriptions of their psychological sufferings. Many of these stories provide indubitable evidence of the author's talent; they were noticed by the critics and were greeted with general approval. A. Serafimovich wrote a benevolent preface to one of the first collections of *Tales from the Don* in which he made a prediction. 'Everything points to the likelihood of comrade Sholokhov turning out to be a valuable writer.'[6] At the same time, as the critic I. Mashbits-Verov rightly points out,

in the strictly literary sense Sholokhov's first stories do not represent a significant achievement. Stylistically they are for the most part undis-tinguished, they are average, semi-realistic, semi-naturalistic narratives. It is not their artistic finish which interests the reader but the living material within them. Nevertheless even among these stories there are one or two which are truly significant in the literary sense (*The Azure Steppe, Shibalok's Seed*).[7]

Similar critical comments are to be found in many contemporary exa-minations of the work of the young Sholokhov. For example, Semyon Babayevsky writes as follows: 'In the early Sholokhov a deliberate stylisation is apparent, a syntactical construction which puts the verb at the end of the sentence. Later on, in *The Quiet Don* there remains not a trace of this deliberate verbal ending which is so imitative of Russian epic ballads.'[8] I. M. Kurilenko also properly observes that 'Sholokhov's first stories are gloomy, monochromatic, linear compositions designed to bring out the brutality of human relationships.'[9] It is this critic's opinion that these stories make wide use of the currently fashionable 'clipped' prose consisting of short sentences without verbs. The heroes' characters generally remain unexposed and there is no well-motivated conflict.

Although the *Tales of the Don* do include plenty of Don Cossack sayings, they contain absolutely no Don Cossack dialect, not of the kind which permeates *The Quiet Don*. It is interesting to note that when the young Sholokhov refers to the handles of a plough he uses the Russian word *poruchni* whereas in the Don Cossack dialect everyone would say *chapigi*, as do the heroes of *The Quiet Don*. This certainly does not mean that the language of *The Quiet Don* and that of the *Tales* have nothing in common. In both you will find expressions like 'the tousled feather-grass', 'the plates of his cheek-bones' and the frequent metaphorical use of the word *gadyuka*, an adder. In the *Tales*, for instance, we read that 'the road winds uphill like an adder', in *The Quiet Don* the mist descends 'like a headless adder', the front extends 'like a winding adder' over hundreds of kilometres, and a column of Kornilov's troops 'crawled along, winding like a fat, black adder'. In a recent study Anatoliy Kalinin reveals a number of similar phrases common to both works. A good example is the description of Grigori Raskov in the story *The Way and The Road* who 'ground his teeth in his sleep, turned over on to his other side and said sadly but distinctly, "You know, mate, death's nothing to laugh about."' In *The Quiet Don* Grigori Melekhov 'turned over on to his side, said distinctly in his sleep, "It's in Olshansk" and then stopped talking'.[10]

Similarities between two works are also to be seen in the attitude of the author to the events described. Thus, for example, in some of the early stories, as the first critics observed, 'class-consciousness is replaced by a general awareness of humanity; a biological urge, love for the living and the desire to propagate the species, defeats the concept of class'.[11] This is mentioned as a defect by the modern Sholokhov expert L. Yakimenko:

At times the young writer seems to stop to wallow in hesitation before the brutality and the drama which is occurring. He seems not to be able to see clearly who is right and who is to blame. At these points in some of the early stories we hear that ringing note of compassion and abstract humanism which gives rise to the idea that circumstances are too strong, that they are more to blame than the will of men.[12]

However, these occasional similarities cannot obscure the deep underlying differences in principle between the early Sholokhov stories and *The Quiet Don*.

The main heroes of the *Tales of the Don* are Young Communists, grain-requisitioners, the representatives of the new order. In the *Tales* there is no admiration for the Cossacks and their way of life. Only on one or two occasions do we encounter Red Cossacks. Otherwise the Cossacks are enemies, bitter and vicious enemies. Indeed Sholokhov uses the word 'Cossack' as a synonym of the enemy of Soviet rule on the Don. The Cossacks torture and execute the muzhiks who have been bold enough to seize land from the Cossacks or other owners (*The Azure Steppe*); Cossack gangs murder and hack down the grain-requisitioners and the chairmen of village soviets and farming associations. When a young Cossack stands up for the Soviet government he is murdered by his father or his brothers and in one story a young Cossack-born grain-requisitioner executes his own father.

This attitude to the Cossacks is in accord with the young Sholokhov's actual experience in real life which we discussed at the beginning of this chapter. This very experience, limited as it was at the time, is embodied in the *Tales of the Don*. It would therefore have been very odd to imagine that this callow Young Communist writer was incubating the scheme of a vast epic work dealing with the Cossacks and the terrible tragedy which befell this race of men devoted to warfare and the cultivation of the land, a tragedy due to end with their official liquidation by the year 1925 according to special pronouncements from the upper echelons of the Soviet Government. It would have been even stranger for this writer to have accepted the tragedy of the Cossack people as his very own.

Mikhail Sholokhov was undoubtedly familiar with many other aspects of life in the region of the Don. I have been told by one writer who used to meet him frequently in the early 1930s that he was taciturn and even shy at all meetings, yet lively and cheerful amongst his friends. He had a great fund of amusing and tragic Don Cossack stories, knew a lot about Cossack folklore, and often sang Don Cossack songs. It would, nevertheless, have been very odd to expect from a twenty-five-year-old writer without a systematic education behind him the sort of encyclopaedic knowledge of every nook and cranny of Cossack life that we see even in the first book of *The Quiet Don*. In any event there is no sense of an encyclopaedic education in *Tales of the Don*. These are in every respect

63

the stories of a capable, perhaps talented, writer, but a beginner. He is still taking his first steps in mastering the Don Cossack popular dialect and the Russian literary language. The portraits of the heroes are as yet very unexpressive, the dialogue is weak, the most complicated psychological collisions are simplified in their portrayal. In almost all the early Sholokhov stories the hero is acting in a tensely circumscribed situation but we do not yet see that skill in the depiction of acute psychological conflict which will be evident in the earliest chapters of *The Quiet Don*. Thus, for instance, the story *Red Guards* (known as *The Turncoat* in later editions) describes for us the split in a Cossack family. The father, Pakhomych, and the two brothers, Ignat and Grigori, side with the Bolsheviks, whereas the third son, the cornet Mikhail, supports the Whites. Afraid of being called up, Ignat, Grigori and Pakhomych flee to join the Red Guards in Kalinov. Grigori is killed in battle and Ignat and Pakhomych are taken prisoners. Just then Mikhail is eating his dinner at home.

He sat at the table and twisted his well-greased flaxen moustache. 'Mum, I've been made a lieutenant because of my work in stamping out Bolshevism. Nobody messes me about. One, two, and you're up against a wall.'

'Oh, Misha, yes, but what about our own family? What if you come across them?'

'Mother dear, like an officer and a true son of the quiet Don I must ignore all family ties. It might be Dad or one of my brothers – I'll have to hand them over for trial.'

'My dear son! Mishenka!...Where do I stand?...My breast fed all of you. I'm sorry for you all.'

'No need to feel sorry!' He turned his stern eyes to Ignat's baby son. 'Get that puppy away from the table. I'll wring his neck, communist misfit...Look at him with his wolf cub's eyes...Little swine, he'll grow up a Bolshevik just like his dad!'

When Pakhomych and Ignat are brought to the village under escort the following conversation ensues between Colonel Chernoyarov and Mikhail.

'I thought I'd better hear the decision from you, lieutenant. Naturally they'll have to be shot, but, after all, it is your father and brother...What if you were to take on the job of pleading for them before the appointed military ataman?...'

'Your honour, I have served truly and with good faith and I shall continue so to serve the Tsar and the Great Don Cossack Army...' He made a tragic gesture.

'Lieutenant, you have a noble soul and a courageous heart. Allow me to embrace you in true Russian fashion in honour of your selfless devotion to the throne and our native people.'

The sound of three kisses, then – a pause.

'What do you think, lieutenant, is our execution likely to stir up trouble among the poorer Cossack classes?'

Lieutenant Mikhail Kramskov was silent for some time, then he said thickly without looking up, 'There are reliable lads in the escort...They can take them down to the Novocherkassk prison...those lads won't breathe a word...But, people under arrest sometimes attempt to escape...'

'I take your meaning, lieutenant!...You can look forward to being made a captain. Let me shake you by the hand.'[13]

One need hardly add that this sort of scene has nothing in common with the depiction of Cossacks in *The Quiet Don*. Suffice it to recall the manner in which Panteley Prokofyevich, a Cossack of the old school, meets his son Grigori on his return home after having been wounded in the battle against Kaledin's men. Grigori is a Podtelkov man, his father a supporter of Kaledin. Nevertheless he rides to meet his son in Millerovo.

There was a sense of estrangement when he met his father. Panteley Prokofyevich had been listening to Pyotr and he looked sullenly at Grigori. His darting, shifty glances were filled with concern, the awareness of inevitable trouble to come. That night he asked Grigori a lot of questions about what was going on in the province and was clearly dissatisfied with his son's answers. He chewed at his grey beard, stared down at his leather-soled felt boots and snorted. He was reluctant to start an argument but he worked himself up in Kaledin's defence. At the height of his temper he shut Grigori up as he had done in days gone by and even stamped his lame foot.

But on the way home Panteley Prokofyevich cools down and just before entering the village the following evening he asks Grigori,

'Doesn't it bring tears to your eyes?'

'It does. Oh yes, it does.'

'Your own home means a lot, you know!' said Panteley with a sigh of satisfaction.

He was heading for the centre of the village. The horses were running downhill, the sledge was bouncing along swaying from side to side. Grigori guessed what his father was doing but he still asked, 'What are you going down the village for? Drive down our road.'

Panteley Prokofyevich turned and winked, smiling through the hoar frost on his beard. 'I sent my sons off to war as privates and they've risen to become officers. Why shouldn't I drive my son round the village? Let them all look and be jealous. My heart's going like mad!'[14]

Even Grigori's brother Pyotr gives him a warm, friendly welcome and, when they embrace, he only says, 'You were forced to leave then? You should have come home ages ago.'

Perhaps Sholokhov's greatest successes in the *Tales* are his landscapes, though even here we do not yet enjoy the high colours or that delight in the natural scenery of the Don which will emerge in *The Quiet Don*. The landscapes of the *Tales* are invariably arid and joyless. We see the 'thin mirage of the water-meadows', 'the heavy-browed frowning hills', 'the charred soil', 'a grey-haired, unwelcoming mound', 'the steppe spattered with the brown pimples of marmot holes'. One morning 'the steppe was covered with mist like a scabby horse' and 'the woods were hunched over the thin palisade of telegraph poles'. 'The blossomy meadow' is for some reason likened to 'the flush on the cheeks of someone eaten away with consumption'. Here, for example, is autumn on the Don:

The sun peeped out, embarrassed, from behind the storm-clouds with a pitiful, helpless air. Cascades of rain fell one after the other in a long line through the awful, clinging mist...The stooks had sunk down and were covered in brown dust; they looked like sick people.[15]

Here is a spring landscape:

A consumptive dawn. A herd has just passed along the levelled track. Dust clouds hover above the steppe wormwood. Ploughing on the hill. People swarming there like worms, bullocks crawling along harnessed to their ploughs.[16]

Here is a summer landscape:

There we lie, old Zakhar and me, under a blackthorn bush on one of those bald patches burnt by the sun on the hillside, looking down at the Don. A brown kite wanders along the scaly ridge of the hills. No cool comes from the blackthorn leaves gaily spattered with bird-droppings. Our ears ring with the burning heat. Looking down at the curly rippling water or the wrinkled melon skins just below, your mouth fills with a sticky spit and you can't be bothered to spit it out. In the hollow the sheep huddle together by the pool which is steadily drying up. They shake their back-ends lethargically, ruffle their trailing fleece and sneeze their hearts out with the dust.[17]

The critic Goffenshefer is correct in his judgement that, in the *Tales*,

Sholokhov deliberately 'lowers the tone' in his pathetic descriptions of the steppe which consist of a gloomy naturalism. The faded, melancholy, dirty-looking steppe – it is the backwoods rather than the true steppe – has a depressing effect. The people who struggle through their lives here die 'with a revolting simplicity'...We refer advisedly to a deliberate 'lowering of the tone'. In his *Tales of the Don* the author deliberately overdoes things, 'laying bare' reality with naturalistic emphasis. This is, however, nothing more or less than the price that has to be paid for literary polemics, artistic fervour and inexperience as a writer.[18]

Sholokhov himself, incidentally, has acknowledged the artistic imperfections of his *Tales of the Don*. In a conversation with K. Priyma he once said,

From the point of view of artistic skill and writing experience the *Tales of the Don* were certainly a trial run, a testing of the pen, a testing of my literary powers and to that extent they were predecessors of *The Quiet Don*. But you shouldn't look for pre-history where it doesn't exist. The only person who could call the *Tales of the Don* an artistic pre-history of *The Quiet Don* would be someone who can't tell night from day.[19]

But where and when did Sholokhov discover his artistic skill? He was, after all, only twenty years old when he began to write *The Quiet Don*. How are we to explain the enormous, unfilled gap which exists between the author of the *Tales of the Don* and the author of *The Quiet Don*? Sholokhov studies have provided no answers to these questions. Referring to *The Quiet Don* – and that included the first books which were published by the Don Cossack writer at the age of twenty-three – V. Petelin exclaims pathetically,

Sholokhov's talent is infinitely many-sided. In his depiction of men from the lowest levels of society and his revelation of their lives in all their fullness and complexity, this writer with equal power creates both tragic and comic natures, penetrates the secrets of life and death, descends to the deepest inner regions of man, and unfolds a broad picture of the events and circumstances of his outward life. He has access to the reflections of mature men, the deepest experiences of women and the world of children. We never experience the slightest doubt about the authenticity of whatever is being portrayed as we follow the development of the diverse feelings and thoughts of the heroes of his works.[20]

But how did all of this arise in a twenty- to twenty-three-year-old writer? No comment from Petelin, who continues,

From the towering heights to which a Soviet writer is raised by Marxist–Leninist thinking Sholokhov was able to capture real life in all its dimensions and to re-create the truth of his day and age in its genuine outlines.[21]

Petelin seeks an explanation of the phenomenal achievements of the young Sholokhov in his profound assimilation of Marxist–Leninist thinking, but another writer, Aleksey Bragin, prefers to turn to a religious or mystical solution of the problem. Recalling the years 1928 and 1929, he writes,

The young people and the intellectuals of Novocherkassk became engrossed in *The Quiet Don*. The face of the author, young and dark-skinned, seemed to peer out at us from the portrait of this 'newspaper novel'. When the third part of Book One appeared, entitled *The Cossacks at War*, the older people in the town spread their hands in disbelief. How could he know so much? He must surely have been an officer? There were arguments about Sholokhov's age and his biography. Legends grew up. Some people accidentally-on-purpose put about false and wicked rumours. It never occurred to the supporters of the old way of life on the Don that a miracle had truly occurred, for one can relate the appearance of a talent like that to nothing short of a miracle.[22]

Another supporter of the miracle theory is S. Babayevsky, who writes, 'One can only assume that Mikhail Sholokhov never sat up for nights on end reading a "Teach Yourself Novel-Writing". Everything he needed to know as a writer he already had within himself as if it were a gift from nature.'[23]

Of course, the mysteries of Sholokhov's artistic biography consist of more than the mere fact that he was young when he wrote the bulk of *The Quiet Don*. The history of literature includes a number of examples of a very young writer creating a significant work which made its mark not only nationally but even in world literature. The famous play *Die Räuber* was written by Schiller at the age of only twenty-one; he wrote another equally famous play *Kabale und Liebe* when he was twenty-four. Lermontov produced his most mature works between the ages of twenty-three and twenty-six, including *A Hero of our Time* which is one of the masterpieces of Russian literature. Other writers who began very young include Fadeyev, Furmanov, Gaydar and Ehrenburg. Before writing *Die Räuber* Schiller had, it is true, received a degree from a university (albeit a rather poor one) where, in particular, he had taken a course in philosophy. Lermontov was exceptionally well educated first at home, and then in a noblemen's boarding-school in Moscow, and he went on to study at Moscow University. Fadeyev attended the Vladivostok College of Commerce for seven years and spent two more in the Mining Academy. Furmanov and Ehrenburg were also quite well educated.

However, there are further examples available. Sergey Yesenin completed only a few classes at his church school where, we are told by one of his class-mates, not only was there no library, there were no books at all other than text-books. Despite this, Yesenin began to write original poetry at the age of sixteen. By the year 1918 when Yesenin was still only twenty-three he was an accepted poet, the author of many remarkable narrative poems and lyrics and when he performed in public, crowds of young people thronged to hear him. Mayakovsky wrote of his own 'education': 'chucked out in the fifth form. Knocked about the Moscow prisons...', and yet by the age of twenty-two he was a fully-fledged poet with his own inimitable style of writing. From a work on social choice I should like to quote the following passage:

Did Leonardo da Vinci or Shakespeare suffer from their relative lack of education? It seems not. Apparently the spirit of curiosity moved them more freely for being unburdened with a load of knowledge. Was either Leeuwenhoek the watchmaker or Hofmeister the bookseller excluded by his profession from doing excellent work as a scientist, any more than their contemporaries lulled by inactivity and educated by Wise Men? Quite the reverse. How often it turns out in reality that the sons of great people who have the very finest opportunities produce the worst results.[24]

I have one opponent who is of the opinion that Sholokhov's youth could have been nothing but a help to him in writing *The Quiet Don*. He tells me in a letter,

I am certain that a *talented* man who had lived in the city and several years on the Don between the crucial years from fourteen to twenty *could* have written that way. That is an enormously impressionable time of one's life, in which the personality is formed and character emerges. A man from outside is better able to evaluate and render (or portray) the society into which he has entered by leaving another one (the contrast of transferring!) than someone born and raised in it. Anyway Sholokhov did live in that society. And the conversation!! Nothing but leisure, nothing to do but talk! There never was and never will be such a conjunction of circumstances. You had speech and dialect and a huge mass of information (as they put it nowadays) invariably with its *emotional colouring*...I'm a Muscovite. Fairly often between the ages of fourteen and twenty I used to go down to a town in the provinces to live for a while and I must say that I returned to Moscow to my educated contemporaries *shaken* by the tremendous amounts of wisdom, colour, masses of material, and the surprisingly beautiful language of the ordinary people with whom I had been living. And if at that time I had gone to live in that country town I *could* have written something highly original and uncharacteristic of an educated Muscovite like myself. As it was I came away from the town for half the year or more and forgot everything as I grew back into the grey, monotonous, educated, intellectual society around me.[25]

It is difficult to accept conclusions of this kind. After all, virtually every first work in Soviet literature (like Lermontov's *A Hero of Our Time* and Griboyedov's *Woe from Wit*) were based on artistic generalisations drawn from their author's experience of life. This may be said also of the *Tales of the Don* in which there is certainly more talent than in the stories which Lermontov attempted to write at nineteen and twenty (such as *Vadim*). But *The Quiet Don* is, in this context, a distinctly different phenomenon. It is an epic novel, examples of which are few and far between in any national literature. In Russian literature *The Quiet Don* can be compared only with Leo Tolstoy's *War and* Peace. So far works with such a broad sweep written with such skill have been created only by mature writers who have behind them substantial experience not only of literature but also of life itself. There has probably never been an epic in the whole history of world literature written by someone between the age of twenty-one and twenty-three. Of course the lack of precedents proves nothing in itself. What matters most are an examination of the works preceding *The Quiet Don* and an analysis of that novel itself.

Approaching the problem from that angle we are obliged to state that so far there has been no explanation of the substantial ideological difference between the *Tales of the Don* and *The Quiet Don*. Sholokhov experts in our own country have yet to settle the question why the author of the *Tales* should suddenly have conceived and then created with extraordinary speed a novel dealing not only with Young Communists, Red Army soldiers and grain-requisitioners, but with the Cossacks. L. Yakimenko correctly points out that,

In Sholokhov's early stories there are virtually no middle peasants. There are on the one hand the poor, the farm-labourers, ex-Red Army soldiers and partisans, and, on the other, the prosperous kulaks. The conflict between these two worlds in the country is depicted by the writer as a clash between the more active representatives of two irreconcilable camps defined by class.[26]

In his book *The Way of Sholokhov* I. Lezhnyov also writes that in the *Tales of the Don* there are no Cossacks and no middle peasants with an ambivalent attitude to the Revolution. Lezhnyov continues:

Only in *The Quiet Don* do we see the appearance of a Cossack whose spirit is buffeted by social and psychological inconsistencies.
The ambivalence of spirit of the middle peasant, underacknowledged by Sholokhov in 1925, emerged with clarity for him at the end of 1926 and in 1927 when he wrote the first volume of *The Quiet Don*. This naturally prompts the question – what is the reason behind this dramatic change which occurred within a year or eighteen months?[27]

Lezhnyov seeks the answer to his own question in the influence which may have been exerted upon the young writer by the resolution on the peasant question arrived at by the Central Committee of the All-Russian Communist Party (Bolsheviks) in fighting off opposition from the left in 1925–6. But this is too lightweight and unconvincing an explanation. It seems strange that Lezhnyov, a literary critic, whose job it is to understand the nature of artistic creativity, when called upon to explain a dramatic change in Sholokhov's career as a writer, turns without the slightest embarrassment to...a resolution. We might well assume that the said resolutions of the Central Commitee compelled the young writer to *reflect* more deeply on the problems of the middle Cossacks. But this explanation is too insubstantial to account for the way in which these problems clarified themselves socially and artistically in the space of a year to the extent that Sholokhov was then enabled to write a genius's epic on that subject. We must also take into consideration our earlier conclusion that the problems themselves are decided emotionally and politically in a spirit quite different from that of the resolution referred to by Lezhnyov.

At the beginning of this study we considered what P. V. Paliyevsky had to say about certain questions of literary technique and form which critics, experts and specialists have to face in relation to *The Quiet Don*. These would seem to be anything but rhetorical questions. Paliyevsky, however, does not presume to answer them but avoids the issue by remarking that it would be ungrateful to pose questions like that about Sholokhov. Nevertheless the study of literature is unscientific if it runs away from such problems.

The question of personal involvement in the events described in *The Quiet Don* is of particular importance. We have already considered the comment of I. Lezhnyov to the effect that readers are surprised that Sholokhov, who was too young ever to go to the front lines in the First World War, should have described the military action there with such truth and accuracy. In an attempt to dispel the readers' doubts Lezhnyov writes that in 1914 the nine-year-old Sholokhov spent about nine months in Dr Snegiryov's Moscow eye-hospital. Some soldiers back from the front were being treated in the same hospital. Lezhnyov adds, 'The stories of the war told by those grown-up soldiers must have made a deep impression upon the nervous lad. He retained a vivid recollection of some of the incidents.'[28]

The ludicrous nature of an explanation like this must be obvious to all. The brief biographical episode Lezhnyov mentions did in fact find a certain reflection in *The Quiet Don*. We have in mind Chapter 23 of the third part of Book 1 of the novel which tells of the time spent by Grigori Melekhov in that very eye-hospital. It is here that Grigori meets the Ukrainian Garanzha who explains to the young Cossack how the current war is against the interests of the people. However, the whole of that chapter has about it an artificiality which hardly corresponds to the logic of the work as a whole. The conversations which occur between Grigori and Garanzha are out of character for September 1914 when the war was just beginning. Equally uncharacteristic is the trick apparently played by Grigori Melekhov on the 'member of the Imperial family' who makes an inspection of the hospital. A Cossack and recent St George medallist might conceivably make a rude reply to an officer but it is quite impossible that he could have asked a woman of the Imperial family for permission to 'leave the room'. The whole of this scene is false and unconvincing. No less unconvincing are the thoughts which are said to have swirled through his head at that moment:

'The swines! Damned parasites! Look at them, lice biting into our backs ...Are they the ones we did it for? Trampled down the enemy's corn and killed the people? And the terror we felt!...Damn the lot of you ...I wish I could send you there. Get you on horses, at the wrong end of a rifle, chuck lice all over you, feed you on rotting bread and maggoty meat.'[29]

In August and September 1914 the Cossacks were not being fed on rotting bread or maggoty meat. But, what is of greatest significance (and this is pointed out with justification by 'D') is that all these thoughts

71

have completely disappeared from his mind the moment he arrives home on leave. The impression is inescapable that Chapter 23 was a subsequent interpolation in Part 3 of the first volume which is written in a different key.

Lezhnyov mentions a number of military escapades in which Sholokhov had taken part as a young grain-requisitioner. But these had already been reflected in the *Tales of the Don*. They are too slender to form the basis of the pictures of grandiose battles and bitter conflict which follow one another in all four books of *The Quiet Don*.

It also remains unexplained how Sholokhov managed to portray in such breadth and depth life in the White camp, the Don Cossack Army, the Volunteer Army and the insurgent forces. How did he manage to draw such accurate portraits of the main leaders of that camp whom he never met in all his life? Written memoirs on that subject were, after all, scarce and not widely known, especially in the provinces. 'I am describing the Whites fighting against the Reds not the other way round; that's why it's so difficult', Sholokhov said in one conversation.[30] For a Soviet writer that certainly was a difficult assignment. When this theme was taken up by writers like Alexey Tolstoy and Mikhail Bulgakov it was understandable; they were writing from experience. For people who had ended up as émigrés it was quite natural to write novels about the White movement. An ex-officer of the Whites, Roman Gul, wrote an interesting novel, *The Arctic Campaign*, and the book was published in the USSR in the mid-1920s. The ex-ataman P. Krasnov wrote a number of novels and stories about the Cossacks after he became an émigré. Neither Gul's book nor those of Krasnov can begin to rival the quality of *The Quiet Don* but one does sense in them a knowledge of the relevant material. However, it would seem to have been quite beyond the capabilities of a Young Communist writer at the start of his career who had never taken part in the White movement to create such a vast canvas depicting the conflict between the Cossack insurgents and the White Army on the one hand and the Red Army on the other. Thus far our experts on Sholokhov have given us no convincing explanation of how it was that Sholokhov dealt so brilliantly with this assignment.

The *Tales of the Don* are utterly subjective. They have no trace of that calm objectivity and ostensibly dispassionate attitude which we have determined as a typical feature of *The Quiet Don*. How are we to explain such a *volte face* in the narrative manner itself?

Soviet literary critics do not stint their praise of *The Quiet Don*. I. Yermakov, for instance, writes as follows:

Sholokhov, as befits the writer of an epic, 'poses' nothing and 'settles' nothing. He calmly unfolds a wide panorama of life as it is, in all its objectivity, with his own special brand of logic. Then when he has read

through to the last page of this 'unproblematic' novel the reader per-
ceives that before him has passed real life with all its intricate and varied
set of problems, questions, delight and drama...Just as through an
ancient epic we can come to know the subjective standards and objective
laws of another world, the conditions under which people lived and their
customs, the poetry and wisdom of another age, so *The Quiet Don* is at
once the product and reflection of its time, a philosophical key enabling
us to penetrate the innermost recesses of an awareness of the historical
crisis with all its problems and questions in all their objectivity...Before
him have passed all the classes in the country, history itself.[31]

In 1950 when Yermakov's article was published it is doubtful whether
even Stalin's works were so highly evaluated in our press. Even if this
praise of *The Quiet Don* contains some exaggeration it is not without a
significant grain of truth. But how did the 'philosophical key' to the
secrets of a revolutionary age find its way into the hands of a twenty-
year-old youth with as yet little experience of life and a very modest
education? Yermakov makes no attempt to answer this question.

It is also a strange thing that this young Soviet communist writer
should hold the populist views and political sympathies which appear
unmistakably in *The Quiet Don*, apparently against the author's will.
Neither the many reservations made on this account in the novel nor
the subsequent utterances of Sholokhov scholars can obscure or transcend the artistic logic of the novel itself, the language used by its
characters and the general emotional impact made by its pages.

There is significance in the fact that many of the first readers and
critics who were far from being members of the RAPP group were very
annoyed by this coloration of the *attitude* of the author of *The Quiet Don*
towards the events which he was describing. In his appraisal of the first
two books of the novel which had just been published, the celebrated
Soviet critic S. Dinamov, a specialist in western literature and editor-
in-chief of the journal *International Literature*, wrote as follows:

Sholokhov has not gone over to the 'uncivilised' camp. He clearly wishes
to portray the Whites without any kind of exaggeration. And yet it has
turned out that he does exaggerate. Up to the very end of the second
book Sholokhov has failed to produce a single White who is distingui-
shable in quality from the heroes of *The Days of the Turbins*. Sholokhov
tells us that Kornilov is weaving the web of a black plot but all this is
not shown with the necessary shattering hatred. Sholokhov lacks the
white-hot commitment to class-conscious antithesis; his characters do not
boil with indignation in their denial of the enemies of the Revolution.
While fully realising the responsibility of these words one has to pro-
nounce them; this must be affirmed for the good of the future career
of Sholokhov. For him the Whites are enemies, but they are nevertheless
heroes. The Reds are friends but they simply do not compare with the
Whites. According to Sholokhov it turns out to be not the Whites who

committed atrocities but the Reds. He has not bothered to depict the Whites in this way; the Reds, 'a force disintegrating under the influence of criminal elements', he has. He found the patience to delineate the figures of Kornilov and Alekseyev, but there is no Red character in the novel to equal them in their roles. The Whites are thick columns, the Reds are slender piers. A strange indifference runs through his depiction of the struggle against the counter-revolutionaries.[32]

Another characteristic comment by Dinamov is this one from an article entitled 'Reactionary Romanticising': 'The strength of Sholokhov's talent lies not only in his ability to describe horse-manure in such a way that we enjoy reading about it...in his work Sholokhov presents our enemies to us and makes us...experience along with our enemies whatever he wants us to.'[33]

The author Nikolay Ostrovsky adopted the same critical attitude towards Sholokhov. Following the publication of Book 3 of *The Quiet Don* Ostrovsky wrote the following dedicatory inscription in his own book, *How the Steel was Tempered*:

To my friend and favourite writer, Misha Sholokhov. I shake your hand warmly and wish you every success in writing Book Four of *The Quiet Don*. I sincerely hope for victory. May the Bolshevik Cossacks rise and take our hearts. Debunk those over-romanticised heroes of yours who have shed the blood of the workers on the Don steppe. I greet you as a Communist! N. OSTROVSKY.[34]

Our critics adopted a particularly acrimonious attitude to the sixth part of Book 3 of *The Quiet Don* which describes the beginning of the Veshensk Uprising. Grigori Melekhov turns up not in the camp of the Reds, which was what many critics were anticipating but as commander of an insurgent division. It was due to the highly critical attitudes adopted by our 'internal' reviewers that the publication of the third book was delayed for three years. Sholokhov created quite a fuss. He argued, wrote to Serafimovich and Gorky, and organised readings from Book 3 in various halls. The journal *Na Pod'yome* contained an account of one such reading. The reading was followed by a discussion:

'What are the feelings which strike us in *The Quiet Don*?' asked, for example, one participant in the discussion by the name of Berkovskaya. 'It has to be said that they are not the ones we should call desirable. This is particularly true of the passage which has just been read about the death of White officer Pyotr Melekhov. After this evening I am going to be asked by the workers, "What comes next? What is Sholokhov writing?" What can I tell them? I shall have to say that Sholokhov was sorry for the dead officer.'

Sholokhov himself, significantly enough, accepted the justice of this criticism as he wound up the discussion: 'I keep trying to discover the root cause of my being translated everywhere abroad and the Social

Democrats' positive comments on the novel...The influence of petty-bourgeois society is taking its toll...I understand this and I am trying to battle against the spontaneous pacifism which keeps creeping into my work.'[35]

It must be said that under the influence of this kind of criticism subsequent editions of *The Quiet Don* have undergone a good deal of editorial correction and have suffered all kinds of textual amendment. For this reason our greatest interest centres around the text of the first edition of the novel. The most superficial knowledge of that first edition raises a lot of unanswered questions relevant to this very issue, the *attitude* of the author to events described in the novel and to many of his characters. We shall examine this in more detail in the next section, but one or two quotations are worth consideration here. (Words omitted by Sholokhov from later editions are italicised.)

Describing a meeting between the leaders of the White Don Cossack Army and the Volunteer Army the author wrote: 'Bogayevsky leaned on the low window-sill, looking *with pain and pity* at Alekseyev's *utterly weary* face. It was as white as a plaster-cast' (Part 6, Chapter 4. These omissions were made only in the editions of the 1960s). Of the meeting between the Generals Kaledin and Kornilov at the State Conference in Moscow he wrote, 'An hour later the ataman Kaledin announced to a hushed auditorium the *historical* declaration of the twelve Cossack regional assemblies' (Part 4, Chapter 14. The omitted word survived in all editions up to 1949). Every edition of the novel up to 1941 said this about General Dukhonin: 'Dukhonin, crushed by the weight of rapid developments *and realising now for the first time the enormous responsibility he had taken on by assuming overall command*, hesitated.' Describing the retreat northwards of the Cossacks from Khopersk and Ust-Medveditsk, the author wrote: 'The Cossacks of the lower regions pursued them and harassed them to the very borders of the district, *battling to liberate every last inch of ground.*' For some reason the October Revolution is constantly referred to in the text of the first editions of the novel as '*the upheaval in Petrograd*'.

The manuscript of Book 3 deposited with the editors of the journal *Oktyabr'* included the story of the Red Cavalry's entry into Tatarsk in January 1919, the moment which the Cossacks who had left the front line and their families had been eagerly awaiting. The Cavalrymen rode into the village. The manuscript said: '*The riders bobbed awkwardly up and down, shaken all over the place in the dragoons' saddles.*' The editor objected violently to this sentence. At first Sholokhov offered stout resistance. He wrote to Gorky, attempting to explain that he wanted the sentence in question to underline the inability of yesterday's workmen and peasants to cope with a horse and saddle. His explanations were, however, rather unconvincing. The words used, 'bobbed awkwardly up and down' and 'shaken all over the place', suggest a contemptuous attitude towards poor riders, the view of a Cossack who is himself a skilled horseman. In one of the *Tales of the Don* the same Sholokhov, incidentally, had described the arrival of the Red Army in a village as a joyous occasion: 'They suddenly saw them: a long snaking line of Cavalrymen coming down the road to the village on their bob-tailed horses, the wind rippling the red flag and broadcasting the sound of their voices, their laughter, the words of command, and the snow crunching under the runners.'[36] It seems significant that Sholokhov finally agreed to alter the description of the arrival in Tatarsk. The sentence quoted has survived only in the letter to Gorky which is frequently referred to by Sholokhov scholars.

The author of *The Quiet Don* never misses an opportunity to indicate how his various heroes sit their horses. Stepan Astakhov, for example, 'sat in his saddle as though he had dug himself in', whereas Shtokman, setting out in search of Grigori with a group of militiamen, 'rode alongside Koshevoy, bouncing about in his dragoon's saddle. The great bay steed beneath him was constantly restive, doing its best to bite the rider's knee.' Even in the four-wheeled carriage (*brichka*) belonging to Fedot Bodovskov Shtokman continually 'bobs up and down and sways about in the seat'.

The chronology of the Veshensk Uprising is something else which remains unclear. To judge by the first editions of *The Quiet Don* this revolt began at the end of February 1919. In actual fact it began on the night of March 11/12 of that year. Perhaps Sholokhov is using the old calendar, as was the custom in all the documents of the White movement. If this were so, however, one would have expected an explanatory footnote, especially since all the other historical dates in the novel are given according to the new calendar; for instance the Red Army breakthrough achieved by the striking force of General Sekretov and the start of the offensive carried out by the Red Army group commanded by Shorin, etc. (Part 7, Chapters 5 and 20).

All editions have retained the descriptions of Rostov and Novocherkassk when taken by the White Cossacks in May 1918.

Rostov and Novocherkassk, the rear of the Volunteer Army, were swarming with officers. There were thousands of them, speculating, working in innumerable institutions well away from the front, sheltering cosily with friends and relations, lying about in military hospitals with forged documents about fake wounds...All the bravest men had died in battle, or from typhus, or from their wounds. Those who were left had lost all sense of honour and conscience over the years of the Revolution and had skulked like jackals miles from the front. They were the dung, the filthy scum floating on the surface of those storm-tossed days. These men were the still untouched, unexercised officer personnel denounced and put to shame by the fulminating Chernetsov in his call to the defence of Russia.[37]

Again it seems strange for a Young Communist author to adopt *this attitude*, calling the officers who were reluctant to fight the Bolsheviks 'filthy scum', and referring to those who fought the Bolsheviks to the death as the bravest of Russian officers who had kept their honour and conscience. The reference by such an author to Chernetsov is incomprehensible. There are many more examples like these of an incomprehensible *attitude* adopted, apparently, by a Young Communist and a RAPP member.

All things considered, the personality of the twenty-three-year-old Mikhail Sholokhov is strikingly at variance with the author's 'personality-pattern' which might have been extrapolated from *The Quiet Don* if the novel had appeared anonymously in the late 1920s. If, for the sake of argument, our analysis of the text of *The Quiet Don* had produced *fifty or sixty* principal distinguishing features belonging to the author of the work, the personality of the young Sholokhov, to judge by the *Tales of the Don* and what we know of the writer's biography, would coincide with that of the author of *The Quiet Don* at no more than five or six points.

4

IF 'THE QUIET DON' HAD APPEARED ANONYMOUSLY...FYODOR KRYUKOV AS A POSSIBLE AUTHOR

In Chapter 3 we decided that if *The Quiet Don* had been published anonymously in 1928 it is highly unlikely that any Soviet literary experts would have named Mikhail Sholokhov among the possible authors of this magnificent epic work. In the context of this analysis what can be said of Fyodor Kryukov? Could the experts and historians studying the anonymous work have arrived at the proposition that Kryukov was the author?

We have already looked at some information about this man and the controversy which broke out in 1965–6 around his name. It is clear to us that Kryukov was a progressive writer, the main theme of whose work was the life of ordinary people. Despite this, Soviet literary criticism has maintained a stolid silence with regard to his work. For instance, in a textbook by K. M. Novikova and L. V. Shcheglova, *Russian Literature of the Twentieth Century (Pre-Revolutionary period)*, which is used on courses in Arts Faculties, Kryukov's name is not mentioned. For all that, at the beginning of this century Kryukov was quite well known in democratic circles both as a writer and a public figure. Although the attention of the reading public at that time was for the most part focused upon works by various representatives of Modernism (so much so that one leading literary expert at the beginning of the century, A. G. Gornfel'd, wrote, 'No one nowadays is tempted by simple, old-fashioned, honest realism') Kryukov did have his readers in Russia and on the Don. In 1911 Kryukov became an influential figure on the journal *Russkoye Bogatstvo* and by 1913 had become co-editor of the Fine Arts Section along with Vladimir Korolenko. Since Korolenko was the general editor and publisher of *Russkoye Bogatstvo* Kryukov became in practice co-editor of the journal as a whole, managing the Fine Arts Section along with A. G. Gornfel'd. These were the years during which *Russkoye Bogatstvo* strengthened its position as the artistic centre of Russian literature.

Maxim Gorky once wrote that Russian literature drew its material predominantly from the central Russian zone and ignored whole regions outside it, non-Russians and Cossacks from the Don, the Urals and the

Kuban.[1] Kryukov was one of those who helped Russian literature to fill that gap. His literary output was very extensive. No less than 44 works by this writer appeared in the 60 editions of *Russkoye Bogatstvo* between 1903 and 1917. Taking account of the stories and tales which he published in other journals between 1892 and 1902, his numerous newspaper pieces and also works published in the Don Region press in 1918–19, the overall total of essays, stories and tales which came from the pen of Fyodor Kryukov probably comes to not less than 200. Collected together they would fill at least 9 or 10 volumes, a not insignificant contribution to Russian literature. Despite this the name of Kryukov is not to be found in the Academy reference work *The History of Russian Literature at the End of the Nineteenth and Beginning of the Twentieth Century: a Bibliographical Directory* (Moscow, 1963) which mentions hundreds of writers many of whom wrote no more than one or two novellas and a few stories. Vol. 10 of the ten-volume *History of Russian Literature* (1954) is devoted to literature of the period 1890–1917. Kryukov's name appears neither in the general survey of Russian realist prose nor even in the section on the theme of the Russian peasantry in early twentieth-century prose, although a writer like I. Surguchev, for example, who also took no part in the October Revolution and who died an émigré, is accorded one-and-a-half pages. Only in the section dealing with the *Znaniye* library established by Maxim Gorky do we encounter a brief mention of Kryukov's novella *Autumn Furrows*. It says, 'F. Kryukov, describer of the Don scene, presents in his novella *Autumn Furrows* a vivid picture of the stratification of Cossack society and the antagonism existing between the poor people and the Kulaks' (p. 446).

Naturally, if we search hard enough, we can discover in Soviet literature a few more brief mentions of Kryukov's name. They appear in *A Description of Korolenko's Letters* (Moscow, 1961), a book by B. D. Letov, *Korolenko the Editor* ((Leningrad, 1961), p. 32), in the third volume of Korolenko's *Selected Letters* (Moscow, 1936), and in a selection of letters from Korolenko to young writers (*Voprosy Literatury* (1962), No. 4). But on these occasions only Kryukov's name is mentioned; there is no discussion of his work. Even in certain articles and sections devoted specifically to the Cossack theme in Russian literature it has proved impossible to find a mention of Kryukov's name, though references are made to Gogol's *Taras Bul'ba*, Leo Tolstoy's *The Cossacks*, Chekhov's novella *The Steppe* and story *The Cossack* and Trenev's novellas and stories (which are predominantly concerned with 'outsiders'). In some researches into 'Cossack' literature it is possible to find the name of I. Nefedov, a writer who died before the Revolution or R. Kumov, who died in 1919, and also the Don Cossack poets A. Leonov and A. Petrovsky, although in scope and significance the work of these Don

Cossack writers and poets bears no comparison with that of Fyodor Kryukov.

A short but reasonably accurate notice about Kryukov was included for the first time in the Soviet period in the papers of an intercollegiate conference held in Volgograd in 1963 in celebration of the hundredth anniversary of the birth of A. S. Serafimovich.[2] In a short address to the conference a university professor from Tambov, B. N. Dvinyaninov, told of the friendship between Serafimovich and Kryukov. These two writers were not only both closely attached to the Don region from childhood onwards, they went to the same high school and studied together in St Petersburg, though in different institutions. Serafimovich and Kryukov were colleagues in Gorky's *Znaniye* Publishing House and for a number of years both were correspondents on the liberal Moscow newspaper *Russkiye Vedomosti*. They met frequently and wrote to each other between meetings.[3]

In the Volgograd conference papers Dvinyaninov published two of Serafimovich's letters to Kryukov which deal mainly with the former's appraisal of some of his own works. In a short note accompanying this publication Professor Dvinyaninov wrote:

The tragic fate of the Cossack writer F. D. Kryukov may be compared with the fate of Grigori Melekhov in Sholokhov's *The Quiet Don*. Behind the complex and inconsistent character of F. Kryukov lies, deeply hidden, the social phenomenon of the 'Melekhov' syndrome. Industry, humanity, truthfulness, a love of his native region, the 'quiet Don', is combined in him with social instability and the lack of a definite place in the revolutionary struggle. His prolonged vacillation, his search for a 'third way' during the Revolution, brought Kryukov to a dramatic spiritual crisis after 1917.[4]

According to Dvinyaninov (whose evidence agrees with that of Molozhavenko which we have already mentioned) Kryukov lived on the Don in 1917 and 1918 and worked at a novel about the Don Cossacks.

A biographical summary of Kryukov's life may be seen in Vol. 3 of the Soviet *Literary Encyclopaedia* which went to press on 17 December 1965, that is before the publication of A. Podol'sky's article in the newspaper *Sovetskaya Rossiya*. From this it can be established that Kryukov was born in 1870 in the Don Cossack village of Glazunovsk, the son of the village ataman. After high school Kryukov studied in St Petersburg at the Institute of History and Literature from which he graduated in 1892. Until 1905 he taught Russian literature in several provincial institutions. He began to write and to be published when he was still a student, his short 'everyday-life' stories appearing in *Peterburgskaya Gazeta*. The year 1892 saw the publication of two long novellas by Kryukov, *The Cossack Village Courts* (*Severnyy Vestnik* (1892), No. 4) and *The*

Revellers (*Istoricheskiy Vestnik* (1892), No. 10). The main theme of Kryukov's novellas and stories was the colourful way of life of the Don
Cossacks. He became a popular Cossack writer on the Don. In 1906 he
was elected Deputy in the First State Duma, representing the Don
Cossack Military Region. He was a founder-member of the party of
'Popular Socialists'. Both in and out of the Duma he spoke out strongly
against the use of the Cossacks in Tsarist government attempts to quell
the revolutionary movement. When the Duma was dissolved he was
arrested and imprisoned for several months. Once released he was for
some time refused permission to return to his province on the Don.
When his right to work as a teacher was withdrawn, he turned to full-time
literary work. Influenced by the revolutionary movement and writers
such as Korolenko, Serafimovich and Yakubovich, who were also his
friends, his work turned more and more noticeably towards social
themes. Korolenko wrote: 'Kryukov is a real writer, with no affectations,
no loud-mouthed ranting, but with his own tone; he is the first to have
shown us the real colours of the Don'. During the Civil War Kryukov
was secretary to the Military Assembly and editor of the newspaper
Donskiye Vedomosti. He died in 1920.[5]

The author of this notice is the literary critic V. Proskurin (not to be
confused with the author P. L. Proskurin who has written tales and
stories of Soviet country life). This critic published a long article 'Towards a characterisation of the work and personality of F. D. Kryukov'
in the journal *Russkaya Literatura*, (No. 4 (1966)).[6] We shall return to
discuss this later. Occasional references to Kryukov have cropped up
here and there since 1965 and 1966, after running the gauntlet of the
censors. Vol. 6 of K. Chukovsky's *Collected Works* contains the sentence,
'We must respect the memory of F. Kryukov.'[7] An extremely flattering
note about Kryukov, written by the celebrated historian of the Russian
social movement, M. K. Lemke, appears in the book *History and
Historians*[8] and an assessment of Kryukov by the poet N. I. Rylenkov is
included in the book *A Noble Soul*.[9]

Kryukov has not been forgotten by his local press, especially in Rostov
and Volgograd. On 21 January 1971, for instance, an article by V.
Davydov, 'The Writers from the River Azure', was published in the
Volgograd newspaper *Molodoy Leninets*. Davydov, a retired local teacher
wrote warmly and well about the essential character of Kryukov's work.
Here is an extract from his article:

The heroes of Kryukov's stories, tales and sketches are freedom-loving,
rebellious, questing people. They suffocate in the stale and stuffy atmosphere of petty bourgeois society with its falsehood, denunciations, trea-
chery, obsequiousness and servile allegiance. Such a man is the history
teacher Shishkarev who is dismissed as unreliable. He asks sorrowfully,

'Is there any justice at all?...Of course, I ought to know by now that times of grovelling servility and cruelty are nothing new in our country ...They even write about it in text-books. Yes...but even though the mind can take this in, the heart...well, it weeps for the affront and it rebels' (*Travelling Companions*). But if Shishkarev is still doubtful about the root causes of this vile life, the veterinary assistant Chekomasov, generally considered the best speaker in his regiment and disinclined to speculate philosophically about the problem, gives an irrefutable answer: 'All Russia has been taught how to suffer, keep quiet and be scared. Because of that we were licked by a tiny little country like Japan; we put up with anything that came along, we are like terrified slaves, we keep quiet, we daren't open our mouths' (*Marking Time*). Any kind of dissident thinking is suppressed, especially freedom of speech; denunciation and spying on other people thrive. The deputy village ataman bellows at a Cossack, 'Popov! Don't say a word more than you need to ...Just remember: you've got free will, only don't let your tongue run away with you. You aren't given free will to worry the authorities' (*Marking Time*). Kryukov remarks bitterly, 'Even here in the backwoods I know there are terrible dramas being played out. Arbitrary rule is at work in all its ugliness. Bitter hardship writhes and cries out in vain for help. Vileness and obscurantism have built themselves a cosy little nest even here' (*On the Quiet Don*).

What is the solution? People can't spend their whole lives in terror; they can't stand permanently on tiptoe. It is unnatural and contrary to common sense, says Kryukov, that even in these out-of-the-way places plenty of young and not-so-young people have been sent to prison or into exile just for possessing forbidden literature or petitions. In a splendid story, *Happiness*, Kryukov tells us of one such lover of the truth, Sergey Bezpyatov. It is told with shattering power.

Davydov makes it clear later on in his article that in Glazunovsk, where Kryukov was born and lived, and in many other villages, young and old alike still retain a great interest in their kinsman. In Davydov's words,

This speaks of the people's deep interest in the fate of this remarkable writer, of an inextinguishable love for their kinsman. They are far from indifferent to Kryukov and his literary legacy and for the noblest of reasons they are attempting to free him from his prolonged and undeserved neglect. And the concern of these people for the tremendous literary legacy bequeathed by Kryukov is perfectly understandable. Hundreds of readers young and old, have asked me to write an article for the newspaper and make enquiries about republishing the works of Fyodor Kryukov.

However, on 9 February 1971 the same newspaper published a resolution from the office of the Volgograd District Committee of the All-Union Leninist Communist Youth League bearing the title 'Concerning certain errors permitted by the newspaper *Molodoy Leninets*'. This article argues, in particular, that V. Davydov's article gave a biased, unprincipled assessment of the political views and the activity of the writer F. Kryukov who was active during the years of the Civil War in the camp of the Don Cossack White Guard rabble. In raising the question of the publication of the works of an active White Guard, F. Kryukov, the author is essentially arguing the case for a political amnesty for an enemy of the Soviet Union who never laid down his arms until the day he died.

According to V. Davydov, at the end of January 1971 he was summoned to the office of the editor of that newspaper where he underwent the kind of interview which made him think seriously that he would shortly be arrested.

The journal *Don* (No. 6 (1974)) has recently published an article by V. Shumov criticising certain research works of historical and local interest. Shumov wrote,

The compilers and authors of works on local history direct our attention to questions of economic and cultural development in the area but say not a word about literary life on the Don. Could it be that there is nothing to write about? No. Before the Revolution the Don region had its own poets (A. A. Leonov, A. I. Petrovsky and others) and prose-writers (I. V. Nefedov, F. D. Kryukov, R. Kumov, I. R. Gordiyev) and writers like K. A. Trenev, A. Svirsky and A. S. Serafimovich grew up on the Don (pp. 91–2).

D. Petrov-Biryuk informs us that the editor-in-chief of the journal *Don* was given a severe reprimand for having mentioned the name of F. D. Kryukov in his pages.

We know that the possibility of 'rehabilitating' Fyodor Kryukov was examined in 1965–6 by the Prose Section of the USSR Writers' Union. The decision went against Kryukov, and all proposals to have his works republished were rejected. This decision was arrived at for non-literary reasons. It is hardly surprising that a number of Soviet literary scholars go on claiming today that the first front-rank writer to bring the theme of the Don Cossacks into Russian literature was Mikhail Sholokhov.

All the main stories and novellas written by Fyodor Kryukov were published in the journals *Russkoye Bogatstvo, Russkiye Zapiski* and *Severnyy Vestnik* – journals, in other words, which are eminently accessible to Soviet literary scholarship. What kind of picture of the writer's personality may be extrapolated from these artistic works?

The first quality which is clearly noticeable in Kryukov's works is his deep love for the Cossacks and especially the Cossack farmer, and also the Don region where he was born and raised. Kryukov wrote in 1918:

I do love Russia, all of her, completely, this great and absurd country, richly endowed with inconsistencies, quite inscrutable...But the most sacred, the strongest and surest of my heartstrings are attached to one corner, that region where I was born and raised. I felt so proud of its past, which I saw in a romantic light as a freedom-loving and heroic past, and I idealised the homespun chivalry of ancient times into a history made up of noisy, giddy festivals, intrepid, unarmed outlaws and poor people. I burned with shame for the present day, for the part which the descendants of the glorious Cossacks were now destined to take on in days of bitter conflict. I was perplexed and I fell into lamentation... I loved the Cossack who tilled the fields and who was now condemned to long years of conflict. I could recognise one of our people from far off, the flat cap, the loose striped trousers with their patches, the shoes; my heart filled with laughter at the sound of ordinary Cossack speech and thumped in response to the lazy tune of an ancient Cossack song.[10]

In the story *From the Diary of the Teacher Vasyukin*, Vasyukin writes as follows:

I myself was born and raised in a plain Cossack family. My father ploughed the land. When I had grown up a little I used to help him in the fields in summer. I know the Cossack way of life. I love my people, those among whom I grew up and whom I still serve. My daydreams are about their happiness. My heart sorrows for them. I think I can state with all confidence that I am a son of the people.[11]

Elsewhere in this clearly autobiographical story we read:

I love listening to our Cossack songs. I love singing the ones that I know. The melodies are rather sad and monotonous but they are full of character and originality and they correspond remarkably well to our monotonous steppe and our strange Cossack life. There is something dear to my heart and strangely sad in the changing tones of these songs telling of the broad open road, leafy groves, clear blue streams, grey-winged eagles and the sadness of being away from home.[12]

And indeed there are many Cossack songs to be found in the pages of Fyodor Kryukov.

Kryukov has a special soft spot for Cossack women:

How I love them. They are cheerful, bold, witty, sometimes deliberately on the coarse side and yet they can also be tender and elusively attractive... There is something in them which does not exist in the cultivated women that I know, a quality of freedom and forthrightness, a delightful wildness which speaks of the joyful pleasure of being alive and the loveliness of free will.[13]

In Kryukov's work we come across very many ordinary Cossack girls. The hard lot of Cossack women is the subject matter of the novella *Cossack Girl* and several stories including *The Officer's Wife* and *Mother*.

Kryukov invariably depicts the life style of the Cossacks from the democratic and popular point of view. He rails against the increasing impoverishment of Cossack farms and the heavy burden imposed by prolonged military service. Several of his stories and tales are devoted to the as yet unacknowledged spontaneous revolutionary ferment which occurred in the Don Cossack villages in the period 1905–7 and after-wards, when the rest of Russia had settled into a period of reaction. Kryukov's novella *The Squall* is a typical example. In a speech to the Duma opposing the use of Cossacks in the police force Kryukov spoke as follows (and his words received a warm response on the Don):

A Cossack values his Cossack title and he has good reason to do so. He values it instinctively, perhaps, uniting with it those distant but still unextinguished traditions which entered his awareness with his mother's milk, the legends of his grandfathers and the words and melancholy strains of old Cossack songs. His remote ancestor escaped at an earlier time down that lonely road to the Don, escaped from feudal imprison-ment, from cruel governors and unjust judges who cut punishment into his back with the knout. He had no rights before and no rights when he ran away. He had to fight to win that most precious, most exalted and purest quality, a human personality with all its virtue and privileges. He then bequeathed to his descendants his fighting spirit and hatred of oppressors with a call for them to defend not only their own rights but those of all oppressed people.[14]

His opposition to the use of Cossacks in the police force is expressed in a number of works by Kryukov (see *The Villagers*, etc.). One of his heroes says,

'What kind of service is that? Dealing with riots. It's shameful! Beating up peasants...guarding the way...I don't blame them for rioting...' No-one could give any satisfactory answers to Anton's questions. And at this point Anton felt a vague and unconscious stirring of indignation. The sacrifice made by the Cossacks was not going where it ought to go, it was being put to an impure and completely unjustifiable purpose, and they were walking into it like a lot of sheep.[15]

The stories *At the Window, Worldly Snares, Daydreams* and *Autumn Furrows* are devoted to the way of life of the ordinary Cossack farmer. A number of Kryukov's stories recount the lives of provincial teachers, clerks and clergymen, Cossack officers and village heads. In anything concerned with the Cossacks Kryukov displays a profound, all-round knowledge. He is familiar with all levels of Cossack society and the natural scenery of his home region. He knows about Cossack military service, all forms of agriculture, horses and riding and he is particularly well versed in Cossack ceremony. In his stories we are present at Cossack weddings and funerals, we watch Cossack fist-fights in the village, we go to the fair, hear the call to military service, watch the allotment of meadowland, and so on (see *The Villagers, In the Lower Stream, Father Nelid*).

Kryukov was still a student when he became convinced that the Russian reading public was ill-informed about the Cossacks. For this reason, when he returned to the Don he began serious research into

Cossack life the result of which was a series of sketches published in *Russkoye Bogatstvo* ((1898), Nos. 8, 9 and 10) under the heading *On the Quiet Don*. At the beginning Kryukov writes,

What is a Cossack? What kind of life does he lead? These questions have worried me for a long time....The Russian public has long been accustomed to think of a Cossack as a special kind of soldier wearing a fur cap tipped to one side, riding a little horse, carrying a lance and wearing long hair combed back behind the ears. The public possibly knows a few Cossack jokes and has vaguely heard about Cossack people living in villages called *stanitsas* out in the border lands, lying about in vineyards swilling down wine and singing Cossack songs. Some of these people might be interested to know that everything they see on that soldier from the top of his cap to the soles of his boots, and also his horse and armour – all of this is not State property, it belongs to him, it was bought by his own hard-earned money...In his home life and on workdays the Cossack does not have the sort of showy appearance which you see when he is on parade. He does wear a cap and it has a red band, but it looks like a well-greased pancake. No uniform, but a black homespun coat or an old tight-fitting jacket. No boots, but light shoes. No loose red-striped ceremonial trousers but ordinary bags. You could sum him up by saying he is a sunburnt, weather-beaten man forever burdened by his duty to the land, by poverty and the unending need to work hard all the time. And he bears one more burden, even in his home life, the obligation to stand ready at a moment's notice to go forth fully armed, riding his own horse, and defend his fatherland against the enemy (pp. 123–4).

The broad scope of the problems touched upon in these sketches may be glimpsed even in the main section-headings: 'The Village and its Administration', 'The Village Assembly', 'Punishment', 'Cossack Intellectuals', 'Trading People', 'Don Cossack Wines', 'Village People of Culture', 'Historical Relics of the Cossack People', 'Fishing on the Don', '"Upper" and "Lower" Cossacks', 'Don Cossack Women', 'Novocherkassk', 'Cossack Self-government', 'Cossack Military Training Courses', 'The Poor People'.

Fyodor Kryukov never married but he did have an adopted son, Pyotr or Pavel.[16] For twelve years he lived and worked as a teacher outside the Don region. He was, however, a great lover of farm-work and every summer he used to return to the Don to help his unmarried sisters work their land. In his stories and tales the work of the Cossack farmer is always spoken of as a hard but happy occupation. For example, this is how Kryukov describes the villagers beginning their work in the fields:

And the whole steppe, now roused from its sleep but still exposed and feeling chilly, stirred and rang with multicoloured voices, like a widely spread camp with waggons, horses and bullocks...And it gave you a happy sensation to feel yourself an independent participant in this, the proud and mysteriously meaningful first day of work on the all-providing land, in the bosom of nature.[17]

In many stories one senses a kind of cult of the land as a mother-provider. Even the poor man Terpug in *Autumn Furrows* is far from considering his hard work, which brings him such a meagre living, a repulsive occupation. Quite different thoughts enter his mind when he is out at work:

There was in those eight acres of overdug, exhausted land something overpowering, almost inexorable. The land concealed its boundaries, blurring the lines between neighbouring plots; it stretched itself out far and wide, before and behind, to right and left, reaching across to the smoky-blue skyline all furrowed and dug into wandering, quavering strips.[18]

Elsewhere there is mention of the 'tender touch of the all-providing land'.

Kryukov's stories and novellas rarely attracted the attention of literary critics, but the few critical articles which were written invariably noted the author's deep knowledge and clever mastery of Cossack popular speech. A. G. Gornfel'd wrote in 1908:

Kryukov lacks geography and misuses folklore but his stories do transport us into the atmosphere of the locality which is breathed into every word of the story – and especially every word spoken by the characters ...Cossack speech is particularly difficult to render. It does not make crude grammatical mistakes; it is basically the Great Russian language slightly tinted, slightly amended in meaning and construction. Kryukov has the ability to present all this to us with loving care and an artist's sense of amusement.[19]

It is indeed true that the comic element which enriches Kryukov's work stems mainly from his skilful rendering of popular speech.

When Kryukov's first volume of stories was issued in Moscow in the middle of 1914 the journal *Severnyye Zapiski* had this to say in a review of the selection:

Writing about Kryukov one cannot resist a feeling of annoyance on behalf of this talented artist who is unfortunately not yet known to a wide circle of readers...Kryukov is known to few, but those who do know him have already acclaimed this writer for his tender, inborn feeling for nature and for people, his straightforward style, his descriptive powers, his precise but picturesque language. He knows what he is writing about and thus avoids the false tone of hack writing which some people mistake for artistic creativity.[20]

Kryukov avoids describing the psychological experiences of his heroes, although these experiences are quite obvious to us from their behaviour, their gestures and their speech. As S. A. Pinus rightly suggests:

Kryukov's love of the ordinary way of life, especially that of the Cossacks, expresses itself in the form of the strictest realism free of all strain and grotesque exaggeration. An expert in true-to-life description, Kryukov permits himself not the slightest artistic transformation of actuality. When it comes to the art of portrayal one is hard put to think of any contemporary writer who is the equal of Kryukov. The special artistic quality which is unique to him is his remarkable ability to reach the heights without wild flights of fancy and plumb the depths of life without using any psychology.[21]

Elsewhere Pinus continues,

Kryukov's realism is fearless in a positive way. Not only does he frequently decide to deal with the awful, crude lower depths of life but he often does the opposite, working at themes which have nothing awful, remarkable or exceptional about them at all, apparently nothing which could be of any interest to an artist, yet out of this living nothingness the author creates an indisputably lovely world, and he does it using the very simplest means.[22]

Similarly exalted assessments of Kryukov's artistic skill are to be found in an article published in 1966 by V. Proskurin, who writes, 'Kryukov the narrator uses a very special language, artistically slight, precise, poetic and yet straightforward, a kind of limpid prose. Special attention must be drawn to his skilful organic re-creation of the abundant riches of Cossack speech.'[23]

Proskurin cites a number of accounts of Kryukov's work written by noted Soviet writers and journalists of the older generation. One journalist, critic and literary expert, D. I. Zaslavsky, wrote this to him:

As a regular reader of *Russkoye Bogatstvo* I was naturally a regular reader of Kryukov. I retain an impression of him as one of the most brilliant contributors to that journal. I believe him to have been the most brilliant portrayer of the ordinary Cossack way of life before Sholokhov . . . He was a talented writer. I could never put his works down.[24]

From Kryukov's stories, sketches and articles it is clear that he took part not only in the revolutionary movement of the 1905–17 era but also in many other ideological movements between 1907 and 1917. The failure of the first Russian Revolution did not persuade Kryukov to abandon his populist thinking or his struggle against an omnipotent bureaucracy and a centralised state. His form of socialism was, of course, utterly remote from that of Marxist thinkers, and Kryukov's attitude to Bolshevik doctrine was one of hostility. Just as the populists of the 1860s and 1870s had seen the germ of socialism in the peasant commune (the *obshchina*), so Kryukov observed the embryo of his desired social structure in the incorporation of the *obshchina* into the system of Cossack villages (the *stanitsa* and the *khutor*) which was a stronger construction than its rural Russian counterpart. He writes with some satisfaction in one sketch (*In the Lower Stream*) that the Cossacks rejected Stolypin's land law which would have hastened the destruction of what remained of the rural *obshchina*. The break-up of the *obshchina* into independent farms and holdings occurred in very few of the rural regions within the Don Cossack Province.

One of the sketches written by Kryukov in this period attracted the attention of V. I. Lenin. This was *Without Fire*, an essay published in the first number of *Russkoye Bogatstvo* in 1912. In it Kryukov tells of his meeting with a young priest, Mikhail Kratirov, who describes to him the mood of the country people among whom he has been serving. In his article 'What is happening in Populism and what is happening in the country'[25] Lenin gives a detailed account of this story, permitting himself a whole-page quotation from 'this authentic description of country life'. Lenin writes:

In Mr Kryukov's article *Without Fire* a sugary little priest tells us about the peasants, their life and their psychology. He depicts the peasantry just as it always has been and still is. If the depiction is a true one then Russian bourgeois democracy (as personified by this very peasantry) is destined for activity of vast importance historically which, given anything like propitious circumstances, has every chance of turning out victorious.[26]

'Peasant democracy in Russia...this kind of democracy is still alive', Lenin continues. 'The story about the countryside told by that sugary priest of Mr Kryukov's confirms this.'[27] Lenin's attention had been caught by Mikhail Kratirov's story about the people's attitude to the Church and religion. When Kryukov remarks on the moral decline of the Russian Orthodox Church his companion rounds on him sharply. 'There is no decline', he says,

When you're down in the dust there is nowhere to decline to. What's new about this? This obsequiousness and cowardice has always existed! ...The difference is that there has never been such a terribly peaceful, silent falling away from the Church as there is nowadays...It's just as if the spirit of life has gone out in the Church. I keep telling you: it's not just the intellectuals who've gone away, the people have gone too, we must acknowledge that. I should know; I was a country priest for two years.[28]

At this point Lenin breaks off the quotation but we shall prolong it, since Kratirov's words give us a better impression both of Kryukov's thinking and of Kratirov's own character – he is anything but a 'sugary little priest'. Kratirov continues:

As far as the shameful subservient role of spiritual pastors is concerned, well hasn't that always existed? I don't just mean sponging on the people in times of terrible poverty...Cowardice and servility and all sorts of sucking up to powerful people – that has gone on, as they say, from time immemorial...Look in any elementary history book...Go back to, say, Ivan the Terrible or his father Vasiliy III. It became necessary for Vasiliy to hide his perfectly legal wife, Solomoniya, away in a convent and get married to someone else. The high-up pastors of the church fixed it for him...Everybody's going on about the Patriarchate now-adays. They think they've got something to hold up, something to praise. Look at your history. The first patriarch of the Russian church behaved with such vile shamefulness that the Muscovites – the devout Musco-vites! – thrashed him in the Uspensky cathedral and dragged him across the floor to his disgrace and execution. Who did? The devout people of Moscow! And they did it at a time when no one had ever heard of nihilists...Yet the Church remains the Church! The only place that can give refuge to a troubled spirit, bring all people together and pacify them...heal their sores...However much it has been soiled by the craftsmen of the guild of clerics it is still the only place which contains a grain of holiness and the spirit of life; in it the spirit of the whole truth shall never die.[29]

In his article Lenin is highly critical – not always with justification – of the populist intelligentsia to which Fyodor Kryukov certainly be-longed at the time. He wrote as follows:

The populist intelligentsia lean towards the conciliatory phrase embrac-ing the whole of humanity. The liberal in these people always makes his presence felt. They are organically predisposed against the viewpoint of the class struggle. They are thinkers. They are taking the democratic peasantry backwards, away from the living, direct struggle against their class enemy, towards that misty, forced, feeble phrase-mongering which masquerades as socialism...Even in Europe any half-educated petty bourgeois will encourage any amount of this wordy, phrasey, so-called socialism (populist, not proletarian). But if ever it comes to 'hating' rather than 'loving' – that's that. Socialism of the humanitarian phrases? – in favour. Revolutionary Democracy? – no, we're against that ...Populist socialism is rotten, stinking carrion. Peasant democracy in Russia, if Kryukov's sugary little priest gives us a proper picture of it, is a living force. It cannot be anything but a living force as long as the Purishkeviches are in charge and people are starving by the thirty million.[30]

At the very start of the First World War Fyodor Kryukov went to the front line, at first as a writer and war correspondent. He stood in front-line positions, marched in columns and in echelon, stopped at the halts. On the Don he observed Cossacks being transported to the front, visited hospitals and held conversations with prisoners. He became familiar with all the various different aspects of military life but his chief interest was in the Cossack regiments and batteries, especially the life and the thoughts of the ordinary Cossack soldier. In his long series of sketches and notes from the front line called *Close to the War*, Kryukov wrote:

Who are they? Who are these people in greatcoats and battle-dress tops?...What is going on right now in their spirits? Where are their thoughts? What is the reason for their silence? What do they live by in their hard and harsh little corners? What hopes light up their hearts? What gives them the strength to bear those heavy burdens and privations? How do they walk to meet their death? How do they accept it? ...Yet throughout the long period of time which I spent in action alongside the Russian soldier this secret remains a secret, unrevealed. It was clearly not enough to be alongside, nearby, to listen and look, to live in curiosity, knowing full well that at any moment if things started to get rough and circumstances became unbearable, you were free to go away, have a rest, be alone. You have to swallow down the soldier's lot through direct experience, find out for yourself.[31]

To judge by Kryukov's dispatches in *Russkiye Zapiski* and the liberal Moscow newspaper *Russkiye Vedomosti* he spent August and September 1914 mainly at the front in the Caucasus. He made several subsequent return trips to the front as a member of an ambulance unit. Some of Korolenko's letters and the article by V. Molozhavenko suggest that in the summer or early autumn of 1916 Kryukov was called up as a Cossack officer. At that time there was a serious shortage of officers and Kryukov, like all other Cossacks, was prepared for war – though he did enjoy certain privileges, as a teacher rather than a writer, with regard to military service. His chance had now come to 'find out for himself' about life at the front. According to his invariable custom, he made detailed notes of his impressions there.

The first book of *The Quiet Don* ends with a description of events at the front in August and September 1914 and the second book begins with a picture of the front in October 1916. Thus, in our examination of the hypothesis that Kryukov could have been the author there can be no doubting his personal involvement. All the events occurring at the front and described in *The Quiet Don* Kryukov could have seen with his own eyes.

After the February Revolution Kryukov made an extended tour of the Don region. He studied the situation on the Don, the influence of the revolutionary events upon the Cossacks, the changes which had occurred in Cossack provinces and villages and the appearance there of new, frequently by no means better, people. He made detailed notes and published notices about everything he saw.

What was Kryukov's attitude to the Revolution developing in Russia? Beyond any doubt he felt no sympathy for the autocracy which had collapsed. Neither did he for the Provisional Government. The Don region was not prepared for revolution; there was no revolutionary situation there, and this deeply disturbed Kryukov. He went around speaking at revolutionary meetings, referring to the destiny of the country, the need for constructive work, and he called for people to put their shoulder behind the mother country. His addresses were well received but Kryukov himself noted the absence on the Don of any significant new forces in which people could place their confidence; he referred to the creative impotence of 'the new Russia as represented by our corner of the steppe'.[32] He claimed that,

The collapse of the Tsarist throne, which occurred at a great distance from here, caused no one any pain and was accepted almost with indifference. Everyone, old and young, had overheard on all sides that the Tsar was a bad man and his ministers were being bribed. Very well then, a point was reached when the old ones had to be changed and new ones elected, good, firm people, more on the Orthodox side if possible, not of the German faith. Maybe then the wandering coach of Russia would go smoother and faster.[33]

However, after travelling the whole of Russia several times from north to south and back again he looked warily at the excess of passion and controversy.

You might say that Russia is sinking in a boundless sea of controversy. Millions of voices beat upon the air, some of them pleasant ones, caustic ones, clever and practical ones but more of them senseless, ringing with empty rhetoric, tedious, stupid, dark or viciously embittered. Empty words are being scattered over everything like seeds from a pod. It is happening everywhere from the church porch to platforms in the remotest little village.[34]

In a long sketch entitled *New Things*, concerning the events of the 1917 revolution on the Don in February and March, Kryukov likens this revolution to the spring floods.

Incidentally the very elements seem to have conspired to rise up this year, to do things on a grand scale in the revolutionary manner. They have filled the quiet villages of the steppe and the remotest settlements with the roar and thunder of destruction... It was a broad, splendid, unprecedented overflow. A modest little river like the Medveditsa changed before the amazed eyes of those who have lived near her from time immemorial. She took on an undreamt-of beauty, an unexpected power, a strange mightiness. But this power was offensive, blind and savagely destructive. It brought nothing but damage and loss... It carried away the grain from the barns, the hay and straw from the store-houses, it smashed down the fragile homes, overturned the fences and the hedges, carried away hundreds of acres of woodland, carved out great holes and ruined the roads... Worst of all it divided the people from each other. It enlivened nothing, fertilised nothing, gave no life. It stopped all creative work and hindered normal, necessary dealings between people. And when the flood waters receded that same pathetic little shallow river was left behind, blocked with sand amid scoured banks, sad strips of bare land and islets suitable for nesting sandpipers and wagtails. Mountains of sand had amassed on the scoured, ruined meadows...We cannot begin to guess what amounts of sand will have been left in people's lives in the quiet corners of the steppe by the Revolution. It will doubtless have left behind potholes and runnels, ploughed-up roads, shattered dams and devastated institutions of ancient standing. It surged up here as unannounced and unexpected as the River Medveditsa. It dumbfounded, bewildered and confused the peaceable, law-abiding inhabitants. At the same time it washed up on to the crest of the troubled waters a few smart, shrewd lads with a single slogan on their lips: smash everything and everyone![35]

At the end of May 1917 there were elections on the Don for the Cossack Military Assembly, the organ of Cossack self-government, an ancient institution abolished by Peter I after the revolt led by Kondrat Bulavin. All the political factions of the Don Cossacks stood for election to the Assembly which was the Cossacks' own form of parliament. About 700 representatives of all Don Cossack villages and regiments attended the first session. They were predominantly officers, including many monarchists. But the Bolshevik Cossack V. S. Kovalev and the communist sympathiser F. Podtelkov were also among the delegates. M. Bogayevsky was elected chairman of the Assembly. Fyodor Kryukov was chosen to represent the village of Glazunovsk. Although his own role in the decisive events which occurred on the Don between June and December 1917 was a modest one he was able to observe directly everything that went on during those months in that region, in the ataman palace and in Novocherkassk. He could have seen with his own eyes the negotiations between the Military Government headed by the Don Cossack Ataman and the Regional Military Revolutionary Committee, the collapse of the government and the Assembly, the suicide of the Don Cossack Ataman Kaledin, the start of the formation of the Volunteer Army on the Don, the retreat from Novocherkassk of the active-service Ataman Popov, his negotiations with Kornilov and Alekseyev, as well as many other events described in the second book of *The Quiet Don*.

Kryukov apparently greeted the Soviet victory on the Don with hostility. In the Bolsheviks' political plans and agrarian programme he saw a threat to the very existence of the Cossacks as an independent people. He feared the destruction of their unique life style and their traditions. When the atrocities perpetrated by Red Guard units throughout the whole of the Don region led in April 1918 to a Cossack revolt against the Don District Council of People's Commissars Kryukov joined the insurgents. Already an elected member of the new Military Assembly he now accepted nomination as its secretary. In 1918 and 1919 many of the resolutions and statutes passed by the Military Assembly were signed not only by the newly elected Ataman General P. Krasnov but also by the secretary of the Military Assembly, Fyodor Kryukov.

The article by V. Proskurin refers to a most significant incident in the history of the first collisions between the Red Army units established in the northern regions of the Don and detachments of the Don Cossack Volunteer Army forming under the command of General Krasnov. When a Red Army detachment took the village of Glazunovsk Kryukov escaped into the steppe but was captured and taken under escort to Mikhaylovka, where the headquarters of the Ust-Medveditsk military sector was located at the time. The commander of this sector and all Red Army units concentrated in that area was Filipp Kuz'mich Mironov who had gone over to the Bolsheviks and the Soviet Government soon after the October Revolution. Mironov knew Kryukov well. As early as 1906 and 1907 they had both participated in the movement of protest against the use of Cossacks to quell workers' and peasants' revolutionary demonstrations. Mironov had spoken out on the Don while Kryukov was doing the same in the State Duma. After the formation of the People's Socialist Party, when Kryukov and his like-minded colleagues were drawing up the party's programme, he made use of the Ruling of the Ust-Medveditsk village which had been written and adopted with the active participation of Mironov and then presented to the Duma by Mironov himself and a Cossack Sergeant, Konovalov. In this Ruling, adopted at a general village assembly, the villagers had delivered an emphatic protest against the mobilisation of Cossacks of the second and third priority groups for service in the interior. It included also an enumeration of the democratic and agrarian reforms directed towards worsening the position of the Cossack workers. It was then that Mironov and Kryukov had met for the first time. After the February Revolution it was Mironov's turn to establish a branch of the People's Socialist Party in the district of Ust-Medveditsk. Their future paths were, however, to diverge. Mironov, without being in full agreement with the Bolsheviks, decided to support their party programme, whereas Kryukov supported the anti-Bolshevik movement. When Kryukov was taken under arrest to Mironov's headquarters in May or June 1918 the two erstwhile comrades spent the whole night in friendly conversation with Mironov persuading Kryukov to abandon his allegiance to the anti-Bolshevik struggle. Although Kryukov gave him no assurances on this count, next day Mironov ordered Kryukov's release and safe-conduct home.[36] Kryukov, however, ignored Mironov's blandishments and rejoined the insurgents.

June 1918 saw a celebration on the Don of the silver jubilee of Kryukov's career as a literary and public figure during which the Don Cossack writer S. Arefin had this to say in the journal *Donskaya Volna*: 'He [Kryukov] took part subsequently in the organisation of the anti-

Bolshevik uprising in the district and then apparently in the uprising itself. He did not like to talk about his activity but he once grinned and said to me, "I had to play the part of a general on a white horse."'[37]

In 1918 Kryukov played an active part in the work of the new Don Cossack government and also helped to create several different organs of the press. He did not change his opinions during these months and thus ran into a good deal of conflict through his involvement with the Don Cossack press. The newspaper *Byloye* wrote: 'The Rostov press had to undergo a double censorship at that time, that of the Germans and that of General Krasnov...the newspapers were having a hard time of it. The editor of *Donskiye Vedomosti* in Novocherkassk, the late F. D. Kryukov (who also worked on *Russkoye Bogatstvo*) preferred to stop working for the paper.'[38]

There is evidence (admittedly unconfirmed) that in 1918 Kryukov worked for a time as headmaster of the Ust-Medveditsk High School. He had been invalided out of the army but took part nevertheless in action against the Red Guards (and later the Red Army). In the opening chapters of the third book of *The Quiet Don* there is a brief but accurately specified description of the military action of the Veshensk regiment, in which Grigori and Pyotr Melekhov are serving against the retreating Reds. In one episode the regiment is covered by a Cossack battery which has just moved up into position and Melekhov makes the acquaintance of a Cossack artillery officer, Poltavtsev. It seems relevant to point out that during those same weeks and in approximately the same places (see Book 3, Chapters 8–10 of *The Quiet Don*) Fyodor Kryukov himself saw action on the side of the Don Cossack Army as an artillery officer, was concussed and was ill for months afterwards.[39] Kryukov was undoubtedly in sympathy with the Upper Cossacks whose uprising began in March 1919. In April *Donskiye Vedomosti* published an article by him appealing to the Upper Cossack insurgents as follows: 'The hour of victory is near. Take courage, brother Cossacks. Stand firm.'[40] In another appeal Kryukov said:

The hour of retribution is at hand. The ardent spirit of the Cossack will flare up and will burn with the flame of holy vengeance. Young blood will boil. The courage of bygone days will be remembered and a mighty assault will smash the Red dam beyond the Donets. Everyone then shall feel the weight of the Cossack's hand. They shall know it, feel it and remember it unto the seventh generation.[41]

The fourth book of *The Quiet Don* (Part 7) includes a description of the battle for the village Ust-Medveditsk in which, along with the division of General Fitzkhalaurov, Grigori Melekhov's insurgent division takes part (following the celebrated clash between Fitzkhalaurov and Melekhov). Again it seems relevant to remind ourselves that in the

95

various battles for Ust-Medveditsk of September 1919, (the village changing hands several times) Fyodor Kryukov, who had previously volunteered for the Ust-Medveditsk guard, was a participant.[42]

After the retreat from the Don Kryukov went to the Kuban in the double capacity of correspondent for *Donskiye Vedomosti* and Cossack officer. In the obituary published after his death in the newspaper *Utro Yuga* S. Svatikov wrote:

When the war against the Reds came to the Don Fyodor Dmitriyevich abandoned his parliamentary work and joined the forces. He refused to stay in the rear. He used to say, 'No one must ever be able to reproach us with calling others to arms and remaining at the rear ourselves.' He would not leave the ranks of the army even during the hard times of the retreat from the home territory of the Don.[43]

Within the Military Assembly Fyodor Kryukov sided with the 'leftist' delegates. Thus it may be supposed that the newspaper *Donskiye Vedomosti*, in whose publication Kryukov took an active part, stood out from the other newspapers published on the Don, though it too bore the unmistakable stamp of anti-Bolshevik opinion. Moscow libraries, however, do not hold this newspaper; complete sets of it are to be found probably only in a few houses in Rostov or Novocherkassk. I have been able to familiarise myself with only a single copy of *Sever Dona* in which there was a long article by Kryukov entitled 'The Foundation Stone'. This is written from the populist standpoint and we can see from reading it that Kryukov considered that Civil War to be the people's tragedy, the tragedy of the great mass of the Cossack people. He accepted this tragedy as his very own. The article describes a long transport column on its way to the front.

Down over the rim of the land went the reddening sun through a mist of jewels. Wide open, deserted, empty spaces...the long, long, monstrous shadows of waggons, people, horses and camels wandered away from the road into the dry, brown steppe-land and were lost in its undulating distance. The wind swirled the sand into twisting patterns ...Old and young had come to the service of their native soil... Someone had mixed the people up, banged their heads together, divided them into enemy camps, fired them with bitter hostility. Millions had been driven out of their old familiar haunts and had become stupefied from poverty, hunger and bloodshed...Work had ceased and dozens, hundreds, thousands of people laboured now on an endless treadmill in infinite futility. They were all weary, their strength was sapped, they were paralysed by grief, deprivation, filth and exposure. Life sometimes seems like an awful dream in which the heart looks forward to a new awakening when the weary spirit will find rest in the old familiar way of living, simple and peaceful, the everyday way of things so well known and so dearly loved. A white-haired old chap with worm-like eyebrows strides along at my side. He is a great talker but a sense of tact and respect will not allow him to weary gentlemen with his chatter. However, from time to time he does ask a wary question or voice his own thoughts, in which one senses the same inability to understand life's ways which I myself suffer from too. 'Ah, there's so much ill-will about nowadays. Ill-will,' he tells me with a sigh. 'They've all got stuck into each other.'[44]

Anyone who knows his literature should be able to detect here without too much difficulty the undoubtedly Tolstoyan undertones which are also clearly appreciable in *The Quiet Don*. From the article by V. Molozhavenko we learn that in 1919 Kryukov tried for a time to leave politics, turned back to his neglected farm, bought some oxen, a pair of horses and some cows, and laid out his garden.[45] As early as the early summer of 1919 Kryukov had written to his friends on *Russkoye Bogatstvo*, 'I feel a longing to return to my writing. I'm overflowing with more than enough material. I shall try to get down to it.'[46] It is probable that in the weeks and months away from public work Kryukov arranged his notes and continued the writing of the novel on Cossack life which he had begun before the war.

In 1973 there occurred the death, at the age of eighty or so, of Prokhor Ivanovich Shkuratov, a man from the same area as Fyodor Kryukov who knew him and all his family well. Shkuratov had led a difficult and complicated life. The son of a priest, he joined the populist labour party headed by Kryukov. He was sentenced in 1921 for his part in anti-Soviet action on the Don but was amnestied in 1927 in connection with the tenth anniversary of the October Revolution. He was, however, rearrested in 1937 and rehabilitated (for 'lack of any evidence against him') as late as 1957. Shkuratov lived out his last years in Tadzhikistan. He maintained a vigorous correspondence with many writers and literary scholars with an interest in the theme of the Cossacks and at the same time worked at an autobiographical novel, *Pavel Kurganov*, which was never completed. In many of his letters Shkuratov wrote about Fyodor Kryukov. For example, one such letter to V. Proskurin on 14 October 1970 recalls his meetings with Kryukov's sister Mariya with whom he had an affair, and quotes her words:

Fedya [Fyodor Kryukov] just writes on and on. He's afraid to go out even in the garden...Letters keep coming but he hands them over to me unread. He says, 'Answer them, Masha, if you have to, but, better still, burn them! I'm busy writing and I don't want to know about anything. I've got quite enough on at the moment.'

Shkuratov himself remembers being received very reluctantly and curtly by Kryukov who said, 'If you want to stir things up, stir things up. I'll wait for a while just now. I just feel like writing and my writing is going well.'

In a letter of 2 June 1970 to A. V. Khabrovitsky, a literary scholar employed as an archivist in the Lenin Library, Shkuratov wrote: 'I well remember the edition of the Ust-Medveditsk newspaper *Spolokh* in which they published Kryukov's reply to correspondents and Kryukov gave a detailed account of his new novel, *The Quiet Don*, the first book of which he said he had just finished.'

Shkuratov informs us that the same newspaper also published seven of Korolenko's letters to Kryukov. 'I can remember almost word-for-word one paragraph of a letter from Korolenko to Kryukov'; he says, 'Vladimir Galaktionovich wrote: "You are wrong to worry about not having a theme. Your region is the Don Cossack Military Region. Write about that, your own region. We are waiting for you to do it."'

However, Kryukov did not manage to complete his work. Following the defeat of the Don Cossack and the Volunteer Armies in the Moscow approaches they began to beat a swift retreat southwards. Kryukov retreated along with tens of thousands of other Cossacks. On the way he fell ill and left the general retreat. In several letters Shkuratov has described the illness and death of Kryukov. At the age of eighty he may have been betrayed by his memory, because there are some inaccuracies of detail and his letters sometimes contain different versions of the same event. Nevertheless Shkuratov's story is certainly not to be dismissed as a 'piece of fiction' as it has been by some literary scholars who have studied this question.

According to Shkuratov, when Fyodor Kryukov fell ill during the retreat he flatly refused to see a doctor. He lay on a bullock-cart with everything possible stuffed under him to protect him from any jolting. At Kryukov's side during those days only a few people remained; his sister Mariya Dmitriyevna, his daughter-in-law, Aleksandra Grigoryevna Kryukova, P. I. Shkuratov and one or two Cossacks. When the sick man recovered a little from time to time he talked a great deal about literature and even managed to raise himself up. Looking out across the Kuban, Kryukov said, 'How can we leave all this behind? Living abroad! Damn the idea! I'm staying in Yekaterinodar. I'm going to work in the high school. The headmaster's a friend of mine.' Kryukov was hoping that the Cossacks would manage to halt the advance of the Red Army at Yekaterinodar.

But the condition of the patient soon began to deteriorate and they had to stop at a little place in the region of the village of Novokorsunsk not far from the road to Yekaterinodar. This was where Fyodor Kryukov died and was buried by the Cossacks and his family, near to the village on a little rise not far from some kind of convent. Shkuratov wrote on the cross in red paint 'F. D. Kryukov' and on a strip of tin-plate nailed to it he put 'MY NATIVE SOIL – For you I have shed bitter tears of love and of hatred.' Kryukov's grave is now lost. The Krasnodar writer G. Stepanov wrote to A. Khabrovitsky: 'Kryukov's grave is lost. Last spring I went to the village of Novokorsunsk and I interviewed all the old-timers. There is no trace of the convent. Thus it is impossible to find even the approximate place where this well-known poet and writer lies buried. We shall have to reconcile ourselves to this sad fact.'

Naturally the question arises – what happened to Fyodor Kryukov's archives?

In 1963 at the Volgograd conference devoted to the memory of Serafimovich, Professor Dvinyaninov announced that Kryukov had left the whole of his pre-Revolutionary archive material in the charge of his close friend, a man from the same region, Professor N. P. Aseyev, a celebrated metallurgist. Shortly before his death Aseyev had handed over some of this material (mainly letters from famous writers to Kryukov) to Dvinyaninov. Of particular interest are several letters from Gorky to Kryukov which were received by Dvinyaninov, none of which has ever been published. (Dvinyaninov informs us that Gorky wrote in one letter: 'You are a young man, and a serious-minded one. There is no doubt about your love of the Russian natural scene and you have a nice lyrical touch, not a rhetorical or professional literary style but one that is intimate, sincere, Russian.') The greater part of Kryukov's archives, however, remained with his niece, Mariya Akimovna Aseyeva who lived in Leningrad. For a long time no-one knew of the existence of this material since those entrusted with it kept it secret. Only when the question of the rehabilitation of Fyodor Kryukov arose, along with the related issue of the possible republication of his work, did the existence of the archives come to light.

From 1963 to 1969 many people approached M. A. Aseyeva with requests to consult Kryukov's archives. They included literary scholars and archivists from the museums in Rostov and Novocherkassk. Mariya Akimovna allowed some of these visitors to consult part of the archives (for which there was no inventory) and she told some of the others that she had burned everything. According to her the visitors also included 'ambassadors' from Sholokhov who offered to buy the archives for large sums of money but she refused to sell. However, she did pass on or sell certain items from the archives to some researchers (almost exclusively letters from great writers to Kryukov at the beginning of the century). In the late 1960s Mariya Aseyeva became very ill and suffered two or three heart-attacks. There arose the question of the future destiny of Fyodor Kryukov's archives. From my correspondence with P. I. Shkuratova, whose acquaintance I have made, it emerges that her husband, Shkuratov, firmly insisted that Mme Aseyeva must hand over the whole of Kryukov's archive material to the Manuscript Department of the 'Pushkinsky Dom' in Leningrad. He also wrote on the subject to Professor K. D. Muratova, the head of that department, suggesting that she should make every effort to purchase all the archive material in Mme Aseyeva's possession. Contrary to this, the biographer of Kryukov, another man from the same region, insisted that the archives should be given to the Manuscript Collection of the Lenin Library in Moscow. It seems likely that the Lenin Library offered Mme Aseyeva the larger sum. At all events she accepted Proskurin's suggestion. In the summer of 1971 Mme Aseyeva brought the Kryukov archives to Moscow and deposited them in the manuscript section of the Lenin Library. This is established by the testimony of A. V. Khrabrovitsky who works in that section, and yet the yearly publication 'Notes of the Manuscript Section', in which new acquisitions are registered, makes no mention of this acquisition. The Kryukov archives were in all probability removed immediately to the special depository. At the present time no literary scholar or historian has access to these archives.

Setting aside the pre-Revolutionary archives, Kryukov amassed a whole new set in 1918 and 1919. This new material he took with him in a large metal box during the retreat, as is confirmed by P. I. Shkuratov. The fate of this part of the archives has never been fully explained. In a letter of 24 April 1971 to V. Proskurin, Shkuratov tells that, following the death of Kryukov, the box containing the manuscripts remained with his sister, Mariya Dmitriyevna Kryukova. In the chaos of the retreat Shkuratov was separated from the cart in which she and Aleksandra Grigoryevna Kryukova were travelling. When they ran into trouble with the driver and had a great argument with him, he dumped them there in the middle of the road and Mariya Dmitriyevna later explained that she had handed the box of manuscripts to a group of Cossacks from Veshensk who had agreed in return to take her and Aleksandra to their relatives in Rostov-on-Don. Mariya Dmitriyevna was of the opinion that Kryukov's archives had found their way from the hands of those Cossacks apparently first of all to Gromoslavsky and then to Sholokhov. In many of his letters Shkuratov insists that in both sets of archives, those in Leningrad and those lost on the Don, he personally saw extracts from, and rough drafts of, *The Quiet Don*. Naturally, all this testimony needs further verification.

Let us return, however, to the published works of Fyodor Kryukov. We have already mentioned the artistic merits of his stories and novellas. Many of the literary devices used by Kryukov are similar to those used also by the author of *The Quiet Don*. There are also thematic similarities; in both we see the life and destiny of the people, specifically the general mass of working Cossacks. On the other hand when we compare our impressions of Kryukov's stories and novellas with *The Quiet Don* it cannot escape our attention that the artistic level of the latter work is noticeably higher than that of Kryukov's early prose. Critics have already pointed out that the plots of the stories and novellas are on the grey side, that they contain little movement and that Kryukov has 'no great figures which stand out in relief and assume a general human significance, no great problems, no clues to help solve problems of psychology, no real heroes'.[47] But the truth of it is that at the end of the nineteenth and the beginning of the twentieth century on the Don there were no dramatic or ominous events occurring, not like the ones which would comprise the main theme of *The Quiet Don*, which produced men of strong character from among the Cossacks, which created and hardened these characters and spawned such a large number of extremely tense and complex situations and conflicts. It was war, revolution and civil war throughout Russia and on the Don which evoked those passions of unprecedented turbulence and that awareness of a direct involvement in one of the great movements of history. These in turn were the vital prerequisite for the creation of an epic, for the transformation of a writer close to the people not merely into one who could depict novel events but into a writer of quite new artistic creativity who operated on another level of artistic quality.

For such a transformation Fyodor Kryukov had had an adequate 'trial run', and he did have the necessary knowledge of his material. He had in addition to this a conscious awareness of the tragedy which the people had suffered and were still suffering and, as an honest and courageous writer, he wished to record an impression of this awareness for future generations. Historical tragedies change both the views and even the character of the people involved in them; some they bring down and destroy, others they assist towards a hastily assumed maturity and exaltation. A tragedy, particularly a historical one, which a writer embraces as his own tragedy can kill him off in the physical or moral sense; it can also raise talent into genuis. We see an example of this in A. I. Solzhenitsyn who dreamt of becoming a writer when he was a young man and might well have become a reasonably good writer even without his ten years of incarceration. But only the historical tragedy which he experienced and interpreted as his own personal tragedy allowed him to create works like *One Day in the Life of Ivan Denisovich*, *Matryona's House*, *Cancer Ward*, *The First Circle* and *The Gulag Archipelago*. Anna Akhmatova is another example. Even her pre-Revolutionary poetry was not without talent and up to a certain point in time she proved to have real ability though without becoming an outstanding poet. However, in *Poem with no Hero*, *Requiem*, *Northern Elegies* and other cycles of poems Anna Akhmatova turned out to be a poet of genius. For that transfer to another level of artistic creativity she paid in full measure through her own suffering.

The events which impelled the author of *The Quiet Don* towards the creation of that great epic were so grandiose and dramatic that this itself could not fail to be reflected in the style and language of the work. The very genre of the epic dictates that the author be extremely laconic and economical in his expressiveness and selection of material in order to accommodate in the comparatively small compass of the novel material of colossal dimensions. Nevertheless neither the plot, nor the characters, nor the details of everyday life, nor the various situations, nor the descriptions of nature in a new work produced by a writer of long standing can divorce themselves entirely from what has gone before, especially if he is writing on a single predominant theme, like that of the Cossacks. It therefore follows naturally that we should compare some pages of *The Quiet Don* with some pages from the early stories and novellas of Fyodor Kryukov.

Probably everyone who has read *The Quiet Don* will recall the conversation between Aksinya and Grigori when they meet among the sunflowers after Stepan Astakhov's return from military training:

Their eyes met. Without replying to Grisha's question she burst into tears.
'I can't go on...I'm finished, Grisha.'
'What's he been doing?'
Viciously Aksinya wrenched open the collar of her jacket. Out tumbled her pink and firm young breasts covered in cherry-blue bruises.
'Don't you know? He beats me every day. He is sucking the blood out of me!'[48]

Here is a scene from Kryukov's *Autumn Furrows* in which one night on the river bank a soldier's wife, Ulyana, meets the Cossack Terpug who is in love with her.

'My father-in-law...he beats me, so much for him being so nice! Just look here...' In one swift movement she undid the buttons and and dropped her shirt down over her left shoulder. Her naked young body gleamed milk-white in the moonlight and her small, supple breasts with their dark nipples shone before him...He glanced quickly at two dark marks on her left side and looked away again immediately.
'Bastard! What did he do that for?'[49]

In the novella *The Officer's Wife* the description of a country abortion and the way in which the mother who is losing blood says goodbye to her two children immediately brings to mind the death of Natalya in *The Quiet Don*.

Returning to *Autumn Furrows*, the evening get-togethers at Pamfil's house are somewhat reminiscent of the evening meetings with Shtokman at the home of one-eyed Lukyoshka. Here is an extract from *Autumn Furrows*:

They sat with Pamfilych the locksmith in his workshop, Ryabokonev, Terpug, the one-armed Grach, looking thin and morose, and the host himself. Then the clerk Mishatkin came along...They often used to drop in on Pamfilych, especially at holiday times. He was a lonely chap, a widower. The years were catching up with him and he did not do much work now. His son, who was his pride and joy, had sent him a hundred or so quite fascinating books and by now he had almost read his way through them...Around these books a motley assortment of book-lovers had formed for a short time, including, on the one hand, the sectarian priest Konon and the clerk to the village council Mishatkin, and, on the other, such proletarian figures as Grach and that simple soul Agafon ...They came to visit Pamfilych to have a chat, or sometimes to have a little game of cards and see off half a bottle of something...They had long discussions and arguments and they got pretty heated...The new times had opened up a strange new world in which there was an inexhaustible source of material for discussion, argument and indignation.[50]

The events in *Autumn Furrows* relate to the period 1906–7 and in one of these get-togethers we later hear Yegor Ryabokonev speaking of the need to arrive at a more sensible, genuine and correct way of living and, what is more, the need to start some sort of party in the village. It is not clear from the context, however, whether he means the Social Democrat or People's Socialist Party.

It is interesting to compare the art of portraiture in *The Quiet Don* with that of Fyodor Kryukov. In most of the portraits of Kryukov's heroes we encounter also a precise description of the various details of clothing, including colours, and the author directs our attention to the impression created by a particular character, often pointing out a trivial but characteristic detail such as an ear-ring or a little cross (one thinks of the silver half-moon ear-ring worn by Panteley Prokofyevich Melekhov in his left ear). Here are one or two examples:

She went out walking in that tripping, fancy way of hers. He went with her as far as the front steps and for some time he watched her walk away admiring her tall, strong, shapely figure.[51]

From under the bushy black eyebrows, like hairy caterpillars, a pair of grey eyes peered out at him...A long, black beard salted with some grey seemed to begin right up under the eyes themselves. It hid the facial features. Yellow teeth bared themselves in a friendly smile which appeared from underneath grey moustaches.[52]

...an old man dressed in a blue cloth smock and broad baggy striped trousers. He put one in mind of a sturdy old tree and it was a pleasant experience to look upon this fine face with its handsome black eyes and the well-combed-out beard in which the grey had begun to dominate the black.[53]

Before me stood a middle-aged Cossack with a round beard, dressed in a canvas jacket with a high collar, baggy cloth trousers with stripes and gleaming boots.[54]

The master walked the balcony in solitude, a tall man with a staid and serious air which did not quite suit his young face with its square beard and lively black eyes. He wore a fawn-coloured silk cassock which neatly encompassed his well-kept figure...And he held himself in a somehow youthful way, standing tall, smoothing his moustaches and thrusting out his chest on which a little silver cross hung near the left shoulder.[55]

An ancient old woman with an aquiline nose and a pointed chin, bent over into a half-moon, in an old blue dress with a dark apron.[56]

His face was not of the ancient type; it was round and full, bright as a new brick, a gentle Russian face with dancing little grey eyes, a balding head and a quite splendid bright-red beard curling under at the bottom.[57]

He was a bony little old man with a little beak of a nose and a scanty beard, a little chap always grumbling. He champed his lips, and shook gently and monotonously like a cracked old sieve.[58]

Our research has a particular interest in comparing the landscapes in *The Quiet Don* and in Kryukov's works, especially since both are primarily concerned with the natural scenery of the northern Don region. In order to illustrate some indisputable similarities and some equally indisputable differences between Kryukov's works of the period 1912–18 and *The Quiet Don* we must now turn to certain descriptions of the Don Cossack natural scene taken from various stories and sketches by Kryukov and from *The Quiet Don*.

Spring. The flooding of the Don and the Medveditsa (Fyodor Kryukov)

The village was wrapped in the twilight of a fresh April evening. The bleached walls of the huts blurred into one vaguely drawn line but the black roofs were etched sharply on glassy pink as the fires burned down in the evening sky. The air was damp and resonant. The sharp call of wild geese rang out with alarm in the chilly, unseen heights above...The ground had stored the heat of the day and now breathed out a moist warmth filled with the aroma of the drying dung-hill and the clinging perfume of the first young shoots of spring.[59]

The river, seen from the mound, looks very wide just now, majestic even, with its sharply rippling light-brown surface and the wind whipping up curly white crests. In the summer she dries up a good deal, grows over green and runs down shallow, leaving behind broad, snow-white sandy strips. Now she is like a sea. Across on the other side, scarcely discernible on the sturdy bank, is a thin purplish haze – a little grove of naked oaks. Behind that rises the sloping hillside, a great blue bank climbing into the distance with the little village church at its foot. The sky covers everything like a vast tent of grey, drained of bright colour. They seem to be drawn in miniature like tiny toys. They hunch together against the bitter wind, as if frozen into immobility.[60]

The scent of the moistened earth mingled with the smell of damp smoke rising from the dung-fuel fires. The smoke crept up from the chimneys in blue-grey streaks, lingered in leisurely contemplation over the thatch and then dropped reluctantly to wind silently down the street before enveloping the willows at the end of the village in a veil of bronze. Against the gentle blue of the sky above, the sun was climbing between the tousled locks of blushing clouds.[61]

The flooding Don shone with a flat whiteness in the twilight just before dawn. Somewhere far, far away the birds of the Don called across the silvery mists of the hollow with their ever-changing cry, gentle and free ...Down in the hollow, flooded now with the waters of spring, shadows of the curly-topped clouds stole across the silver needles of the rippling surface. Purplish hills stood on the distant skyline. Remote open spaces, free and tenderly welcoming...[62]

Spring. The Don ('The Quiet Don')

Smoke rose from the fires of dung-fuel and gathered in layers above the village. By the cinders piled up at the roadside the rooks cawed as they flew to their homes.[63]

The ashen sky was pierced in places by a few early-morning stars. The wind blew from under a bank of dark clouds. Mists reared up over the Don, gathered in layers above the chalky hillside and crept down the slopes like a grey headless serpent. The whole left bank of the Don with its sands, backwaters, shallow stony creeks, and dewy woodlands, shivered in the numbing cold of the dawn. The sun was still hidden, as yet too tired to rise.[64]

As evening approached a thunder-storm built up. Dark clouds piled up over the village. The Don, dishevelled by the wind, sent wave after foaming wave against her own banks. Across the meadows dry lightning seared the sky; every so often thunder rumbled across to crush the ground. Right up under the storm-clouds wheeled a large hawk with outspread wings, pursued by cawing crows. The chill of the clouds breathed down the Don from the west. The sky blackened ominously beyond the water-meadows, the steppe waited in silent expectation. In the village shutters closed with a bang. Old women hurried home from evening service, crossing themselves.[65]

Summer on the Don (Fyodor Kryukov)

The smooth waters of the murmuring Medveditsa gleamed with silver and flashed with sparks. Birds called across the air in joyful excitement while down below the denizens of the river, singers and musicians all, kept up a dull humming hubbub to the gentle buzzing of the little bees and flies of springtime...By mid-day the spring sunshine had immobilised everything in an enervating, intoxicating heat. The floor of the oak grove was a smooth soft bed, dark covered with the grey mould of last year's chestnut-coloured leaves through which tiny spikes of new grass poked up here and there striving towards the sunlight, so tender in the first days of their life. The shy, spreading wormwood, velvet streaked with grey, put forth its shoots like tiny green files, miniature oars, greeny-gold spears. The sky was a brilliant blue. It hurt the eyes to watch the lively little swallows diving away into the fathomless depths with their quick, shrill cries.[66]

Summer on the Don, and early autumn ('The Quiet Don')

The sun poured its yellow heat down upon the whole steppe. A smoky yellow dust hung in the inlets between the ripe, uncut wheat. The metal parts of the reaper were too hot to touch. It was too bright to look up at the white-hot linen of the yellow-blue sky. A saffron spread of clover began where the wheat ended. Occasional puffs of wind sailed up floating from the Don and flapping up the dust. The stinging sun veiled everything in a burning haze.[67]

The day was in slow decline, lulled by the indescribably sweet and peaceful stillness of autumn. The hazy blue sky had now lost the fullness of its summer gleam. Apple-leaves blew over the ditch from some unknown place, scattering a rich purple hue. The road wound away, forking over the crest of the undulating hills, luring the people to stride forth over the dreamy, misty, emerald skyline out into the unimaginable spaces beyond, but all in vain. The people were shackled to their homes and their daily activities. They toiled away sadly, exhausting themselves with the threshing, while the road, that deserted, melancholy track, cut through the skyline and flowed away into the unknown. Down along it came the wind with heavy tread, scattering the dust.[68]

February. The days before spring on the Don (Fyodor Kryukov)

Everything looks grey, uncaring, exposed in all its poverty. A sharp breeze sears the face with its dry cold, whistling through the curling branches of the steppe-land apple-trees, bare and red like frozen fingers, gusting through the prickly grey mesh of blackthorn, rapping on the empty windows of the huts. The vaguely outlined shadows of clouds steal across the black mats of ploughed ground, over the tiny tresses of greenery which look down into the hollows, past the old, brown weeds swaying on their spires of clay. The stubble of yesteryear, where it has escaped the plough, looks up with its faded, dead, golden stare and the wisps of old-man's-beard stand out on the ploughed ground like thin red hairs on a pock-marked face.[69]

February on the Don ('The Quiet Don')

An easterly wind came riding like a Cossack across his native steppe. The snow had piled up everywhere, levelling all the hollows and depressions, hiding every road and track. The windswept plain in its white nakedness stretched away in every direction. The steppe looked dead. Now and again a crow would fly across, as ancient as the steppe itself, as ancient as that burial mound standing up in the meadow and decked out with a snow bonnet trimmed with a princely, beaver-fur collar of wormwood. Flying over, the crow would shatter the air with its swishing wings and send down a low, hoarse, moaning cry. The wind would carry its call far and wide so that it re-echoed sadly over the steppe like a bass string plucked accidentally in the stillness of the night.

But beneath the snow the steppe lived on. Where the ploughed ground stood up in frozen waves silvered by the snow, where the soil had been locked into rippling stillness since the autumn, the winter rye lay there swamped by the frost, grasping at the soil with its greedy, animated roots. Silky green, covered in teardrops of frozen dew, it huddled, shivering, into the crumbling black earth, nurtured itself on the life-giving black blood and waiting for the spring sunshine before rising and breaking through the gossamer-thin bejewelled crust of snow to a new life of lush green in May.[70]

Home. A poem in prose (Fyodor Kryukov)

Home. Like a mother's caress, like her tender tones above the cradle, thus do the magical sounds of familiar speech touch my heart with a warm glow of pleasure. The gentle light of evening is beginning to fade, the cricket chirps under the bench in the nook, the young moon etches a silvery pattern on the pane. Scents of dill from the garden. Home. Crosses on the graves of my kinsfolk, over the meadow smoke rising from fires, little white houses making patches in the green frame of the willow-groves, the furious clamour of the threshing floor, the crane standing in idle contemplation, this stirs my heart more deeply than all those wondrous countries across the seven seas where the beauty of nature and art have united to create a magical world. I love you, my home soil...the sedge by the still waters, the silver of the sandy water-meadows, the lapwing calling from the rushes, the singing and dancing in the evening, the bustling market-place at holiday time and the Don, so old and so dear – I would not exchange this for all the world... Home...The lazy tones of an ancient song, the gentle melancholy, the bold spirits, the magnificent revelry, the infinite sorrow, all this touches my heart with pain and sweet sadness of a closeness and intimacy beyond the power of words...The silent wisdom of the grey-topped burial mounds, the call of the blue-grey eagle across the sky, blurring in a jewelled vision of the knights of old shedding their young blood, scattering their Cossack bones over the dearly loved open spaces of the steppe ...Are you not my home?[71]

Home on the steppe: a lyrical digression ('The Quiet Don')

The feather-grass had ripened. For miles around the steppe was arrayed in swaying silver. The wind would rush along, bending it down springily, rustling it, piling it high, chasing it south, chasing it west, in opal-grey waves. Whenever a flow of air streamed across, the feather-grass would bow devoutly, leaving a blackened trace along its grey-topped crest.

Grasses had come into multicoloured bloom. The faded, joyless wormwood drooped on the hilltops. The short nights mouldered away rapidly. After sundown stars without number stood in the coal-black sky. The moon, the Cossacks' 'baby sun', waned towards darkness with a pallid white gleam; the wide-ranging Milky Way mingled with other starry ways. The acrid air was close, the wind dry and bitter with wormwood. The earth, saturated too with the all-pervading scent of the wormwood, yearned for cool. The proud starry ways, untrodden by hoof or foot, trembled and died away slowly, a scattering of wheat grains on the arid black earth of the dark heavens which never took, never brought the joy of new shoots. The moon was a parched salt-marsh. All over the steppe the grass was withered by drought. Overhead the quails kept up their unceasing silvery tinkling, against the metallic ring of the grasshoppers...

O steppe-land of mine! The bitter taste of the wind that settles the manes of the mares and stallions. The salty tang of that wind, the dry snorting of those horses. Breathing in that bitter, salty scent, they champ their silken lips, whinnying at the taste of wind and sun. O steppe-land of mine, under the low skies of the Don! The winding ravines, the dry valleys, the red clay slopes, the wide open spaces covered with feather-grass, with overgrown hoofprints looking like little nests, the burial mounds standing in silent wisdom, keeping watch over buried Cossack glory...I bow down low and, like a good son, I kiss your sweet earth, O ever bright, blood-soaked steppe of the Don Cossacks![72]

One can hardly fail to notice the similarities in style and mood of the author, or authors, of these extracts. Both Kryukov and the author of *The Quiet Don* look upon the natural scenery of their native ground through the eyes of the Cossack farmer. Both are moved by the 'silent wisdom' of the burial mounds keeping watch over 'buried *Cossack* glory and *Cossack* bones'. Both are moved by their native steppe soaked in *Cossack* blood. All the descriptions of nature are saturated with metaphors. In Kryukov we have the moon etching a pattern and the earth breathing. In *The Quiet Don* the wind comes 'riding like a Cossack', the earth yearns, the sun is 'too tired'. Both writers have a fondness for verbs formed from adjectives, and nouns formed from adjectives and participles.* In both we come across lofty confessions of the author's affection for nature.

Nevertheless the differences in literary style between the landscapes which we have considered are substantial enough to call for an explanation. Kryukov's landscapes are more cloying, more 'literary', less disciplined, less precise than those of *The Quiet Don*. This is particularly noticeable in the latter extracts with Kryukov's use of expressions like

* Noticeable only in the original Russian. (*Translator's note.*)

'home soil', 'tender tones', 'magical sounds', 'gentle light of evening', 'young moon', 'wondrous countries across the seven seas', 'still waters', 'lazy tones', 'infinite sorrow', 'pain and sweet sadness', 'grey-topped burial mounds', 'blue-grey eagle' and so on. True, Kryukov's poem in prose was subtitled *A Cossack Prayer* and it was written for assimilation by the simplest of minds. Even in our own day, when one literary scholar of my acquaintance read this to the old Cossacks that he met as he toured the villages of the northern Don, many of them wept. They had their own individual interpretation of simple phrases like 'scents of dill from the garden', so different from that of the present-day city-dweller – or countryman for that matter.

Various differences between Kryukov's works and *The Quiet Don* do clearly exist and are not to be ignored. Of course, after embarking on his literary career in 1892 Fyodor Kryukov continued to develop as a writer, and as the years went by his artistic gifts strengthened and matured. If you were to ask me whether Kryukov could have created *The Quiet Don* I personally should answer – though not without reservations – that he could have done. It is my belief that if *The Quiet Don* had appeared anonymously in the late 1920s Fyodor Kryukov is the man who would have been named by many literary critics as the most likely author of the bulk of this remarkable novel.

However, *The Quiet Don* did not appear anonymously. It was published as the novel of a twenty-three-year-old Young Communist writer by the name of Mikhail Sholokhov. The arguments and hypotheses so far adduced are, of course, insufficient to challenge his authorship today. On the other hand there are no grounds for claiming that the personality of Kryukov at the age of forty-five or fifty markedly fails to match the 'personality-pattern' of the author which might have been extrapolated from *The Quiet Don* had it appeared anonymously. Of the *fifty or sixty* main distinguishing features belonging to the author of *The Quiet Don* it is possible to point to forty or forty-five which coincide with the personality of Fyodor Kryukov as reconstructed from his work and what we know of his biography. There is no 100% correspondence, and it is therefore too early to arrive at any definite conclusions.

5

'D's' BOOK 'THE MAINSTREAM OF "THE QUIET DON"'

The book with the title *The Mainstream of 'The Quiet Don'*, written by a literary critic referred to as 'D' and published by Alexander Solzhenitsyn who also supplied the preface, is in fact nothing more than the rough draft of the first section of a research project conceived on an extensive scale. The proposed plan consisted of three chapters; all we have are some sections of the first one ('Analysis') and some of the opening pages of the second ('Detective Work'). No more than the theme of the third chapter ('Politics') is indicated. It is also clear from the letter by 'D' included in the preface that this plan underwent substantial amendment as the work proceeded. The section on the poetics of *The Quiet Don* was to have been developed into a whole chapter. The author informs Solzhenitsyn that 'during the spring and summer' he had got to the end of three new chapters of the 'historical part' but had not quite finished 'trimming and smoothing' them. None of this half-finished material found its way from 'D' to Solzhenitsyn, who observes that there is no certainty that 'these half-finished sections and the labours of the last months have not perished'.[1] Nevertheless Solzhenitsyn decided to publish these 'fragments written at different times and belonging to different sections' since 'D' had died 'not among friends' and without being able to carry out his intentions.

The main thesis and thinking of 'D' are summarised in a brief prologue to his work. He writes as follows:

An analysis of the structure of this work and also its ideology and political thinking establishes the presence in it of two quite different, but coexistent, authorial principles. The standard to be used for the separation of the two is established in the first two books of the novel which belong wholly to the pen of the author who may be considered the creator of the epic. A distinguishing characteristic here is the poetic interpretation of the folk theme which determined the actual 'series of ideas' (Tolstoy), that is, the poetic scheme of the characters and heroes in the work. One finely expressed quality of this historical chronicle is its true-to-life, documentary exactitude which stems from a sound understanding of history and, in this particular case, also from the

author's obvious personal involvement in the events and organic connection with the way of life he is portraying.

Turning to the spiritual content of the epic we observe the existence
of that rather diffuse, but exalted humanism and love of the people
which characterised the Russian intelligentsia and Russian literature in
the period from 1890 to 1910. Politically the novel possesses an obvious
leaning towards separatism, but the idea of this is, if we may use the
term, eroded and ennobled by the flow of poetry through the novel,
the concepts of freedom incorporated in its folklore. A stylistic characteristic (in the narrow sense) is the combination of two literary manners:
the delineation of everday detail with ethnographic authenticity on the
one hand, and the pictorial freedom of impressionism on the other.
Uniqueness of language is arrived at by the author limiting himself to
the Don Cossack dialect freely employed both in the characters' own
direct speech and in his own narrative idiom. The vocabulary and
phraseology of this dialect have been totally assimilated and they show
not the slightest sign of contrived stylisation. This popular language is
blended skilfully with the writer's intellectual style of expression. By
applying the standard of the author's poetics it is a simple matter to strip
away the speech of the 'co-author' which has none of the characteristics
outlined above...

The contributions of the 'co-author' are strikingly different from the
text written by the author who was the original creator. These contributions are characterised by a complete independence from the creating
author's scheme of poetics, and no poetical 'series of ideas' is introduced
to compensate for the omission of this primordial design. He has no
poetics. There is merely a naked political formula which serves as a
starting point for the 'co-author's' later developments of plot and
character. This formula (namely that the great ideas of communism in
Russia must override separatist reaction) stands in stark contrast to the
thinking of the creating author. The 'co-author' is an agitator and a
journalist to the same extent that the creating author is an artist. The
'co-author' expounds rather than portrays events; he indulges in open
argumentation rather than describes his heroes' movements and
thoughts. The 'co-author's' language does not square with the creating
author's unique use of phraseology and vocabulary; it suffers noticeably
from poverty and even helplessness, from the absence of professional
fluency and literacy. It is typical of the 'co-author' that he makes his
own presence felt as he attempts to stylise himself in imitation of the
creating author. He has no command of the dialect; his characters speak
a constrained kind of language embracing expressions belonging to
everyday vernacular and to journalistic literature of the 1920s. When
stylising his descriptions of nature in imitation of the author's descriptive
sketches the 'co-author' frequently creates an illiterate caricature or
absurdity which – and this is the main point – lacks any connection with
the heroes and the events, whereas in the case of the creating author
these pictures become an individualised symbolic commentary on what
is occurring. The 'co-author' puts so little thought into his phraseology
that even when quoting popular sayings and proverbs he fails to rein-

terpret them and even mistakes their meaning. . . Such are the facts, the result of our analysis.

In those parts of the text which belong to the creating author this analysis reaches the following conclusions:

Books One and Two represent a completed section of the novel which, however, has come down to us only after suffering some omissions (several chapters). This may be established by considering a number of gaps in the story-line which is generally distinguished by its leisurely and profoundly exploratory epic development. Besides gaps in the narrative text there are some interpolated chapters, stories and characters, of a style which makes them protrude from the background of the normative chapters like alien passages having nothing to do with the author. There is also a series of normative chapters and fragments in Books Three and Four which are of an impressively high artistic order and which belong to the creating author. However the treatment of these chapters and the overall arrangement of material in Books Three and Four indicate that the 'co-author' who produced them had in his hands only occasional bits and pieces, drafts and preparatory materials, part of the original, never fully completed, design. The fact that the connecting links and the whole concluding section of the novel were written by the 'co-author' is suggested by the lack of co-ordination on occasions between chapters and the disastrous inability of the interpolated sections to accord with the underlying scheme. This inconsistency has distorted the artistic design of the whole epic. The need to rearrange the work (in all its parts) so that it might accord with an ideology alien to that of the creating author compelled the 'co-author' to resort to omissions and insertions and thence to the fabrication and eventual utilisation of some extremely valuable materials in this historical chronicle connected with local ways of living, events in the Russo-German war, the two revolutions and the Civil War. However, neither the omissions nor the insertions have robbed the work of its 'series of ideas' which in a work of art finds expression not in direct pronouncements but in the general overall portrayal.

. . . It emerges from a textual analysis that the activity of the 'co-author' occurred in the following fields:

A. The (ideological) editing of the author's text through the omission of chapters, pages and occasional lines which did not correspond to the ideological purpose of the 'co-author'.

B. The incorporation in the text of several chapters of the 'co-author's' own work which thus created a special ideological zone within the novel.

C. The compilation of chapters and fragments of the author's text by binding them together with 'co-authorial' work.

D. The use of the author's material (historical documents, summaries of events and a variety of notes and rough drafts) in the 'co-author's' text.[2]

'D' considers the Russian writer Fyodor Kryukov (died 1920) to be the most probable author of *The Quiet Don*. Mikhail Sholokhov is considered by 'D' only the principal co-author; he holds the opinion that some chapters of *The Quiet Don* as they now stand may have been written by Serafimovich. In the prologue to his researches 'D' actually gives the approximate proportions of authorial and co-authorial text. He suggests that in the first two books about 95% of the text belongs to the author but that in the third and fourth only about 75% of the text belongs to him. He gives an inventory of those chapters which, in his opinion, *certainly* belong to the author and an inventory of those which *certainly* belong to the co-author.

What is there to be said about the principal propositions advanced by 'D'?

There can be no doubt that the draft manuscript written by 'D' and published by Solzhenitsyn has produced an important, fascinating and even very plausible *hypothesis*. In the study of literature, as in all other disciplines, the proposal and justification of hypotheses is an important part of scientific advancement. But a hypothesis always includes something incomplete; it is usually far from explaining all the facts; it contains as a rule a good number of unproved propositions. 'D's' book possesses all these characteristics of a hypothesis. Many of the propositions in the book seem to me to be convincing and correct. However, a good number of the other propositions made by 'D' are not only doubtful or contentious but actually and obviously wrong.

For example, the differences between certain chapters of *The Quiet Don*, differences in style, language and all other artistic means, are not open to doubt. There is a strikingly obvious distinction between the language of the concluding eighth part of the epic and that of its first parts. In the last 150 pages of the novel both the speech of the heroes and that of the author are virtually devoid of Don Cossack vernacular expressions. Only one or two dialect words are used here and there. The fifth part also contains many chapters which use an impoverished form of language, especially in the descriptions of fighting in Rostov and the relations between Bunchuk and Anna Pogudko. This is, incidentally, a point which has been made by several previous commentators. For instance, K. P. Spasskaya in her article, 'Some observations on the vocabulary of works by Mikhail Sholokhov',[3] states that,

the author of *The Quiet Don*, in an attempt to stress the uniqueness of the life of the Don Cossacks, makes wide use of Don Cossack speech especially in the first and third books of the novel. Don Cossack speech is used abundantly in dialogues and in descriptions of the home life of the Cossacks and their agricultural work, and also in descriptions of nature.

In that period, Spasskaya observes, 'Sholokhov creates his own individual literary style.'[4] The concluding chapters are a different matter; these, according to Spasskaya (who gives examples) 'are written in a language *which is quite new to the author*'. She shows convincingly that even in many chapters in the fifth book of the novel, 'the dialect expressions take on a quite different character. They are there, but they are generally accessible; their meaning does not have to be looked up in a special Don Cossack dictionary. Anyone can understand them. They do not go beyond the normal literary vocabulary.'[5] Although Spasskaya completely contradicts her own premises by proceeding to the conclusion that in the final part of *The Quiet Don* the author took a new step forward in the development of his language, moving in the direction of a cultivated literary language purged of vernacular expressions, her article has nevertheless been sharply attacked by many Sholokhov scholars. These people have usually asserted that such investigations do nothing at all to advance the study of this great novel. However even as prominent a Sholokhov scholar as L. Yakimenko was compelled to indicate that in the fourth book there are virtually no dialect expressions either in the author's speech or in that of his characters. Yakimenko's contention is that in this book poetic language and popular speech are used 'with extreme economy and circumspection'.[6] It is clearly no accident that Soviet literary scholarship has left the language and style of *The Quiet Don* virtually unresearched. Sholokhov scholars have limited themselves to occasional examples which illustrate the wealth of the author's language; they have carried out no comparative analysis.

The events in Rostov and the whole of the short-lived affair between Ilya Bunchuk and Anna Pogudko are dealt with superficially and in most unexpressive language. We have stated above that Anna Pogudko does not compare as a character with any other female personage in the novel. The love between Anna and Bunchuk is portrayed far more feebly than the capabilities of the author of *The Quiet Don* would seem to permit. The characters who emerge in these chapters of the fifth part of the novel, such as the Bolshevik Abramson, are lacking in colour and quite unmemorable, despite the fact that we know from the first and second books all about the author's outstanding ability to bring out the personality of even episodic Cossack characters.

However, none of these differences in the use of language and other artistic devices can be taken as proof of 'D's' version of the truth. Even in the novels of Dostoyevsky we come across not only chapters of impressive profundity and magnificent penmanship but also examples of superficial, hurried scribbling. This is particularly true of *The Devils*; yet no one has so far called into question Dostoyevsky's authorship of this novel.

Far greater significance attaches to the infringements of the general artistic and poetic scheme of characterisation in *The Quiet Don*. Natalya, for instance, says practically nothing in the first two books of *The Quiet Don*. We read that Grigori says 'wearily' to her, 'You are sort of remote

...You are like that moon; you give no warmth or cold. I don't love you, Natasha dear – don't be angry with me...I'm sorry for you. We've been together all this time but I don't feel anything inside...Just an empty feeling...like the wide-open steppe...' But Natalya 'looked up at the inaccessible starry pastures and the ghostly shadows of the veil of clouds drifting above. She said nothing.'[7] She remains silent even when Grigori returns home after leaving Aksinya. The author tells us only that 'in the doorway, hanging on to the door to avoid falling, stood Natasha, on the point of collapse, white-faced, forcing out an agonised smile, lacerated by Grigori's quick, off-hand glance'.[8] When Grigori returns after serving briefly with Podtelkov and Golubov, Ilyinichna, reproaching him for having stayed away so long, says, '"Even your wife will give up soon at this rate. We've been trying to find her another husband." Grigori turned playfully to his wife: "What's this I hear, Natalya – eh?"' Even now Natalya says not a word. 'She coloured up, fighting down her embarrassment in front of the family, went over to Grigori and sat down. Her eyes, infinitely happy, lingered upon him, drinking in the whole of him, while her hot, rough hand stroked the dry skin of his brown arm.'[9]

In days of happiness and days of friction Grigori and Natalya do no more than exchange a few phrases from time to time. The poetic design behind the character of Natalya is revealed in her letter to Grigori when he has left for Yagodnoye with Aksinya.

Dear Grigori Panteleyevich,

Write me how I am to live and is my life lost for always or not? You left home without saying a word to me. I haven't done you any harm and I have been waiting for you to untie my hands and tell me you have gone for good, but you have just gone off as silent as the grave. I thought you'd gone away in a temper and I expected you back but I don't want to split you up. Better me trampled in the dust than two of us. Have pity on me now and write to me. I want to know which way to think or else I'm in the middle of the road. Don't be cross, for the sake of Christ.

Natalya[10]

Many Sholokhov scholars have underlined these characteristics of Natalya on more than one occasion. Yakimenko writes:

The drama of Natalya's life is portrayed by Sholokhov in a deeply moving way. From his pages rises the serious and sorrowful figure of a lovely Russian woman, strong and wholesome in her moments of passion and suffering. Carefully and subtly the writer exposes the secret, stormy life of a woman's heart; he renders the agony and the ecstasy of love with touching passion and power. In the figure of Natalya one is moved by the combination of moral strength and determination in suffering on the one hand with an inability to cope with life, a defencelessness on the other... The principal features of Natalya's character are chastity, purity and a reticent shyness. These are what invest her figure with such winsome charm.[11]

Later, however, Grigori returns home for a short spell at the height of the Veshensk Uprising and following a month of vicious fighting. There ensues between him and Natalya a conversation which is worth quoting almost in full:

Natalya stopped and bent down ostensibly to tie up her shoe-lace but actually to hide her face from Grigori. She asked him, 'Well, why don't you say something?'

'What have we to say to each other?'

'Oh, there's plenty...You could tell me about getting drunk near Karginsk, running after whores...'

'Oh, you've heard about that?...Well, if you know, what's the point of telling you about it?'

'You haven't changed, have you?'

'Oh, shut up, Natalya!'

'You're never satisfied, you damned hound! Why are you torturing me again?'

'You ought to pay less attention to the rubbish you hear...I'm not all that guilty, you know...Life's to blame, Natasha...Living on the verge of death all the time...'

'You've got children, you know. Aren't you ashamed to look them in the eye?'

'Oh yes, shame! I'd just forgotten about shame. How can you think about shame when all your life's been mucked up?...You have to go out and kill people...You have no idea what all this mess is about... You can't understand it! You just let your woman's fierceness flare up. You don't stop to think about me eating my heart out. My heart bleeds sometimes! Yes, I did turn to vodka. A few days back I had a kind of fit; my heart just stopped and I went cold all over my body...'

'Oh, don't try all that fancy talk on me! You've treated me bad and you've admitted it. Now you want to blame it all on the war. You men are all the same! You've put me through it time and again, you devil. It's a pity I didn't finish myself off that time before...'

'There's nothing else for us to say. If you're in a bad way have a cry about it – tears are always a comfort to women when they're unhappy. I can't console you just now...'[12]

This conversation is so far from corresponding to the character of Natalya that it leaves even Yakimenko nonplussed. Commenting on this clash between Grigori and Natalya he mentions that the reader is surprised by Natalya's 'sudden crudity' and the 'inward-looking egoism of her feelings'.[13]

A couple of months later, however, Grigori, who has taken up with Aksinya again in Veshensk calls in at home for a day on his way to the front.

They arrived in Tatarsk at dawn. Nearing his gate Grigori put on a spurt, then left the reins to Prokhor and hurried anxiously towards the house. Natalya, half-dressed, happened to come to the doorway. At the sight of Grigori her sleepy eyes lit up in such a brilliant surge of delight that his heart jumped and his eyes suddenly moistened. Natalya *said nothing* as she held her only love and pressed her whole body against him. Grigori realised from her shuddering shoulders that she was crying.

Grigori spends the whole day around the home, helping his father on the farm and talking to him, Darya and Dunyasha. Natalya stands beside him all the time, pleased to see him, but she says nothing.

Just before sunset Grigori stopped work and went indoors. Natalya was alone in the best room. She had decked herself out as if there was something to celebrate. She wore a neatly fitting dark blue woollen shirt and a light blue poplin jacket with an embroidered bodice and lace cuffs. Her face was a delicate pink and it shone slightly because she had just washed it with soap. She was rummaging in the trunk but when she caught sight of Grigori she put the lid down and straightened up with a smile. Grigori sat down on the trunk, and said, 'Sit yourself down for a while. I'm off tomorrow and we shan't have had time for a talk.' She sat down obediently at his side and looked at him sideways-on, her eyes almost afraid of him. But he suddenly took her hand and said tenderly, 'You're lovely and smooth. You'd never know you'd been ill.'
'I'm better...We women have got nine lives like cats,' she said, smiling diffidently and looking down.[14]

Here we have 'reverted to type'.

Old Grishaka is another example. This centenarian with so much experience of war behind him is by way of being a symbol of Cossack tradition in the novel. When Soviet power comes to his village in the winter of 1919 Grishaka puts on his ceremonial Cossack uniform.

His sheepskin coat was flung open to show all the crosses and medals he had won in the Turkish war. Red tabs shone defiantly on the high collar of his ancient uniform, his loose, striped trousers, floppy from old age, were neatly tucked into his white stocking-tops and he had pulled a cockaded cap down over his massive waxy ears.

Panteley Prokofyevich is alarmed at the sight of him and he asks him to remove the insignia. The old man replies:

'I have served my White Tsar in faith and truth, my lad. This power does not come from God. I do not acknowledge them as having power. I took my oath to Tsar Alexander and that's that!' Old Grishaka champed his pallid lips, wiped the foliage of his moustaches and waved his staff in the direction of the house. 'You've come to see Miron, haven't you? He's in. We had to let Mityusha go, Heaven protect him...Your lads have stayed behind, have they? That's them all over – right Cossacks they've turned out to be! They've taken an oath, too, but now the army needs them they've stayed with the women!'[15]

We see Grishaka again at the secret funeral of Miron Korshunov who has been shot.

Petro led Old Grishaka by the hand down from the attic. The old man was wobbling as though the floor under him was as unsteady as a quagmire. But he went gamely up to the table and stood at the top end. 'Now then Miron! So this is how we meet again, old son!...' He crossed himself and kissed the cold brow dirtied with yellow clay. 'Mironushka, soon be my turn...' His voice rose to a wail. As if he was afraid of making a fool of himself Old Grishaka raised a hand to his mouth in a gesture that was anything but an old man's, and flopped against the table.[16]

And yet one month later Grigori Melekhov, commander of an insurgent division, comes to the village for a few days and comes across Old Grishaka. The following conversation ensues between them:

'You'll be all right, grandad. Mouth full of teeth.'
'Teeth? Don't be stupid, lad,' said Old Grishaka angrily, 'Teeth'll not keep body and soul together – not when the soul's ready to go. You're still at it, fighting are you? Useless lout.'
'That I am.'
'Our Mityushka's just the same. Mark my words, there's more than enough evil about. It'll end with tears.'
'There is enough, you're right.'
'That's what I'm saying. What are you fighting for then? You don't know yourselves. It's all God's will. Why did our Miron have to die? Because he went against the Lord and the people have risen against authority. All authority comes from God. Even if it's anti-Christ authority it still comes from God. I used to say to him before, 'Miron, don't you get the Cossacks rising up, don't you incite people against authority, don't encourage them into sinful ways.' He used to say to me, 'No, sir. I can't stand it. We must have an uprising and destroy this authority – it's scattering us all over." And he didn't stand it. Those who live by the sword die by the sword.'[17]

We have already referred to the populist opinions of the author of *The Quiet Don*. This author feels for the Cossack working people whose tragedy he shares. They are in conflict with both Whites and Reds. In the sharp verbal skirmish between Grigori Melekhov and General Fitz-khalaurov all the sympathies of the author and the readers are on the side of Melekhov. But when Shtokman and Koshevoy search the district for Melekhov in order to have him brought to trial and shot, the author and the readers are still on Melekhov's side. The author of *The Quiet Don* clearly indicates that in the conflict with the Reds the Cossacks themselves are not to be blamed, considering their undoubted ignorance, their property-owning prejudices and their allegiance to Cossack tradition and privilege. For a people is what it is, and anyone who wants to attract ordinary people to his side must work on the basis of real life, not political schemes. The author gives no fully developed answer to the question – how could the life of working Cossacks be improved? One method might have been to develop popular self-government, but the author totally rejects the terror by which the Bolsheviks first attempted to impose their authority. However, on many of the novel's pages, especially in the third and fourth books, this underlying ideology disappears from the epic and is replaced by a different one. Let us examine two extracts from *The Quiet Don* which are strikingly at variance in language and in their *attitudes* to the events occurring.

The beginning of the Veshensk Uprising
(from Book 3, Part 6, Chapter 28)

Next morning his host woke him up by rushing into the shed and snapping out, 'Come on! Get up! The ice has broken on the Don!' He giggled with laughter. Grigori jumped down and a great booming wall of dung briquettes rumbled down after him. 'What's happened?'

'On this side Yelansk and Veshensk have risen...I think Kazansk, Shumilinsk and Migulinsk have too. You see which way things are going?' The veins stood out on Grigori's forehead and neck; greenish sparks flashed in his eyes. He could not hide his delight; his voice trembled and his black fingers ran aimlessly over his greatcoat fastenings. 'What about this village here? What's happening?'

'I've heard nothing...come on out of your hole.' They walked over to the hut, Grigori striding out and his host running along, telling him what had happened.

'The first village to rise in Yelansk was Krasnoyarsk. The day before yesterday twenty Yelansk communists went to arrest some Cossacks in Krivsk and Pleshakovsk but the people in Krasnoyarsk heard about it, called a meeting and came to certain conclusions. 'How long are we going to put up with them taking people away?' they said. 'They're taking our fathers and they'll get round to us too.' There were about fifteen of them, good lads all of them. Led by a grand fighting Cossack, name of Atlanov. They only had two rifles, one or two had swords, one or two pikes and staves. They rode across the Don to Pleshakovsk and found some communists having a rest in Melnikov's yard. They galloped in to attack them, but the yard had a stone wall round it. They made one run and were pushed back. The commies killed one of them, God rest his soul. They were being chased back and he fell off his horse and got caught in his noose. The Pleshakovsk Cossacks brought him back to the village stables. There he was, dear lad, with his whip still in his cold hand...it had to be torn out. That moment marked the end of Soviet power. To hell with them!...'

In the hut Grigori wolfed down what was left from breakfast and went out into the street with his host. Cossacks stood around in groups on the street-corners as if it were a holiday. They went up to one of the groups. The Cossacks touched their caps in response to their greeting and answered warily, examining the unfamiliar figure of Grigori with curiosity and anticipation. 'Gentlemen, he's one of us! Don't be afraid of him. Haven't you heard of the Tatarsk Melekhovs? He's Panteley's son Grigori. He saved me from being shot,' Grigori's host said proudly.

They had scarcely begun to talk when at the end of the street which ran off up the beetling white hillside two men on horseback appeared. They galloped down the street stopping at each group of Cossacks, turning their horses, shouting something and waving their arms. Grigori could not wait for them to arrive at their group. 'They're not our lads ...They're messengers from outside somewhere,' said one Cossack without taking his eyes off them. The two riders passed the side-street before theirs and rode up. The leader was an old man with his coat open wide and with no hat on. He was red in the face and sweating. His curling grey hair streaked down across his cheeks. He reined in his horse like a youngster, leaned back as far as he could and stretched out his right hand. 'Cossacks, why are you hanging about on street-corners like women?' he called out, almost weeping. Bitter tears broke up his voice; his livid cheeks shook with emotion. He rode a fine prancing horse, a four-year-old chestnut mare with a white blaze, a fibrous tail and spirited, steely legs. Snorting and champing the bit she squatted back, reared up slightly, pulled at the rein, straining to go off again at a brisk, ringing gallop and feel the wind beating once more upon her ears and whistling through her mane, and to hear the shapely shells of her hooves booming and drumming over the frost-seared ground. Under the mare's skin every vein and ligament twitched and played. All down her neck ran long lines of raised muscle, she breathed out a limpid, pink, quivering steam and her bulging ruby eye, a revolving white orb marked with blood, looked askance at the master with a demanding and malicious urgency. 'Sons of the quiet Don, what are you doing standing there?' the old man cried again looking away from Grigori and towards the others. 'They're shooting your fathers and grandfathers, seizing your property, mocking your faith...and you're chewing sunflower seeds and enjoying yourselves. Are you waiting for the noose to tighten round your throats? How much longer are you going to hide behind the women's skirts? The whole of Yelansk has risen, great and small. The Reds have been driven out of Veshensk, while you Rybin Cossacks... What have you got in your veins, blood or peasants' *kvass*? Rise up! Get your arms! We've been sent from Krivsk to rouse all the villages. Get on your horses, Cossacks, before it's too late!' He turned his frenzied eyes upon one old man whose face he knew and called out with tremendous contempt, 'What are you standing there for, Semyon Khristoforovich? The Reds killed your son at Filonovo and you're lying about on the stove to save yourself!'

Grigori had heard enough; he flew back to the yard. He trotted his horse out of the shed; it had been standing there all too long. He dug down among the dung briquettes, breaking his nails till they bled, dragged out his saddle and was soon flying through the gateway like one possessed. 'I'm off! God be with you!' he managed to call out to his host who was now approaching the gate, then, dropping down over the saddle-bow and leaning into his horse's neck, he lashed him on either flank and put him into full gallop, raising white whirlwinds of snowy dust all down the street. The lacy patterns of snow settled behind him, his feet worked the stirrups, his numb legs rubbed against the sides of the saddle. Beneath the stirrup the horse's hooves drummed in their fast flight. He felt such an enormous, wild surge of delight, such a flood of power and resolution that he gave voice involuntarily to a hoarse, gurgling whoop. Hidden and imprisoned feelings had been unleashed within him. From now on his way seemed as clear as a moonlit track.[18]

Young Cossacks taking part in the uprising
(from Book 3, Part 6, Chapter 46)

Beyond the flooded forest the Cossacks were walking over the dunes; Khristonya, Annushka, Panteley Prokofyevich, Stepan Astakhov and the others...They walked along glumly but with full stomachs and clean clothes...There is nothing like living at home among loved ones! And now they had to walk towards death...and that's what they were doing. Young lads of sixteen or seventeen only recently called up into the ranks of the insurgents walked over the warm sand in their bare feet...War for them was a novelty, a bit like a game with the other lads...Cossacks who had served at the front referred to them contemptuously as 'greenhorns'. And the greenhorn still looked upon the world of war with a beady stare of amazement, still raised his head above the trench burning with curiosity and dying to spot the 'Reds' until a Red Army bullet smacked into him. If he's killed by it the sixteen-year-old 'soldier' is stretched out and no-one would ever guess now that he had even sixteen short years behind him. There he lies, a great child with a boy's podgy arms, ears sticking out and the beginning of an Adam's apple on his slender, immature neck. He is carried back home to his village and buried in a little grave where his grandfathers and their fathers lie mouldering. He is met by his mother, wringing her hands. Long will she weep for her dead one and tear her grey hair. And then after the burial when the clay has dried out on the grave she will go to church in remembrance of her 'slain' Vanya or Semushka, an older woman bent down nearer to the ground by her mother's grief which can never be assuaged.

Or it may happen that the bullet wounds your Vanya or Semushka without killing him. Now at last, and only now, does he realise the ruthless severity of war. His lips with the dark down above them will quiver and contort themselves. Your 'soldier' will squeal like a hare, piping out in his childish voice, 'Mummy, my dear, darling Mummy!' and tiny tears will sprinkle from his eyes. The ambulance carriage will trundle him away over bumpy, trackless ground, aggravating the wound...And your 'soldier' Vanyushka will cry, ask to be taken home, call for his mummy. Should he recover from the wound and find himself back in his company he will now complete his knowledge of war once and for all. A couple of weeks in the ranks, seeing action, facing the enemy, and his heart will harden. Then – take a new look at him – he'll know how to face Red Army prisoners, standing with his legs apart, spit to one side in the manner of a brutal sergeant-major, hiss through his teeth and say in a voice which is just beginning to break, 'All right, you peasant bastard, you've bloody well had it now, haven't you? Ha! You wanted the land, did you? And equality? I suppose you're a commie? Admit it, swine!' Eager to show what a fine lad he is, to demonstrate that 'Cossack spunk', he will raise his rifle and kill a man who has lived and now died on Don soil, a warrior for Soviet power, for communism, for a world in which there would be no more war.

And somewhere near Moscow or Vitebsk, in some out-of-the-way village of the great Soviet Union the mother of a Red Army soldier will be informed that her son 'has fallen in the war against the hated White Guards for the liberation of working people toiling under the yoke of land-owners and capitalists.' She will read the notice and reread it and she will weep...An agony of grief will assail her mother's heart, tears will flow endlessly from her expressionless eyes and not a day will pass from now until she dies without her remembering the one whom she once carried in her womb and brought forth in blood and woman's agony, the one who now has fallen under an enemy's hand somewhere in the unknown region of the Don.[19]

It is, of course, possible to suppose that both these extracts, so different in orientation and language, were written by a single author who deliberately and hastily interpolated into his novel a number of scenes conforming to the views and tastes of those who would have to decide whether to publish it. Soviet literature possesses the peculiar distinction that inside virtually every author dwells his own 'co-author'. Many a Soviet writer has within him a censor and an editor whose influence on the author's work is enormous. It compels him to invent many scenes and introduce into his work characters who are quite superfluous in terms of artistic logic and artistic truth. Even when it is completed a novel or a story is still subject to pressure from without which frequently enforces further corrections and the addition of extra pages. It is well known that after the first publication of his novel *The Young Guard* A. Fadeyev had to insert into it a number of new scenes and heroes. An even better illustration is provided by A. Bek's novel *A New Appointment* which was prepared for printing and accepted by the editors of *Novy Mir* in 1964. It was not difficult to guess that one of the heroes in the novel, Onisimov, was based on a real-life prototype, the late Minister for Ferrous Metallurgy, Tevosyan. He emerges in the novel as a man totally devoted to socialism, scrupulously honest in his work and everyday life, but nevertheless a conservative, a worshipper of blind discipline, an earnest old-campaigner, a 'Soldier of the Party' and a 'Soldier of Stalin', which in Onisimov's eyes amounts to the same thing. Tevosyan's widow did not like the character of Onisimov, nor that of his wife, an unexciting and not over-intelligent woman given to blind subservience to 'orders from above'. She used her influence to prevent the publication of this novel which had already been approved, a work of undoubted ability which in no way infringed the code of so-called 'Socialist Realism'. In an attempt to save his novel Bek added a few scenes in which the Minister Tevosyan appears under his own name as a friend of Onisimov. At one meeting with Onisimov Tevosyan is accompanied by his wife, a woman of charm and beauty. Even this concession failed to satisfy Tevosyan's widow and her friends. Even though it had been set up in type, Bek's novel never saw the light of day during his lifetime and has still not been published in the Soviet Union. Many other Soviet writers have had to introduce new scenes and pages into their works to make them 'passable'. In most cases the interpolations did not contravene the basic logic or the ideological orientation of the original work, but there have been occasions when they did. We now know that before submitting *The First Circle* to the editors of *Novy Mir* Alexander Solzhenitsyn had to exclude some chapters and even change the original 'detective-story' plot which resulted in a substantial alteration in the ideological tone of the novel. It is true that our literature in the mid-1920s was not yet schooled in this kind of doctoring, as Solzhenitsyn correctly indicates in his preface to 'D's' book. On the other hand the philosophies of many front-rank writers of that period were highly inconsistent, so contradictory that they included quite fantastic inter-weavings of the old and the new. The works of Andrey Platonov, for instance, display trenchant criticism of many aspects of Soviet life; they use every available artistic method to reject what is unacceptable. But Platonov by no means rejects socialism in general, or the most important features of communist ideology. All of this was reflected in his artistic work. Similarly the inconsistencies in the work of Mikhail Bulgakov are not an indication of time-serving on his part, they belonged actually to his general outlook, his attitude to the reality around him.

The traces of hasty ideological editing are easily visible in *The Quiet Don*. Let us take a single example. In Chapter 22 of the first part of the novel Grigori and Natalya are married in the village church. '"Now exchange rings", said *Father* Vissarion, looking straight at Grigori with some tenderness.' In the first chapter of the second part the author mentions among the merchant Mokhov's guests *Father* Vissarion who, after the death of his wife, has been living with a Ukrainian housekeeper. In Chapter 16 of the third part the author describes the tribulations of the Melekhov family after they have received the false report of Grigori's death. '"Be brave, Prokofyich. What's the use of falling into despair?" said Vissarion the *parson* encouragingly after the funeral meal.' In Chapter 5 of Book 4 we learn that Panteley Prokofyich has hidden something away during his confession to *Father* Vissarion. In Chapter 23 of the fifth part of the novel Grigori walks past *Father* Vissarion's house. On the last page of Part 6 we learn that Mishka Koshevoy has burned down even the house of Vissarion the *parson* in Tatarsk. And in Chapter 3 of the eighth part we read that 'Vissarion the *parson* married them [Koshevoy and Dunyasha] secretly in an empty church at night.' This lack of correspondence not in the heroes' speech but in that of the author conveys a good deal to the attentive reader. It is obvious that a Young Communist food-requisitioning author of the 1920s could not possibly refer to a priest as 'Father Vissarion'. It was no less impossible for a Cossack writer who respected Cossack tradition and Cossack devotion to the Orthodox Church to refer to 'Vissarion the parson'.

The comments made by 'D' on Shtokman, the pro-Bolshevik Cossacks and workers like Valet, Davydka and one or two others, deserve particular attention. According to 'D', Shtokman, Koshevoy, Valet, Bunchuk (and others) are introduced in the first parts of the novel written by the original author not as positive, but negative characters, alien to the Cossacks and their ancient traditions and therefore incapable of winning the support of Cossack workers and bringing new freedom and happiness to the Don. Podtelkov and Krivoshlykov have a more intimate connection with the Cossacks since their programme involves a transference of power from the Tsarist generals and Russified officers to the mass of the Cossack workers. Podtelkov and Krivoshlykov strive for the autonomy of the Don region within Soviet Russia but their efforts come to nothing because of the intrusion of the demoralised Red Army units. And although Sholokhov, the 'co-author', edited this part of the novel in an attempt to convert Shtokman, Koshevoy, Valet and the others into true heroes, builders of a new, happy life on the Don, the original logic of the novel nevertheless asserts itself and the main outlines of the original sketch are preserved in the text.

Many of these claims made by 'D' are worth serious consideration, since they are based on the attitude of the author towards those particular characters as clearly expressed in the novel. Thus Shtokman (whose name, according to 'D', comes from the German word *Stock*, 'a stick'), when brought to Tatarsk by Fedot Vodovskov, looks round 'blinking myopically' and asks Fedot 'roundabout questions with something behind them'. In the village Shtokman manages to gather round himself only a small group, whose members arouse no sympathy in the author or the reader. We are told of Davydka that he '*idled away* three months'. The study of the Soviet pamphlet on the Cossacks which Shtokman had brought '*dragged on* for three evenings'. In that pamphlet 'the unknown author *openly and maliciously ridiculed the poverty* of Cossack life, *poured scorn upon* Cossack institutions and authorities and on the *Cossacks themselves* who had sold themselves as monarchs' bodyguards'.[20]

There is hidden irony in this very reference since only twenty pages earlier the author has given this description of 'the poverty' of Cossack life in Tatarsk: 'The village had grown fat on the harvest and it lay there wallowing in the diminishing heat of September, stretched out over the Don like a snake of beads across the road. Life went on, full-blooded, bitter-sweet, highly-coloured, distinct and individual in every yard busy with threshing and under every roof.'[21] We shall see later that this was a period when the Cossacks certainly did not seek to be monarchs' bodyguards and the Tsar's expectation of Cossack support in the days of February and just before was disappointed.

Valet is a particularly unattractive character in the novel. The author repeatedly stresses his small stature and physical weakness. He has 'a dirty little hand', 'scarred fingers', 'malicious, close-set eyes'. Even Koshevoy, his friend in Shtokman's group, says to him, 'You're like a dog on a chain, Valet. You'd snap at anyone.'[22] After the skirmish with Grigori Valet speaks to Koshevoy 'in a thin shaky voice'.

His stubbly little mug was white with animosity, his little close-set piggy eyes darted here and there sharply and savagely, even the smoke-coloured hair on his skin seemed to quiver...'That Grisha, your friend, he's a swine. He's insulted me, the bastard! I'd have killed him, only I didn't have a gun...' Mishka, walking along with him, glanced at his scrubby bristly face and thought, 'You would have too, you lousy rat.'[23]

Koshevoy himself, as we saw in Chapter 2, arouses little sympathy in the author or reader. The author never misses an opportunity to show Koshevoy's cowardice. After his flogging, Mishka is sent to work as a drover on a horse ranch where he makes an attempt at agitation among the Cossacks. Meeting a rebuff he is very frightened.

Mishka stopped suddenly, his legs wobbling beneath him and the sweat poured down his back and under his arms...And Mishka began to plead humbly. His jaw trembled, his eyes darted everywhere in panic...'Why did I say all that? If I offended you...for God's sake, forgive me! All right?...' Mishka smiled an abject, pathetic smile in the darkness.[24]

When the Veshensk Uprising breaks out Koshevoy not only attempts to hide away, he behaves like a real coward. When his own mother refuses him sanctuary in his own home Mishka begins to sob, 'slobbering like a child with bubbles coming out of his mouth'. His heart continually 'leaps and plunges down'.[25]

The author of *The Quiet Don* misses no opportunity to stress the weaknesses of Podtelkov. 'Even before his [Podtelkov's] election to the chairmanship of the Revolutionary Committee he had changed percep-tibly in his attitude to Grigori and the other Cossacks whom he knew. His voice already contained chilly notes of superiority and a certain condescension. Here was an ordinary Cossack giddy at the thought of power.'[26] In the first edition of the novel reference was made to Podtel-kov's admiring love of his leather jacket and to the 'full-bosomed blonde girl' with the manners of a whore whom he took around with him as a 'sister of mercy'. As to Shtokman, he remains a demagogue to the last, and one with nothing to say to the Cossacks; it is the ex-officer Voronovsky, not he, who manages to gain the support of the Red Army peasants serving in the Serdobsky regiment.

Here again we encounter the problem of the standpoint of the author, his attitude to 'us' and 'them'. Of all 'D's' arguments against Sholokhov as the author, this is perhaps one of the most serious, amounting almost to an actual piece of evidence. Everything which the author of *The Quiet Don* writes about the everyday life of the Cossacks, their relationships, their appearance, all of this has 'gone right through the author's heart' (Belinsky's expression). He loves the Cossacks, for all their ignorance and weaknesses. Shtokman and his circle in Tatarsk are looked upon with a cold and alien eye and, moreover, *with contempt.* This particular *attitude* to events is more important than the descriptions of the atrocities performed by Shtokman, Koshevoy or Ivan Alekseyevich in the village of Tatarsk or with regard to Cossack prisoners. In his *Red Cavalry* Isaac Babel describes not only the dissolute behaviour of the Red Guards but also their out-and-out savagery (which evoked in its day a bitter clash between the writer and S. M. Budyonny). Babel feels deeply for the victims of this savagery and yet he does not hold the Red Guards in contempt. In his novel *For Whom the Bell Tolls* Ernest Hemingway paints a truly horrific picture of the Republicans executing prisoners in a Spanish town. But the writer does not look on the scene through pro-Franco eyes; his sympathies remain with those who are fighting Fascism, even though there is much in the Republican camp which is not to his taste. In *The Quiet Don* the sympathies of the author are undoubtedly on the side of the Cossacks and Grigori Melekhov at every stage of his tragic destiny.

Even the earliest critics of the novel repeatedly drew attention to this 'weakness' in Sholokhov's depiction of the Red camp. During the first RAPP discussions of the novel in plenary session V. Yermilov said,

When the author is describing the Cossack way of life, the Cossack social structure, in short when he tightens the threads around Grigori Mele-khov, Sholokhov has an abundance of colour and skill and artistically finished detail. When the threads are tightened at the opposite pole, around the worker Bunchuk or Shtokman, these heroes begin to use journalistic language. So does Sholokhov himself.[27]

The critic S. Dinamov (who had no connection with RAPP) wrote,

It is impossible to understand Sholokhov's treatment of the character of the revolutionary Shtokman. If Sholokhov were a proletarian writer

Shtokman ought to have represented the climax of his proletarian writing; this character in the novel ought to have been more solidly put together, more tightly bound in the artistic sense...This is not what has happened. The fertile flow suddenly dries up, the magnificently inter-woven pattern of description suddenly stops, the vivid tonality of depic-tion pales, the sure hand of a genuine master seems to falter... Sholokhov's Shtokman simply did not come out right! Shtokman came out in a grey monochrome and without significance. Sholokhov failed to create the image of a Social Democrat by the name of Shtokman descending like cold steel upon a backward village. Sholokhov had no understanding of the revolutionary, no feeling for him, and he was therefore incapable of creating his image so that it contained blood and muscle...Sholokhov could not find the necessary words; he turned out not to have the right colours...Shtokman does not come to life in these pages. He is upstaged by other strapping figures, full-blooded, artisti-cally realised Cossack characters such as Grigori and Petro, Panteley Prokofyevich and Stepan Astakhov.[28]

S. Selivanovsky claimed, not without justification, that,

Elements of schematism appear in Sholokhov's depiction of the Bolshe-viks. This is a fact which requires the closest scrutiny and explanation. How can it actually happen that in the work of a writer whom we describe as a proletarian the Bolshevik characters are the ones who turn out to be uninteresting and only half-alive when they are compared with the character of Grigori?[29]

Surveying all the books of the novel the critic P. Gromov wrote of Koshevoy that he is an 'unhistorical' hero, 'underdeveloped', 'artificial', 'schematic' and 'of restricted intellect'.[30] At a later date A. Upit said that 'too little space in the novel is occupied by the artistic depiction of the life and activity of those heroes who became the creators of the new life'.[31] The critic A. F. Britikov, examining the character of Shtokman, noted that 'this Bolshevik himself through his indiscreet actions impelled Grigori and the Cossacks into revolt, that he had no tactical flexibility, no profound knowledge of the peasant's heart and soul, no awareness of the real reasons behind the uprising'.[32] The same things were said in all literary manuals and even encyclopaedias in the 1930s and 1940s. For this reason the efforts beings made nowadays by Sholokhov scholars (whose main aim seems, in most cases, to be the vindication of every step ever taken by the author) to prove the all-round merit of Shtokman, Bunchuk etc. as characters have a strange, unconvincing air about them.

However, 'D' is clearly in the wrong when he attempts to show that the 'co-author' or 'double' (Sholokhov) converts Valet into 'a rigid, heroic, truly proletarian personality',[33] that the 'co-author' offends against the author's original design by depicting Koshevoy as the communist 'who proclaims Soviet power in the village of Tatarsk and proudly champions Bolshevik legality'.[34] We see in the second book that Valet was able to do precisely nothing to promote the victory of Soviet power on the Don. Along with Koshevoy he attempts, unsuccessfully, to desert to the Red Army. The Cossacks who capture them simply shoot Valet down. To Koshevoy who is also expecting a bullet in the back these same Cossacks say, 'Come on, that's enough of that. We've killed the peasant but you've been spared.'[35] The whole of this scene is obviously written by the author, not the co-author, of the epic. As far as Koshevoy himself is concerned, the eighth part of the novel, which according to 'D' belongs almost *in toto* to the pen of the co-author, essentially maintains the earlier attitude to this character. Koshevoy also becomes 'giddy at the thought of power'. Scarcely had he been appointed chairman of the Revolutionary Committee when he began 'walking slowly and impressively; his walk was so unusual that one or two of the villagers stopped when they met him and watched him with a smile from behind'.[36] In the quarrel between Koshevoy and Grigori who had just returned from serving with the 1st Cavalry the reader's sympathies once again are not with Koshevoy. When Ilyinichna tackles him indignantly about the murder of Grishaka the centenarian and says 'Killing a peaceful old man, that's war too, is it?', Koshevoy replies,

Of course it's war! I know these peaceful people. A peaceful old chap like him, he sits at home holding up his trousers and he does more harm than anybody else at the front... It's just such as him, old Grishaka, that has set the Cossacks against us. All this war started through them. Who did all the agitating against us? Them, the peaceful ones, they did. And you say I'm a 'killer'... I used not to be able to kill a lamb or a piglet and it's still the same – I know I couldn't.[37]

Even the wedding between Koshevoy and Dunyasha passes off without any songs or any drinking of home-distilled vodka and the happy-go-lucky Prokhor Zykov who was best man walks around disgusted all the next day and complains to Aksinya,

Call that a wedding, my lass?... Do you know what we had for supper? Roast chicken and sour milk. If only they'd given us a drop of vodka, damned devils! No, my girl, that's it, finished. I've been to the last of these new-style weddings. You have more fun at a dog's wedding; at least you get the dogs tearing each other's hair out.[38]

And although the Soviet security has required Grigori to appear in Veshensk in a week's time, Koshevoy sets off for the village himself to insist on Melekhov's immediate arrest so causing him to flee once more.

The logical development of the character of Grigori Melekhov remains intact in its principal features in the eighth and final section. It is also incorrect for 'D' to claim that the main theme of the 'co-author' or 'double' is 'the affirmation of Grigori's consistent leaning towards the

Bolsheviks and his eventual transference to their side'.[39] Without question some of Grigori's 'toings-and-froings' do seem strange. Within a month of becoming commander of an insurgent division Grigori says, in the company of Medvedev, the Commander of the 4th Division, 'We'll kill the colonel. He stayed behind deliberately, Kharlampiy. Let's go down on our knees before Soviet power. We're the ones who are wrong ...I'm only joking, Kharlampiy, drink up.'[40] These words have the air of an insertion made late in the day. But in the concluding part Grigori shows no leaning at all towards the Bolsheviks. He tells Prokhov that it would be better if neither the Soviets nor the Cadets had authority in the village. 'What I think is that there isn't a ha'p'orth of difference between them, my kinsman Misha Korshunov, say, and Mikhail Koshevoy.'[41]

Writers and critics in the 1930s indulged in a good deal of controversy and speculation as to how Sholokhov would bring his epic to a close. In a conversation with Sholokhov Stalin also asked when Sholokhov intended to bring his Grigori round to the Bolshevik side. Sholokhov quipped, 'I keep trying but he won't come.' Everyone closely associated with literature was aware that Stalin was displeased with the ending of *The Quiet Don*. Even the journals which received the manuscript tried to persuade Sholokhov to rework the ending, to 'brighten' it in relation to Grigori's fate. It was suggested that he should come to terms with collective farming and greet it with delight and optimism. But Sholokhov dug his heels in and Stalin gave way, which must have been unprecedented in the literature of that period. The fame of the novel was too great.

Some people, of course, are bound to find the eighth and last section of the novel weaker than its first sections. This is a moot point. But it cannot be described as 'false', as it is by 'D'. In this eighth section we see a picture of the Don region in ruins. Here is Sholokhov's description of spring 1920 on the Don:

A lilac haze hovered over the steppe. The earth had become completely arid, the grass had stopped growing and cracks ran across the fields ploughed the previous autumn. The ground dried out more and more by the hour and hardly a soul was to be seen working the fields near to Tatarsk. In the whole village only one or two very old men were left. Only the frost-bitten and the sick had returned home after the retreat and they were all unfit for work. Women and youths were the only ones who could work the fields. The wind drove dust clouds through the depopulated village, banged the shutters to and stirred the straw up on the roofs of the barns. The old men used to say, 'We shall have no bread this year. Only women in the fields and only one farm in every three doing any sowing. And dead soil won't give birth to anything.'[42]

The year 1920 on the Don was actually a hungry one, with a very poor harvest. For this reason the arrival in the villages of grain-requisitioners confiscating the bulk of the Cossacks' already meagre harvest led to a further outbreak of uprisings. Although the novel makes many reservations about this, referring to 'the kulaks and the prosperous section of Cossack society', we learn that when Fomin makes a call to revolt his *whole* troop responds, except one man who runs away. The reader can hardly blame the author of the eighth section of the novel for telling us of this new outbreak of civil war on the 'quiet' Don soil which has already seen so much suffering.

'D' writes that,

Melekhov ought to have died during the Cossack retreat, somewhere along the road to Novorossiysk or (disregarding all his antipathy towards the Whites) to have boarded a boat sailing for the shores of Turkey. The destiny of Grigori Melekhov, like that of his friends, is clearly fulfilled by Chapter XXVIII of the seventh part (Book Three). It seems quite unnatural for Melekhov, after all that he has gone through and after assuring himself that he would encounter ruthless punishment, suddenly to throw himself on the mercy of the conqueror.[43]

All of this reasoning by 'D' seems to me unconvincing. The demand that Melekhov should at all costs have been brought over to the Whites and even shipped away to the shores of Turkey is not very different from Stalin's insistence that Grigori Melekhov must be brought round to the Bolsheviks. Such an ending would also have been pure propaganda, only in this case pro-White. It is beyond doubt that the familiar present ending is a rich one artistically. Grigori has now lost all sense of discrimination; he can see nothing but his home village and his son. He has lost faith in the Reds and the Whites and he is ready to face death, even the execution from which he once fled. And although Grigori is still alive the novel remains a tragic one, since almost everyone else in the Melekhov family has died, the Don Cossack people has died, or at least the great bulk of it. Aksinya's death and the dramatic scene of her burial by Grigori can never fade from literary memory.

He buried his Aksinya in the bright light of mid-morning. When she was laid in the grave he crossed her dark-skinned arms, pallid now in death, on her chest, covered her face with a neckerchief to stop the earth getting into her half-open eyes with their motionless heavenwards stare and the dullness which had already set in. He said good-bye to her, firmly believing that they were not to be long parted.

Now he had no reason to hurry. Everything was done.

The sun rose high above the ravine in the smoky haze of a hot dry wind. Its rays silvered the thick mop of grey hair on Grigori's uncovered head and caressed his pallid, terribly motionless face. As if awakening from a troubled sleep he looked up and saw the black sky and the blinding, radiant, black disc of the sun overhead.[44]

It is worth considering the question of the 'dropping' of certain characters which 'D' takes to be a consequence of the co-author's revision of the novel. Naturally in a novel with so many characters and of such bulk it would be difficult not to overlook a few of the heroes. Sholokhov scholars have estimated that the second book alone includes about 200 episodic or better documented characters. Sholokhov himself once admitted,

When I started to write *The Quiet Don* I felt sure that with the best will in the world I should never be able to achieve the compositional wholeness and consistency that would be ultimately desirable. It was necessary to rotate a vast number of events, facts and people. This caused an occasional gap when I forgot about a character and he stayed outside my field of vision.[45]

One might also point out that *The Quiet Don* not only 'loses' a few heroes but also 'resurrects' a number of Cossacks who have been killed earlier on. In Chapter 33 of the sixth part we read about the killing of Bigmouth Antip (Antip Ivanovich Sinilin) together with Pyotr Melekhov and some other Cossacks. Yet in Chapter 51 of the same part we watch Grigori Melekhov ride off back to the front after a few days' leave. On the way he comes across a cart loaded with dead Cossacks and he recognises the two escorts as Bigmouth Antip and Stremyannikov. The cases of Atarshchik and Izvarin are not, however, simply matters of oversight. Atarshchik is portrayed by the author with unmistakable affection and therefore his absurd death from a stray bullet in Palace Square has the air of an artificial episode cutting right across the author's original design. It is also difficult to understand the disappearance of Izvarin, one of the theorists behind the Don Cossack separatist movement. Nevertheless, I cannot agree that in *The Quiet Don* the author's separatism is obvious for all to see, and is even 'washed clean and ennobled', as 'D' suggests.[46] The author of *The Quiet Don* is not a separatist but an autonomist, which is something quite different. He loves the Don and the Cossacks no less than Atarshchik but he certainly stops short of associating himself with Izvarin's arguments in favour of the complete withdrawal of the Don region from Russia. We might note in passing that even Fyodor Kryukov, considered by 'D' to be the most probable author of *The Quiet Don*, was not a separatist. The People's Socialist Party, in the formation of which Kryukov was an active participant, advanced on behalf of the Don region no more than a demand for wide powers of self-government and the reconstitution of the Military Assembly disbanded two centuries before which would be elected by all Cossack citizens 'in order to deal with all questions concerning the internal affairs of the Cossacks, as used to happen in olden times'.[47] It was simultaneously proposed that the Cossacks should be given all Don Cossack lands seized in the past by Cossack colonels or else distributed by the government to officers and officials. The popular socialists further proposed that all privately owned lands on the Don should be brought up by the exchequer and handed over to the peasants permanently resident in the district.[48]

It is well known that in 1952 *The Quiet Don* underwent sudden and ghastly 'plastic surgery' which distorted the whole appearance of the novel. This stylistic emendation resulted in the excision of all the more expressive Don Cossack sayings and dialect words, the very phrases which had imparted an inimitable vividness to the language of the book. In his preface to 'D's' study Alexander Solzhenitsyn considers that this correction of the text amounts to a powerful argument against the authorship of Sholokhov. He writes as follows:

One is amazed that he [Sholokhov] was ready to accept the levelling out of vocabulary which was performed in the 1953 edition. Many of the Don Cossack sayings which made such an impression when the novel first appeared have been ironed out and replaced by unexpressive words in general use. The erasure of all the startling colours until everything becomes uniformly grey – is it possible for an author to tolerate this in his own work, his own flesh and blood?[49]

Here, however, we must once again take into consideration certain pecularities of Soviet literature. Unfortunately we have experienced plenty of instances of many and varied cuts and insertions being visited upon books even without the authors' knowledge. Aware of this practice, some Sholokhov scholars have claimed that the stylistic correction of *The Quiet Don* in 1952 was carried out by the editor K. Potapov without Sholokhov's approval. As soon as the literary atmosphere changed following the Twentieth Congress of the CPSU Sholokhov restored the earlier version of the novel. Such claims probably contain more than a grain of truth. Moreover, people close to Sholokhov and those who met him regularly assert that in the 1950s he was suffering from acute alcoholism and receiving no treatment for it. He was said to be remarkably indifferent to the text of his works. Therefore many editorial amendments to *The Quiet Don* were undoubtedly carried out without obtaining Sholokhov's agreement to each individual alteration. I recall that it was in the early fifties, inevitably following a series of well-known articles by Stalin on linguistic topics, that several literary media together with the Writers' Union mounted a campaign against the misuse of dialect. One can only suppose that *The Quiet Don* became one of the first victims of this campaign.

It is also possible to cite many instances in our literature of well-known writers themselves correcting their early works to their detriment rather than otherwise. Fyodor Gladkov took two years to write *Cement*. Over the last thirty years he has continually amended this book and spoiled it considerably. Gladkov has converted the original and elliptical speech of the characters in the novel into 'good literature' by sacrificing surprising metaphorical expressions in favour of constructions which are grammatically correct. The author himself has muffled the dramatic effect of several powerful scenes and changed – for the worse – the character of some of his heroes.[50] Works as well known in past years as V. Ivanov's *Armoured Train 14-69* and L. Seyfulina's *Vireneya, Humus* and *The Lawbreakers* have been revised and corrected several times by the authors themselves. And, as the critic L. N. Smirnova observes, the revised versions of the novellas *Vireneya, Humus* and *The Lawbreakers* which have been so meticulously smoothed out, whittled down and distilled into a new essence have lost much of their original charm in the process.[51] For all that, most of these indisputably damaging emendations were introduced into the texts by the hand of the authoress herself. In 1927 the important Soviet poet Ilya Selvinsky published a narrative poem, *Ulyalyayev's Band*, which was highly original in its use of language and rhythmical verse forms. It was an epic poem which proved very successful, especially with young people. But readers who had committed many of its stanzas to memory scarcely recognised it in its post-war edition. This was indeed a case of the author himself erasing 'all the startling colours' until everything became 'uniformly grey'. The highly individual speech, the vernacular expressions, had largely disappeared from the poem and this whole operation was carried out by Selvinsky himself.

In *The Mainstream of 'The Quiet Don'* 'D' makes the basic assumption that the 'co-author' of the work under analysis is a writer devoid of all talent, a professional weakling, a master of neither dialect nor any form of cultivated literary language. He was apparently capable of nothing more than creating absurd caricatures of description and dialogue and indulging in out-and-out propaganda. This assumption is obviously incorrect. Even in his *Tales of the Don* the young Sholokhov demonstrated an indubitable talent for writing. Therefore, even accepting 'D's' hypothesis, we are bound to admit that both the author and the co-author wrote into *The Quiet Don* many interesting pages and chapters which fit well within the logical plan of the novel. 'D' prefers not to acknowledge any literary ability at all in the co-author, which leads him down many a blind alley and also gives rise to various errors and manipulations. For instance, he does not deny that the co-author's text in the third and fourth books contains a good deal of indisputable literary merit. Yet in one of his propositions he claims: 'Volumes Three and Four. Bits and pieces. Outline material converted by some *literate* person into a continuous text. (Serafimovich's hand here?).'[52] This is an unconvincing and definitely erroneous supposition. The involvement of a writer like Serafimovich in the writing of *The Quiet Don* would have been a difficult thing to hide.

In his notes 'Textual Problems (The Chapters on Typhus)' 'D' writes as follows:

Much in these chapters (descriptive sections, characterisation, etc.) could have been created, but some of them don't fit according to time. e.g. Chapter on evacuation of Novorossiysk...Isn't some of this material connected with those travelling with Kryukov? The priest Shkuratov and his son. Maybe Shkuratov got hold of the archives in that nest (box, etc.) Shkuratov junior (P.I.) – a writer, long-time Gulag inmate – couldn't he have written something himself? He could have been about twenty at that time (1920) (i.e. P. I. Shkuratov, author of *Pavel Kurbatov*).[53]

All this conjecture is quite unpersuasive. It is clear that neither 'D' nor his publisher Solzhenitsyn knows what happened to P. I. Shkuratov, who was twenty-nine, not twenty, in 1920. His typewritten novel is called *Pavel Kurganov*, not *Pavel Kurbatov*. This novel does contain scenes depicting the Cossack retreat into the Kuban but these are quite different from anything in *The Quiet Don*. Naturally Kryukov, who died in the spring of 1920, could not have observed the evacuation of the Cossacks and the Volunteers from Novorossiysk. But by the mid-1930s quite a lot of memoir material describing that evacuation was available in our literature. Moreover, the Cossacks returning to the Don included many amnestied people who either had not succeeded in boarding ships in Novorossiysk or had managed to fight in Wrangel's front line and later have themselves evacuated to Turkey, Bulgaria and other countries. Sholokhov, of course, might also have availed himself of their accounts. There was plenty of time for Sholokhov to have worked on these chapters, since the fourth book of *The Quiet Don* did not appear in print until the end of the 1930s.

'D's' book contains errors of another kind. The first paragraphs of the sixth part of *The Quiet Don* concerning the 'great cleavage' on the Don are confidently attributed by 'D' to the co-author. Let us recall this prologue to the sixth part of the novel. In the 1957 edition we read:

In the April of 1918 there occurred a great cleavage on the Don. The front-line Cossacks of the northern districts – Khopersk, Ust-Medveditsk and to some extent the Upper Don – accompanied the retreating Red Army units, while the Cossacks from the lower districts harassed and pursued them towards the frontiers of the province. The Khopersk Cossacks accompanied the Reds almost to a man, half of those from Ust-Medveditsk did so and only very small numbers from the Upper

Don. It was not until the year 1918 that history finally made a decisive division between Upper and Lower Cossacks.[54]

This paragraph is contrasted by 'D' with the beginning of Chapter 22 of the same section where we are told:

From across the Don, from the upper regions, from every area came news of a broad tidal wave of revolt. It was not just a case of one or two odd villages. Shumilinsk, Kazansk, Migulinsk, Meshkovsk, Veshensk, Yelansk and Ust-Khopersk had risen and formed companies with all haste. Karginsk, Bokovsk and Krasnokutsk were clearly coming round to the side of the insurgents.

Emphasising the words 'the village of Ust-Khopersk' 'D' asks, 'How can this be, since we have been told that the Khopersk Cossacks to a man had left? Does it mean they all came back and revolted?'[55]

Yet there is no inconsistency here. 'D' is suggesting that the village of Ust-Khopersk must necessarily be the capital of the Khopersk district by analogy with Ust-Medveditsk which was the capital of the Ust-Medveditsk district. In actual fact the village of Ust-Khopersk belonged to the same region, the Upper Don, as Veshensk. The administrative centre of the Khopersk district was the village of *Uryupinsk*. In 1917 and 1918 the Khopersk Cossacks did indeed take a most active part in the revolutionary events. The village of Uryupinsk had a strong Bolshevik group and this was among the very first villages to fall to the Soviets. In April 1918 the overwhelming majority of the Khopersk front-line Cossacks retreated northwards along with the Red Army units. In the spring of 1919 the Khopersk district failed to support the Veshensk Uprising even though terror of a criminally excessive kind swept through that area as a result of the directive on 'Decossacking'. Most of the front-line Cossacks were then serving with the Red Army and had little knowledge of what was going on in their district.

Referring to the statement that 'the revolt was kept within the frontiers of the Upper Don district' (Chapter 38) 'D' recalls that we were told elsewhere that the revolt 'flared up in an all-consuming fire', that news of the tidal wave of revolt came in 'from every area' and that 'the revolt flooded across the whole Don region and the steppe country beyond the Don for two hundred and fifty miles around' (also the beginning of Chapter 38). 'D' sees this as an inconsistency, an attempt by the co-author to underestimate the scale of the revolt, and so on. But there is no inconsistency here. The Veshensk Uprising actually involved for the most part the Cossacks of the Upper Don district. All the first documents and addresses of the insurgents were signed by the District Council of the Upper Don. A telegram in early May 1919 from the Lieutenant General of the Don Cossack Army to the Don Cossack ataman and the chairman of the Military Assembly went as follows:

Pleasure in sharing with you welcome news received from insurgent Cossacks of *Upper Don district*. Recent return of courageous airman Officer-Cadet Tatarin dispatched to that district by myself on April 26 with Lieutenant Bogatyryov who had remained there. Uprising in full swing. Insurgents number up to 25,000. Sufficient small arms and machine guns. Ammunition captured from Reds. Morale splendid... News of arrival of our airmen spread quickly throughout insurgent front. Inspired them for long period.[56]

Not that the insurgent Upper Don Cossacks limited their activities to the one district. By skilful deployment of their units they were able to cross the district boundaries, destroy Red Army communications, attack transport, break railway links and so on. Thus there is no reason to accuse the author of *The Quiet Don* of inconsistency. In the sixth part of the novel the size and scale of the Veshensk Uprising are depicted with great accuracy.

Another relevant point is that the first edition of the novel (Moscow, 1933) gives a different version of the beginning of Part 6 from the one referred to in *The Mainstream of 'The Quiet Don'*. This is how it goes:

In the April of 1918 there occurred a great cleavage on the Don. The front-line Cossacks of the northern districts – Khopersk, Ust-Medveditsk and to some extent the Upper Don – *left with Mironov* and the retreating Red Army units. The Cossacks from the lower districts harassed and pursued them towards the frontiers of the province, *battling to liberate every last inch of ground*. The Khopersk Cossacks *went with Mironov* almost to a man, half of those from Ust-Medveditsk did so, and only very small numbers from the Upper Don.

All the italicised words are unusual for 1933, especially the references to the 'liberation' of the province and to Mironov, a Lieutenant Colonel and a well-loved leader of the Cossack workers in the upper districts who was shot in the Butyrki prison and declared an enemy of the Soviet people. It was 1960 before he was rehabilitated. Thus the repeated mention of Mironov's name in the first edition of *The Quiet Don* is somewhat mystifying, especially since that name has disappeared from the pages of the novel in every subsequent edition. If we are to accept 'D's' theory of the presence in the novel of an author and a co-author of the text I should prefer to attribute the beginning of Part 6 to the original author.

By working on the rigid assumption that all the well-written chapters in *The Quiet Don* belong to the author, Fyodor Kryukov, and all the badly-written ones to the co-author, Sholokhov, the critic 'D' opens his work to inconsistency and error. In the chapter entitled 'The Outsiders', for example, 'D' claims that the author of the epic was undoubtedly responsible for Chapter 12 of Book 2 which includes the cruel episode outside the Putilov works and the clash between Listnitsky and the Cossack Ivan Lagutin, a member of the regimental military-revolutionary committee. 'D' even explains what place this extract occupies in the development of the original plan.

Listnitsky is intended to represent the type of Cossack officer whose commander-in-chief was Nicholas himself, and his son and heir, the ill-starred Aleksey. As opposed to commanders like Atarshchikov and Izvarin, Listnitsky is not the least bit concerned about the primordial liberties of the Cossack; he is imbued with the sense of self-importance imparted by that 'special trust' which the autocracy placed in the Cossacks. He belonged to that section of executive Cossack officers who led their companies blindly on any punitive expedition. Listnitsky has come to see in the Cossacks a force always readily available for fighting sedition and revolution. He was in this instance directed not by personal cruelty or fanaticism. Not in the least; here was simply a case of unshakable certainty that this was the only conceivable course of action. Although by temperament slow to react, self-possessed and aloof, when the occasion arose Lieutenant Listnitsky boiled over with the requisite zeal of a scrounging master. As the reader can see, this serviceman's zeal awakens in him only when there is good reason, as in the pre-October days in Petrograd. In those days, inspired by the prospect of the victory of Russian arms under the leadership of General Kornilov and cherishing a hope that the old ways might be restored, Listnitsky even began to think in terms of full identification with the Cossacks...But he remains true to himself and when shortly afterwards he happens to fall into conversation with a Cossack in his company, Lagutin, his first words make it clear that full identification is an impossibility...This dialogue is followed by the cruel incident outside the Putilov works when Lieutenant Listnitsky, forgetting his noble intentions, has his Cossacks thrash a workman with their whips. Thus is the real Listnitsky exposed (and *clearly defined* by the author) as he approaches the border of two revolutions and enters the Volunteer Army ready to save Russia from the Bolsheviks.[57]

But thirteen pages further on in another version of the chapter entitled 'The Outsiders' 'D' ascribes the incident outside the Putilov works not to the author but the co-author and again explains why the co-author had need of it.

It is apparent that the author considers the typical ordinariness of Lieutenant Listnitsky an essential part of his historical chronicle. It is characteristic of the officer class in old Russia and the most frightening thing about it is the complacency of this caste and the consequently complacent anti-popular spirit (soldiers and officers speaking different languages if they get into conversation). It is precisely because, according to the basic plan, Listnitsky's character lacks the ability to transcend ordinary decency that his denunciation of Bunchuk is an impossibility. It does not fit the original pattern; it is something stuck on by the co-author. It was the co-author's opinion as he attempted to touch up the figure of Lieutenant Listnitsky according to his own scheme that such a character must be given the attributes of a double-dyed scoundrel. He must needs appear as a dastardly nonentity (Book 1, Part 3, Chapter XXIV), a villain and careerist of the vilest kind (Book 2, Part 4, Chapter I), and he must at all costs display savage cruelty (Book 2, Part 4, Chapter XII.)[58]

Another mistake made by 'D' is even more illuminating. The second book of *The Quiet Don* ends with a description of Podtelkov's expedition into the northern districts of the province and its tragic outcome. (Part 5, Chapters 27–30). 'D' confidently ascribes these chapters to the original author. His opinion is that the author of *The Quiet Don* sympathises in his own way with Podtelkov, Krivoshlykov and Lagutin since these Cossacks strove to establish self-government on the Don.

Not for nothing does the *author* put real, living Cossack speech into the mouths of his Cossack Bolsheviks and give his Reds typically Cossack habits...The soil of the Don, the Don Cossack way of life, these are Podtelkov's passion and he himself is a typical Cossack of self-asserting, runaway, outlaw stock. Different in type but equally typical, and a 'good Red', is Ivan Lagutin.[59]

For all that, it has been shown that many of the pages of these last chapters in Book 2 of *The Quiet Don* are in fact a literary version of the text of a short pamphlet by A. Frenkel, *Orly Revolyutsii* (*Eagles of the Revolution*) published in Rostov in 1920.[60] Frenkel had been a member of Podtelkov's expedition but had managed to escape during the chaos when it was surrounded by the Cossacks. He later became a member of the Don regional Office of the Communist Party and in 1919 represented the Don province at the Eighth Communist Party Congress. Fyodor Kryukov, it goes without saying, could not have read Frenkel's pamphlet. Parts of this document are worth quoting.

We passed Alekseyevsk and headed for Rubashkino. As soon as we had come down the hill into this settlement we noticed immediately that everybody was running about in panic. Men, women and children were leaving everything behind and running or riding away on horses and carts in all directions. We stopped our own carts and started calling out to them as they fled. A few minutes later an old chap came out of a yard on the outskirts, pale as death, his hair all over the place, cap in hand and trembling like a leaf. 'Well, dad, can't you recognise your own people?' 'We don't know anything. A man rode in before you and he said the Bolsheviks were coming and they'd set up a battery and knock hell out of us.'

We learned from our conversations that our billeting officer had been captured by a mounted patrol of Cossacks and taken away by them. Riders started appearing now and then on the hills to both sides. There was no point in spending the night there so we went back...It was late at night when we arrived in the village of Kalashnikov in the rural district of Polyakov-Nagolinsk. Podtelkov was nervous and anxious. 'We mustn't sleep here,' he said, 'We must move on, anywhere, or they'll take us unawares.' But the Cossacks dispersed to get some sleep. The whole expeditionary force, shattered and weary, broke up for the night. Podtelkov made several vain attempts to muster them and he was very agitated. 'The squad has been wearied by the journey. They're not ready for battle. I can't do anything without a squad. We're done for.' ... Pickets were posted, patrols dispatched and a long, anxious night began full of the agony of expectation...

At dawn we started getting ready to leave. By six or seven a.m. it became known (and with binoculars it was easy to see) that the settlement was surrounded by thousands of Cossacks on every side...

When Podtelkov received the Cossacks' demand that we surrender our arms and when he heard the proposal that we should send out a delegation he thundered in fury, 'What? Why, this is counter-revolution! What kind of talks can we hold with them? We shall fight them. Follow me! Get in line!...'

Podtelkov ran forward followed by thirty or forty men. At the edge of the settlement he was stopped near a rise in the ground by a member of the commission of five, the Cossack Mrykhin. 'Podtelkov, shame on you!' he said reproachfully, 'Against your own brothers...Let's not have any bloodshed, let's talk things over with them.'[61]

Here now are one or two extracts from *The Quiet Don*.

They passed Alekseyevsk. It was drizzling. The sky was overcast. Only to the east a patch of deep blue sky peeped through a break in the clouds, shining under the declining sun. Scarcely had they started riding down-hill into the Tavrichansk settlement of Rubashkin when people began running out in the opposite direction and several carts raced away too. 'They're off. They're scared of us...,' said Lagutin absent-mindedly looking round at the others. Podtelkov shouted, 'Fetch them back! Shout to them to come back, the devils!' The Cossacks urged their carts forward and waved their caps. One of them bellowed, 'Hey! Where are you going? Hang on!...' The carts flew down into the settlement. The wind swirled down the wide, deserted street. In one yard an old Ukrainian woman shouted as she stuffed cushions into her little carriage. Her husband, barefoot and hatless, held the horses steady.

They found out in Rubashkin that the billeting officer sent on by Podtelkov had been captured by a mounted patrol of Cossacks and taken off into the hills. The Cossacks were evidently not far away. After a brief consultation they decided to go back...Podtelkov, walking up and down by a cart, started to point out the advantages of moving on to Ust-Medveditsk, but he was cut short by one of the Cossack agitators. 'You're out of your mind. Where do you want to take us? Straight to the counter-revolutionaries? Stop messing about, my friend. We're going back. We don't want to die just yet. What's that over there? Look!' He pointed up the hill. Everyone looked round. On a rise three mounted figures were clearly outlined. 'One of their patrols!' exclaimed Lagutin. 'There's another!' Horsemen loomed up all over the hillside. They were riding together into groups, scattering again, riding away behind the hills and reappearing. Podtelkov gave the order to set off back. They rode through Alekseyevsk. There, too, the population had evidently been warned by the Cossacks. When they saw the carts of the expedition approaching they began to hide and run away in all directions.

It was getting dark. They were soaked by the persistent drizzle and they shivered, wet through. They walked alongside the carts, rifles at the ready. The road wound away into a hollow, worked its way along and emerged on the far hillside. Cossack patrols came and went on the hilltops, escorting the expedition, increasing the tension they already felt...

'Fyodor, don't expect anything just yet,' whispered Krivoshlykov, calling Podtelkov over to his cart. 'They'll not attack now. They'll wait for night.' 'I think you're right...'

Podtelkov strode on, drinking in the many different scents which mingled together as they rose from the soaking wet grass. Now and again he stopped to wipe clods of mud off his heels. Then he would straighten up and bear his massive body forwards ponderously and wearily, to the leathery creaking of his dripping, unbuttoned jacket.

It was night-time when they arrived in the village of Kalashnikov in the rural district of Polyakov-Nagolinsk. The squad of Cossacks left the carts and broke up, scattering among the huts for a night's sleep. A distraught Podtelkov ordered pickets to be posted but the Cossacks were reluctant to muster. Three men flatly refused to go... Podtelkov looked harassed and alarmed. He only waved his hand. 'They've been wearied by the journey. They're no good for defence. We're done for, Mishatka!...' Somehow Lagutin got a few men together and sent them out on patrol. 'No falling asleep, lads! Or they'll get us!' Podtelkov said encouragingly to the Cossacks nearest to him as he went round the huts.

All night he sat at a table, holding his head in his hands, breathing heavily and hoarsely. Just before dawn sleep overtook him and his great head dropped on to the table... Then came the dawn. Podtelkov went outside... On the hillside through the pall of white mist that hung over the village and the willows in the meadow large numbers of Cossack soldiers could be seen riding up and down trotting, bobbing and galloping, surrounding the village, tightening the ring. Before long the other Cossacks began streaming into the yard where Podtelkov had stopped and coming up to his cart Vasiliy Miroshnikov, a sturdy Ukrainian Cossack from Migulinsk, called Podtelkov to one side, looked down at the ground and said, 'Now then, comrade Podtelkov... Delegates have just arrived from them. They have orders to tell you to lay down your arms and surrender. If you don't they're going to attack.' 'You... what do you think you're saying?' Podtelkov seized Miroshkin by the lapels of his greatcoat, thrust him to one side and ran over to his cart. There he grabbed his rifle by the barrel and turned to speak to the Cossacks in a rough hoarse voice. 'Surrender?... What kind of talks can we hold with counter-revolutionaries? We shall fight them! Follow me! Get in line!' They poured out of the yard and ran in a gang to the end of the village. By the last houses a member of the commission, Mrykhin, caught up with Podtelkov who was breathing heavily. 'Shame on you, Podtelkov!' he said, 'Our own brothers...are we going to shed their blood? Stop, now. Let's talk things over.'[62]

The similarity between these two extracts is so obvious that there is no need to prolong the quotations.

Sholokhov evidently also borrowed two documents from Frenkel's pamphlet which he included *in toto* in Chapter 28 of the fifth part of *The Quiet Don*: 'A list of all ranks in Podtelkov's unit sentenced to death on 27 April 1918' and 'A resolution of the delegates from Karginsk, Bokovsk and Krasnokutsk'.[63] The pamphlet, it is true, gives considerably less detail about the execution of Podtelkov and the members of his expedition. Nevertheless certain details do coincide between the pamphlet and the novel; the rest could easily have been touched in by Sholokhov acting independently.

In his summary of the various 'layers' of the text written respectively by the author and co-author 'D' gives it as his opinion that in Part 5, Chapters 16 and 17, and also 19 and 20, which deal with the destinies of Bunchuk and Pogudko, belong undoubtedly to the co-author, Sholokhov, whereas Chapter 18, which describes the retreat of the Volunteer Army from Rostov, belongs to the author, apparently Fyodor Kryukov. This, however, is doubtful, at least up to the place marked with three asterisks half-way through Chapter 18. Reading the first pages of this controversial chapter one notices a clear similarity to the description of the retreat of the Volunteer Army which appears in N. Nakurin's book *How the Revolution was Fought* (*Kak Srazhalas' Revolyutsiya*), Vol. 1, edited by N. N. Popov (Moscow, Goslitizdat, 1925). In this work as well as in *The Quiet Don* we encounter the error to which we referred when discussing Sholokhov's *Tales of the Don*, a strange one for a Cossack writer to have made. Nazarov, who was elected Don Cossack ataman after Kaledin, is described at the very beginning of the chapter as 'the appointed military ataman'.

The Chapter 'Red Herrings', which occupies fifteen pages (pp. 154–68) of 'D's' book, also fails to withstand critical scrutiny. He cites a letter from Leonid Andreyev to the writer Sergey Sergeyevich Goloushev in which Andreyev informs his friend that 'your *Quiet Don* is being rejected' and then, supported by Solzhenitsyn in a publisher's note, he attempts to show that this letter of 3 September 1917 might have been referring to the first book of Kryukov's novel which Goloushev could have obtained from Serafimovich and sent on to Andreyev on the newspaper *Russkaya Volya*. But this whole chain of complex arguments falls apart as soon as one looks at the other letters written by Goloushev during the summer of 1917 (eight of which, for example, are available in the archives of Pushkinsky Dom). These letters make it quite clear that Goloushev did actually pay a short visit to the Don region that summer and wrote a sketch entitled 'From the Quiet Don' which he offered to Leonid Andreyev for publication. In a letter of 23 August Goloushev writes, 'Here am I sitting in a railway carriage heading for the Quiet, murky Don.'[64] In another letter (undated) we read, 'when I got back my sketch "From the Quiet Don" I was quite simply bewildered, but within a couple of hours I have forgotten my bewilderment. I sent the manuscript to *Narodnyy Vestnik*. They were glad to have it and I even stopped remembering about it.'[65] Sure enough, in *Narodnyy Vestnik* (Moscow, 1917), Nos. 12 and 13–14, of 24 and 28 September, there appeared a sketch entitled 'From the Quiet Don' written by Sergey Glagol (pseudonym of S. S. Goloushev).

What general conclusion may we draw from our discussion of the book by 'D'? First of all we must repeat that it contains no more than a hypothesis. Since this is a question of accusation we might use legal parlance and conclude that the book presents important evidence, but that the circle of evidence is not complete, for which reason the case brought by 'D' against the 'co-author' remains not proven. Alexander Solzhenitsyn, who published 'D's' book, realises this. As he writes in his preface, 'Of course, more than five decades after the event, the chance of any judicial inquiry into this literary mystery has probably gone for good. That is more than can be hoped for now...Not for the first time history had kept jealous guard over a cherished secret.' However, as Solzhenitsyn suggests, 'the possibility of a literary investigation always remains open. It will not be too late for that a hundred, even two hundred years from now.'[66] This is a conclusion with which we can agree. Recently a literary examination of *The Iliad* and *The Odyssey* (epics dating back to the seventh or eighth centuries B.C.) was carried out with the aid of a computer. It was thereby established that both works were written by the same author. The novel *The Quiet Don* is, of course, available for similar examination. Modern methods of literary scholarship and textual analysis allow such work to be conducted at the highest scientific level. To begin with it would be sufficient to compare the language, style, vocabulary and certain other characteristics typical of the first volume of Sholokhov's Complete Works (*Tales of the Don*) with the second and third volumes (Books 1 and 2 of *The Quiet Don*). The official version has it that these volumes were created at practically the same time (in the periods 1924–5 and 1926–8). A mechanical analysis would be able to confirm or refute this with reasonable certainty.

We have already cited an extract from the memoirs of the poet S. Shchipachev concerning the young Sholokhov. Concluding these memoirs Shchipachev writes as follows:

THE MAINSTREAM OF "THE QUIET DON"'

I last reread *The Quiet Don* four years ago...It was in hospital. There was plenty of time for reflection and I started wondering what other works are worthy of having this novel set alongside them. No, Tolstoy's *War and Peace* was not what came to mind on that occasion, although that comparison is fully justified. What came to mind was *The Lay of Igor's Campaign*. It seemed like an unexpected, even arbitrary comparison but I thought it over. Who can tell? Long ages may pass away and the language we speak and write today will be almost incomprehensible so that translations are needed. Will not *The Quiet Don* suffer the same fate as that unfading earlier work, the sole difference being that the name 'Mikhail Sholokhov' will still be known even then?[67]

I find it probably easier to accept Shchipachev's words than 'D's' opinion, on condition that we amend Shchipachev's sentence to read 'the name of one of the authors, "Mikhail Sholokhov", will still be known even then'. For even if we come to the firm conclusion that he had before him the unfinished novel of another author we must also remain convinced that the part played by Sholokhov in the creation of this epic novel was far more considerable than 'D' and Solzhenitsyn believe.

6

FURTHER PROBLEMS IN SHOLOKHOV'S LITERARY BIOGRAPHY

So far we have discussed the basic problem which underlies Mikhail Sholokhov's literary biography – how did a twenty- to twenty-four-year-old writer, fresh from a period of grain-requisitioning and unskilled labour, after the briefest of débuts in *Tales of the Don*, manage to create the epic canvas of a genius, depicting the tragedy of the Don Cossacks in the years of war and revolution?[1] Addressing a conference of young writers, and proposing an increase in the fees offered to people at the beginning of their literary careers, Sholokhov turned to the praesidium and exclaimed, 'I put it to you: what great writer began with works of genius? As a rule, the first works of all great writers have always been mediocre.'[2] Sholokhov himself seems to be an exception to this rule. Virtually without warming up, or one might say with no more than a single-stride run-up, he managed to leap higher than any other Soviet writer. But there are other problems in the literary biography of Mikhail Sholokhov, and an examination of them is likely to assist us in solving the riddles of *The Quiet Don*.

Naturally we turn first of all to the question of *Virgin Soil Upturned*. The first book of this novel was written in some haste in a few months during the year 1930. Its publication was, however, delayed. The editors of *Novy Mir*, having accepted the author's manuscript, insisted upon the excision from it of those true-to-life but extremely cruel scenes of the dispossession of the kulaks which begin the description of collectivisation in the village of Gremyachiy Log (Chapters 6–9). Sholokhov informs us that he had to turn to Stalin for help. Stalin read through the novel and said, 'We weren't afraid to dispossess the kulaks; why should we be afraid to write about it now?'[3] With this kind of support the first book of *Virgin Soil Upturned* was published in 1932, that is simultaneously with the third book of *The Quiet Don*.

No-one has so far called the authorship of *Virgin Soil Upturned* into question. Only Solzhenitsyn has caste any doubt on this, at a press conference in Stockholm in December 1974 when he said,

There is one figure here whom perhaps I should name straightaway. He is Pyotr Gromoslavsky, or Gremislavsky (depending on your local origin). This man Pyotr Gromoslavsky was a third-rate writer from the village of Veshensk. In 1918 and 1919 he worked in Novocherkassk in some capacity on the journal *Donskaya Volna* published by Kryukov. Well, he tried his best, but did not exactly cover himself with glory. However, he was quite capable of hack work. In 1920 he retreated with Kryukov as far as the village of Novokorsunsk where Kryukov died. Thereupon he returned to Soviet territory. As a participant in the White retreat he was debarred from publication but he did marry his daughter to Sholokhov. I shall take this no further but it is possible to imagine that Pyotr Gremislavsky, a literary hack, might well have written a book on the level of *Virgin Soil Upturned*.[4]

But this kind of suggestion cannot even be construed as a hypothesis. Naturally, it is hard to believe that Sholokhov, living under the same roof as (or next door to) his father-in-law and his brother-in-law, who both had some association with literature and some literary education, never consulted them or asked them for help. But there is absolutely no evidence on this score, since the internal relationships within the substantial Sholokhov-Gromoslavsky clan have always been and remain to this day hidden from outsiders. When I was studying this problem I took down the account of one Veshensk Cossack to the effect that in 1930, at the height of collectivisation on the Don, a directive was received concerning the eviction both of the kulaks and also of all ex-White officers. At the time Sholokhov had little influence with the local authorities, and was powerless to prevent the arrest and exile to Siberia of his father-in-law and brother-in-law. It was only in 1932, after the appearance of *Virgin Soil Upturned*, that Sholokhov managed to gain an amnesty for his relatives and permission for them to return to Veshensk. Should this testimony be confirmed, it would utterly invalidate the story of Gromoslavsky's involvement in the writing of *Virgin Soil Upturned*.

There are various views about the literary merit of this novel. Solzhenitsyn, for example, considers it extremely weak in every respect, quite out of line with *The Quiet Don*. Many Sholokhov scholars, on the other hand, consider *Virgin Soil Upturned* a classic work, of no less distinction than *The Quiet Don*.[5] It is our belief that the truth lies between the two extreme valuations. Considering the time when it was written, *Virgin Soil Upturned* was without doubt an exceptional work, and can in no way be considered an artistic failure. It contains a good measure of true-to-life incidents, forcefully written, and some convincing, well-drawn characters, the best of which are probably Makar Nagulnov and Kondrat Maydannikov. One thinks also of the portrait of Dymok who somewhat resembles Mit'ka Korshunov in *The Quiet Don*. Also similar to *The Quiet Don* is the style used for the description of nature (see the beginnings of Chapters 1, 26 and 34). Judging by the draft plan of *The Mainstream of 'The Quiet Don'* the critic 'D' believes that those pages which show similarities with the style of *The Quiet Don* were taken by Sholokhov from a number of 'lost' chapters and other notes made by Fyodor Kryukov (sections 'A Treasure Discovered?' and 'Sweet Leftovers – Still Some Left'). This again is no more than a hypothesis. It differs from 'D's' basic hypothesis in that it remains not only unproved but unprovable.

Virgin Soil Upturned contains pungent dialogue and some sharp clashes of personality. The author is also successful in his depiction of collective labour in the early days of sowing, the 'revolt' of the Cossack women, and in several other scenes. He certainly has a sound knowledge of the events described in his work. Naturally *Virgin Soil Upturned* lacks that merciless truthfulness which so impresses the reader of *The Quiet Don*. The aim is simply to show us some aspects of Don Cossack life in the difficult days of collectivisation. A good deal is passed over in silence and a certain amount is even distorted. For this reason we can nowadays achieve a better and deeper insight into the nature and character of the events of 1929 and 1930 from books by V. Belov, S. Zalygin, V. Grossman, V. Tendryakov and F. Abramov (even though some of their works are not entirely devoted to the theme of collectivisation) than from *Virgin Soil Upturned*. However, in the literature of the early 1930s Sholokhov's novel was the best available work dealing with rural life in the Soviet Union; which probably accounts for its early popularity. (There are scholars who take Panferov's *Bruski* to be a more truthful and powerful work on collectivisation.) Be that as it may, the controversy over the artistic merits of the first part of *Virgin Soil Upturned* is not the most important aspect of our subject. The really important point, which must be fully and clearly discussed, is that it is possible to discern in *Virgin Soil Upturned* the grown-up, and in many ways better educated, author of *The Tales of the Don*, but certainly not the author of *The Quiet Don* itself. Just as there is no ideological or philosophical link between the *Tales* and *The Quiet Don*, there is similarly no connection between the latter and *Virgin Soil Upturned*. *The Quiet Don* appears in some ways to fall outside the author's ideological and artistic course of development.

The Quiet Don is a depiction, many-sided, complex and profound, of the colossal changes which occurred in the Don province during the period of war and revolution. *Virgin Soil Upturned* merely presents a one-sided, simplified and schematic depiction of a radical change of direction in life on the Don. There is more to this than a mere reduction in the scale of events. We know that *Virgin Soil Upturned* describes only the events occurring in the space of a few months in 1930 at a small village on the Don called Gremyachiy Log. It is most striking that this restriction of the visual field is not offset by a compensating depth of penetration into character or the nature of events. The sense of tragedy and the profundity peculiar to *The Quiet Don* are either reduced or deadened in *Virgin Soil Upturned*, if they are found at all, although collectivisation in its Stalinist form was in many ways a social and personal tragedy for the Don Cossacks and the broad mass of the Russian peasantry. People with years and years of work on the Don behind them make it clear that agriculture in the region, which had barely recovered during the NEP period, suffered damage from 1930 to 1933 almost equal to that of the civil war years. We must accept that at the time when the first part of *Virgin Soil Upturned* was being written collectivisation was only just beginning, and it is obviously unreasonable to expect the author to reflect such tragic consequences of this policy as the disastrous famines of 1932–3, the massive repressions, the exile to the north of whole villages, and so on. Nevertheless even the early period of collectivisation produced a great deal of tragic conflict which in this novel is either quickly and easily overcome, or passed over in a few words, or dealt with in an almost humorous manner as in the case of the mass slaughter of cattle in Gremyachiy Log.

There is no character in *Virgin Soil Upturned* to compare with Grigori Melekhov, Aksinya, Natalya and many other personalities in *The Quiet Don*. Perhaps Lushka alone manages to recall a character from *The Quiet Don*, Darya. The language of *Virgin Soil Upturned* lacks the rich tints and the impressive play of nuances in Cossack popular speech which are encountered in most of the chapters of *The Quiet Don*. The clashes between people and personalities which are set down with such skill, succinctness and extreme tension in *The Quiet Don* are not successfully re-created by the author of *Virgin Soil Upturned*. The dialogue is also much weaker in the latter novel; in fact it always tends to shade off into a series of long, wearisome monologues pronounced from time to time by Davydov, Nagulnov, Ostrovnov, Polovtsev and Maydannikov; and this is scarcely affected by the fact that sometimes the monologues are self-addressed. The narrative method in *Virgin Soil Upturned* constantly lapses into a trite journalistic patter quite unimaginable in *The Quiet Don*. Here are a few examples:

Next day, on February 4, a general meeting of the collective farm unanimously passed a resolution to expel all kulak families from the region of the Northern Caucasus. The meeting also confirmed the administrative farm council elected by authorised delegates and consisting of Yakov Lukich Ostrovnov, Pavel Lyubishkin, Dyomka Ushakov and Arkasha, who only just made it. Davydov was a popular and uncontroversial choice for the fifth place. This was no doubt affected by the receipt only the day before of a note from the Regional Agricultural Union to the effect that the Regional Party Committee in Conjunction with the Regional Agricultural Union wished to propose Comrade Davydov, a distinguished party worker and the committee's authorised representative, for the post of chairman of the administrative farm council.[6]

Next day the Gremyachiy Log Party cell, meeting in closed session, unanimously accepted a proposal for the socialisation of all livestock, animals large and small, the property of the members of the 'Stalin' collective farm in Gremyachiy Log. In addition to the animal stock it was decided also to socialise the poultry...It was further resolved and minuted that a powerful propaganda campaign be mounted in favour of the cessation of the harmful practice of slaughtering cattle, to which end all party members took it upon themselves to go round all the farms that very day. With regard to the legal sanctions to be taken against those caught slaughtering animals it was resolved for the time being not to implement them but to await results of the propaganda campaign.[7]

The plan stipulated that an area of 472 hectares was scheduled for ploughing that spring in Gremyachiy Log, 110 hectares being virgin soil. Last autumn 643 hectares had been ploughed by farmers still working individually and 210 hectares of winter rye had been sown. It was proposed to apportion the total sowing area between grain and oil as follows: Wheat – 667 hectares; Rye – 210; Barley – 108; Oats – 50; Millet – 65; Maize – 167; Sunflowers – 45; Hemp – 13. Total – 1325 hectares, plus 91 hectares of sandy ground extending south of Gremyachiy Log to the Uzhachin range where melons were to be planted.[8]

Another example is the sharp clash between Andrey Razmetnov and Marina Poyarkova, who have lived together for many years in love and harmony.

People stopped leaving the farm...The last person to leave was Andrey Razmetnov's common-law wife, Marina Poyarkova. Their life together had run into trouble. Marina had got religious and become all devout ...There was more to this than met the eye. On the 26th Marina submitted her written resignation from the collective farm on the grounds that being in it was 'going against the Lord'...Andrey rushed home from the village council, pale with anger. Wiping the sweat from his scarred forehead with his sleeve he pleaded with her in front of Davydov and Yakov Lukich: 'Marisha, darling! Don't ruin me! Don't disgrace me! Why do you want to leave the farm? You little devil – haven't I loved you and looked after you? You've got your cow back...what else do you want? How can we share our love together if you want to go away and live as an individual again? They've allowed you to keep your hens and cocks, yes and that smooth-necked rooster and the Dutch gander you wept bitter tears over – they're all back with you living in the farmyard! What more do you want? Withdraw your resignation!' 'I will not!' Marina shouted, her slanting eyes narrowing in fury. 'I refuse, so you needn't bother asking me! I refuse to live on this farm! I refuse to go on living in sin with you! Give me back my cart and the plough and harrow!...' 'Marina, think what you're saying. If you don't I might have to give you up!' 'Go to hell, your fair-haired devil. You lecherous dog, damn you! I can see you blinking, you evil spirit. Popping out your beady eyes in anger! Who was it last night standing with Malashka Ignatenkova down that little lane? Not you, was it? You lying swine, you bastard! Give me up! I can live without you. You've been leading up to this for ages, I can see that now!' 'Marisha, my sweet one, where did you pick that up? What Malashka? I've never stood with her, never in my born days. And what's that got to do with the farm anyway?' Andrey clutched at his head and said no more. He had clearly run out of arguments.[9]

Dozens of pages might be filled with examples of this kind of prose from *Virgin Soil Upturned*.

The author of *Virgin Soil Upturned* also lacks the objectivity in describing people who are unsympathetic, or simply bad, which was part of the nature of the author of *The Quiet Don*. Most of the kulaks in *Virgin Soil Upturned*, and especially Polovtsev and Lyatyevsky, are double-dyed scoundrels painted by the author almost exclusively in dark tones. Polovtsev, for example, not only hacks Khoprov to death with an axe, he also strangles Khoprov's wife with his own hands, reflecting as he does so, 'She is a woman, a Cossack woman and I am an officer – I ought to be ashamed...Oh, to hell with it!'

The humour is quite different in the two novels. In *Virgin Soil Upturned* it consists mainly in the ridicule or buffoonery of old Shchukar. The laughter is somehow forced; the author tickles the reader to make him laugh. By contrast there are in *The Quiet Don* no long-winded funny stories or bits of nonsense. The amusing moments are as a rule short, and a gentle flow of folk humour emerges from the hardships of life itself, the day-to-day existence of the Cossacks. For example, the conversation between the two grandfathers at the wedding of Grigori and Natalya, lit up as it is by humour, is so significant in content that the reader has no time for laughter – he is too busy following the meaning.

The difference in artistic strength between *The Quiet Don* and *Virgin Soil Upturned* is beyond doubt. This proves nothing in itself. Thackeray, for instance, wrote nothing to equal his own *Vanity Fair*. Leskov wrote some very weak novels along with his masterpieces. Turgenev's *Smoke* and *Virgin Soil* cannot be compared with his *Nest of Gentlefolk* and *Fathers and Children*.

Sholokhov wrote *Virgin Soil Upturned* after sending the third book of *The Quiet Don* to Moscow. This third book was received with hostility by the editors of *Oktyabr'* and influential literary circles. Many critics had been convinced in advance that Grigori Melekhov would turn up in the ranks of the Red Army, but he becomes first an officer in Krasnov's army and then commander of an insurgent division which is successful in routing Red Army units. Various kinds of political charges began to be brought against Sholokhov. He was now accused of leaning not so much towards the peasantry as towards the kulaks and of vindicating the Cossacks in their counter-revolutionary uprisings. Meanwhile, because of collectivisation, the political atmosphere in the country had become oppressive and critical literature had become virtually unacceptable. Articles appeared in the Rostov press claiming that Sholokhov sympathised with the resettled kulaks and was unhappy about collectivisation. Several high-ranking party workers in Moscow were soon advising him to write a novel about collectivisation, about the rural scene of his own day. The young writer, newly accepted into the party, thought it best not to ignore this advice. In an attempt to clear himself of the then dangerous charge of leaning towards the kulaks Sholokhov dropped everything for a short period and wrote the first part of *Virgin Soil Upturned* within a few months. He did not take much trouble over his selection of material. On his own admission he simply 'scraped together in a heap what was lying about in abundance under his nose'.[10] The use in *Virgin Soil Upturned* of artistic methods simpler than in *The Quiet Don* is explained away by several Sholokhov scholars in terms of an attempt by the writer to make his novel accessible and comprehensible to millions of collective farm-workers. This sort of conjecture probably has more than a grain of truth in it. The important point here is a different one. What is strange is that Sholokhov proves to be weakest as a writer when describing something that he knows very well and ought, it would seem, to have the feel for, and strongest when describing what is alien, unfamiliar and even inimical (the pre-war situation of the Don Cossacks, the First World War, the Cossack insurgent camp, and so on).

It is normal for writers in the fields of realistic literature to conform to a different principle. Maxim Gorky had a magnificent knowledge of merchants, the petty bourgeoisie, the intelligentsia and down-and-out tramps; he had no close knowledge of the world of working men and women, for which reason his novel *Mother* turned out artistically weaker than his other works. Nikolay Ostrovsky wrote a fine, sincere book entitled *How the Steel was Tempered* in which everything had been experienced, fully assimilated, well considered and rendered familiar. But when, in *Children of the Storm*, the same author describes the way of life and the feelings of Polish magnates, the whole thing comes out laughably weak and unconvincing. The first book of Aleksey Tolstoy's *Road to Calvary* (*The Sisters*), is a remarkable work, but the third book of this trilogy, in which the author undertook to describe the workers and peasants of whom he had no knowledge, is a very feeble offering. Even Leo Tolstoy falls below the level of his true genius in *Resurrection* when his heroes include imprisoned revolutionaries. Mikhail Sholokhov violates this principle, and no amount of reference to the hasty way in which he wrote *Virgin Soil Upturned* can explain away the violation. The first books of *The Quiet Don* were also written very quickly, and in these books, for which he did have to *collect material*, the Whites and the Cossack insurgents are creatures of flesh and blood whereas the Reds are pale shadows. *Virgin Soil Upturned*, for which all he had to do was 'scrape together' what was lying about under his nose, prolongs the violation of the principle.

It is not easy to account for the striking inconsistency in philosophy and political sympathies between the authors of *The Quiet Don* and *Virgin Soil Upturned*, the lack of correspondence between their outlooks. After all, it would seem that these two books were created at virtually the same time. We have already shown that the author of *The Quiet Don* advocates a general or 'abstract' humanism affecting all men; he protests against violence visited upon anyone. The author of *Virgin Soil Upturned* clearly and unambiguously rejects the philosophy of general humanism; he adopts what he sees as a class-conscious stance. He begins his novel deliberately with a detailed, naturalistic description of scenes involving the dispossession of the kulaks in Gremyachiy Log. Even though Davydov knows from the Regional Committee that many kulaks were fully reconciled to handing over grain and that under the existing laws there were no grounds for undermining their position, since the renting of land and the hiring of labour were then quite legal, he is totally resolved on the dispossession and exile of every kulak at the earliest possible moment. The dispossession of the kulaks is the very first preoccupation of Davydov when he arrives in Gremyachiy Log and sets to work, although he has no knowledge of peasant farming, or of the peasantry itself, or of the Cossacks; but he has, on the other hand, recently read the speech by Stalin 'at a conference of Marxist, er...what do you call them?...You know...the land question, they, er...Damn it, what's their name? Land-workers, isn't it?'[11] Sholokhov, moreover, is entirely on Davydov's side. The secretary of the Regional Committee, who cannot stomach Davydov's insistence on doubling the amount of grain required from the kulaks and then 'squashing them with our thumbnails', is soon put down as a right-wing opportunist.

Andrey Razmetnov cannot stand it and refuses to take part in the dispossession of the kulaks. He says to Davydov and Nagulnov,

' I'm not doing any more work dispossessing the kulaks...I've had no training for it. I...I...I haven't been trained to fight kids! It's different at the front. You can slash about with your sword there and get anybody ...Sod you lot, I'm not going again!' Andrey's voice rose higher and higher like a tightened violin string until it seemed it must break. But then suddenly Andrey gave a hoarse sigh and let his voice drop to a low whisper. 'Is that the right way of going about it?...What do you

think I am, an executioner?...Do you think my heart's made of stone?
...That Gayev's got eleven kids. When we got there they all screamed
the place down, fit to blow your hat off! My hair stood on end. We
started evicting them...Then I just shut my eyes, put my fingers in my
ears and shot off back to the farmyard. Those women sprinkling water
over the daughter-in-law...and the children...God Almighty, you
...you...'[12]

But Davydov (and with him the author) condemn him for being
'soft-hearted':

Davydov brought his leathery palm up to Andrey's face and ground his
teeth viciously...Then suddenly he brought his black fist crashing down
on to the table like an iron bar and roared, 'You!! How can you feel
sorry for them? Have we got to feel sorry for kicking the kulaks out?
Just think. We're kicking them out so they don't stop us building a new
life without these...so it can't happen again in the future...Soviet
power in Gremyachiy is *you*, and have I got to jolly you up with
propaganda?' Here he gave a forced smile. 'All right, we'll send the
kulaks to hell; we'll send them to Solovki. They won't die will they? They
work – we feed them. When we've finished building the new life those
children won't be kulak children. They'll have been re-educated by the
working class...'

Without even considering what might really have awaited the families
exiled to Solovki, one is surprised at the ease with which the author's
favourite hero speaks of the suffering of children and the certainty with
which he assigns even them to the ranks of the enemy! But Razmetnov's
friend Nagulnov reprimands him in even more abusive terms.

'You swine!' he breathed out in a ringing whisper, clenching his fists.
'Is this how you serve the Revolution? You feel *sorry* for them?...Me?
...Stand them up in thousands, kids, grandads, women...tell me they
need to be ground into the dust...for the sake of the Revolution...
Give me a machine-gun...I'll shoot the lot of them!' Nagulnov cried
out with sudden savagery.[13]

Nowhere in the novel does this very real savagery receive the condemnation it deserves.* In an attempt to convince his assistants of the need
to expel the kulaks and their children to Solovki, Davydov recounts the
tragedy of a friend of his, a worker whom he had known at the front
and whose daughter had been forced into prostitution at the age of
thirteen. But what bearing does this story have on the perfectly innocent
children of Gayev or the other Cossacks? As it happens, we discover
unexpectedly at the very end of the first book of *Virgin Soil Upturned*

---

* The last phrases seem, however, to have been too much for Sholokhov's first
English translator, working in Moscow, who omits everything after the word
'Me?...' See *The Soil Upturned, a novel*, Co-operative Publishing Society of
Foreign Workers in the USSR (Moscow-Leningrad, 1934), p. 85. (*Translator's
note.*)

that Gayev was not a kulak at all but a middle Cossack. His dispossession
was against the law. He returns to the village with his substantial family,
whereupon Davydov, thus guilty of having outrageously exceeded his
authority, calmly discusses with Gayev the possibility of his joining the
collective farm.

At this point we cannot but recall Natalya Korshunov in *The Quiet
Don*. We have already mentioned L. Yakimenko's description of Natalya
as an example of 'delightful Russian womanhood'. Another Sholokhov
scholar writes in similar vein.

Natalya bore within her the high moral qualities so highly prized by
working people. Not, that is, the servile humility of a downtrodden
creature, but the reserved manner of a person of inner well-being and
spiritual strength. It is no accident that Sholokhov emphasises her 'bold
grey eyes' and her proud bearing. Meekness was not the source of her
charm. Natalya is the incarnation of the high moral qualities, the grace,
the loveliness which have been forming in the womb of popular life.
When Sholokhov said that there were a lot of good women on the Don
who could have been prototype characters Natalya was, of course, the
person he had in mind.[14]

Natalya and Mit'ka Korshunov come from the same family. But the
author of *The Quiet Don* does not see them as 'kulak children'; they are
quite different people and different fates await them. For the author of
Virgin Soil Upturned no such distinction exists. Every single kulak family
must be expelled from Gremyachiy Log and sent to Solovki, and that
included Frol Damask's son, Timofey, who differs little from Mit'ka
Korshunov, and all the daughters of the local kulaks, many of whom
were Russian women and girls just as lovely as Natalya Korshunov.

When he learns that the Cossacks are slaughtering their cows Nagulnov seeks to persuade Davydov that an 'unprecedented' number of
them must be shot. When difficulties arise over collecting for the seed
fund Nagulnov announces to his comrades that they should 'not persuade the Cossacks by fine *phrases* but bash them over the head and give
them good *sentences*'. True, Nagulnov does generally show 'leftist' ten-
dencies, though this far from disqualifies him from the author's
sympathy.[15] In fact the author subsequently confesses his love for Makar
Nagulnov. 'And so the nightingales of the Don sang farewell to two men
dear to my heart, Davydov and Nagulnov, the ripening wheat whispered
farewell; farewell sang the nameless stream bubbling over the
pebbles.'[16]

For the author of *The Quiet Don* this confession would be tantamount
to a confession of love for the Commissar of Bukanovsk, Malkin, who
shot the old Cossacks without any reason and ridiculed the peaceful
inhabitants. A 9th Army Regimental Commissar said of this man Malkin

that he was a good lad, though he did sometimes 'oversalt' things a bit.

The totally different approaches of the authors of *The Quiet Don* and *Virgin Soil Upturned* to the problems of humanism have been referred to by Soviet critics, always, one might add, to the detriment of *The Quiet Don*. On the appearance of the fourth book of *The Quiet Don* in which Sholokhov preserved the original logic of the characters as established in the first three books the critic N. Charnyy wrote, 'When you read through the pages of Sholokhov's last book it is difficult to get rid of the impression that the title pages got mixed up in the printing-house and that really the whole of *The Quiet Don*, including the fourth book, was written well before *Virgin Soil Upturned*.'[17]

We have already mentioned that the author of *The Quiet Don* follows the Tolstoyan tradition of placing in the centre of his epic narrative a nature that is original and which evaluates life not according to ideological dogma but through spontaneous feeling and the free play of reason. The main hero of *The Quiet Don* is the people, the Cossack people. *Virgin Soil Upturned* is quite a different matter. Here the centre of the author's attention is occupied not by the people but by a party functionary who forces upon the people, fairly easily it must be said, certain fixed ideas according to which he then compels them to live. These ideas are extremely simple – to lean upon the poor Cossack, to win over the middle Cossack, to liquidate the kulak, and thus build a new and happy life on the collective farm. As Davydov says, 'Comrade Stalin has totted up all this arithmetic.'

Both novels deal with the clash between the elemental nature of man and social planning. Whereas in *The Quiet Don* the author's sympathies are on the side of human feeling unfettered by political prejudice, we see quite the reverse of this in *Virgin Soil Upturned*. Here the natural, elemental principle in the people, and indeed nature herself, are brought without too much trouble under party control. We learn from the novel that the Gremyachiy Log 'Stalin' Collective Farm is behind with the sowing of Kuban wheat. Lyubishkin, a brigade-leader, expresses his fear that the Kuban wheat will not thrive. The farm manager, Ostrovnov, an experienced farmer (and his secret enemy) says to the communist party worker Davydov,

'It won't come up you know. Nothing will fetch it up! You want to sow all year round and still see it coming up...Gremyachiy Log, Comrade Davydov, is not Egypt. We've got to watch our sowing dates very carefully here!' 'What's all this opportunist talk you're putting about?' said Davydov angrily. 'It has got to come up for us! And should it become necessary we shall reap two harvests a year. This is our soil – it belongs to us. Whatever we want we shall squeeze out of it. Fact!' 'Childish

twaddle.' 'We shall see about that. Comrade Ostrovnov, you are displaying a rightist deviation in the way you speak, and that for our party is
an undesirable and pernicious deviation...That deviation is marked
with a special brand and don't you forget it.' 'I'm not talking about
deviations, I'm talking about the land. I don't know anything about you
and your deviations.'[18]

The whole village is anxious about the late-sown wheat. The old
Cossacks ask permission to hold a service in the hope that God might
send a good downpour of rain which is all that can save the Kuban wheat.
Davydov naturally bans all services. But even without God's help the rain
comes and the wheat obliges by coming up. The disgraced Ostrovnov
thinks to himself,

'That devil with a gap tooth! He said it would rain and the wheat would
come up. You'd swear that God himself was on the side of this damned
government. The harvests used to fail and the crops didn't grow and
now ever since 1921 we've been snowed under with grain! All nature sides
with the Soviets.'[19]

This is for all the world like the novel *Bread*, where an engineer says
to Voroshilov that 'every material has its breaking point', and Voroshilov
replies, 'All material things are having to submit to the Revolution. You'll
not convince me otherwise.'

There is a passing mention in *Virgin Soil Upturned* of the fact
that Davydov's first experience of horses came during the Civil War.
Nagulnov despises property-holding and has no farm of his own; he
strives solely for world revolution. Razmetnov cannot even thatch a roof
and his mistress Marina says to him, 'You're a fine thatcher you are!
Old man Shchukar can thatch better than you... You've cost me money.
I've got to have it all rethatched.' And, sure enough, two days later Old
Man Shchukar does the rethatching, 'complaining to her about Andrey's
poor workmanship'.[20] And yet these three men who know so little about
farming and day-to-day peasant work are the ones who set up the
collective farm in Gremyachiy Log and teach the Cossacks how to
organise their work on collective lines.

Another essential difference lies in the fact that *The Quiet Don* avoids
enraptured party rhetoric. Although occasionally certain heroes make
high-flown speeches advocating this or that idea, the author seems to
stand aside, hiding behind the heroes and their situation. In *Virgin Soil
Upturned* the author is obtrusive and given to frequent assertions of his
love for Soviet power.

The story behind the second book of *Virgin Soil Upturned* is worth
some attention. When today we read both books, one after the other,
we are clearly aware how much weaker the second one is in all respects.
It contributes virtually nothing to its well-known predecessor. The

author seems to want no more than to wind up the strands of the plot which were started in Book 1. There are almost no new characters other than the Regional Committee secretary and Varyukha, who are very superficially pencilled in. There is perhaps only one scene which is at all impressive, that in which Ostrovnov murders his own mother. Yet, although Book 1 was completed in eight months, this second book of *Virgin Soil Upturned* occupied Sholokhov for thirty years!

Early in 1933 the newspaper *Vechernyaya Moskva* published an interview with Sholokhov in which he said he was writing the second part of *Virgin Soil Upturned* and that he was going to bring the story up to the middle of 1932.[21] In February 1934, in an interview given to a correspondent of *Literaturnaya Gazeta*, Sholokhov said that his work on the *ending* of the second part of *Virgin Soil Upturned* was being held up by his preoccupation with the final book of *The Quiet Don*.[22] In June 1934 *Komsomol'skaya Pravda* published an interview in which Sholokhov stated,

I have recently been working at the fourth book of *The Quiet Don* and the second book of *Virgin Soil Upturned*. My work on both of these is *all but completed*...Book Four of *The Quiet Don* will be the last one. I shall hand it in between mid-November and the beginning of December. *Virgin Soil Upturned* will be ready at the end of December this year.[23]

Although the publishing-houses, working on assurances like these made by Sholokhov, included the second part of *Virgin Soil Upturned* in their schedules for 1935 and 1936 and 1937 they still did not receive it. In January 1938 Sholokhov gave an interview to a TASS correspondent in which he said 'I am continuing my work on *Virgin Soil Upturned*. At the beginning of next year I shall start writing the second book.'[24] Finally, on 1 January 1939 *Pravda* published an interview with Sholokhov in which, amongst other things, he said, 'During 1939 I propose to complete the final book of *Virgin Soil Upturned*.'[25] Nevertheless *Virgin Soil Upturned* never was completed in this pre-war period.

Throughout these years there was, of course, a great deal to hinder the completion of the novel. In 1931 and 1932 on the Don and in the Kuban, schedules for wheat production on the newly created collective farms were raised beyond all reason. At the same time the actual grain yield on these farms, so recently appropriated from the kulaks, was in most cases lower than it had been before collectivisation. There was a shortage of experience in working collectively, and insufficient livestock and tractors. In addition the prices fixed by the state were very low and failed to cover farm expenses. Protests from collective farms and their workers were met by the authorities with massive repression. In the grain-producing regions arrests of local Soviet and Party workers were carried out virtually everywhere. Even many 'twenty-five-thousanders'* were arrested. (Davydov, the main hero of *Virgin Soil Upturned* was himself a 'twenty-five-thousander'.) The collective-farm workers did not escape the repressions. In many cases whole villages down to the last man were exiled to the north and into their places came peasants from zones with little arable land outside the black-earth region. In the district of Veshensk where Sholokhov lived, more than 300 activists were arrested and more than 3000 families were expelled from collective farm land without having their shareholding returned to them. Some of Sholokhov's own friends, the prototypes of his heroes, had a bad time of it. In 1933 famine struck the Don and the Kuban, not as seriously as in the southern provinces of the Ukraine but still badly enought to take the lives of many people. Agricultural production in the province of Rostov fell markedly. None of this squared with the optimistic picture of collectivisation which was painted in the first book of *Virgin Soil Upturned*. Real events proved to be infinitely more complicated and refused to fit in with Stalin's primitive 'arithmetic' which Davydov used as his guide. Some of Sholokhov's published letters make it clear that he stopped all writing for a long period. What he did at this time was to remonstrate about the fate of his friends, protest against the arbitrary methods of the state organs of grain procurement in Veshensk, demand that a commission be sent to the Don by the Party Central Committee and importune Stalin himself.

Mass repression continued on the Don and in the northern Caucasus right up to 1937 and 1938. Sholokhov himself lived under the threat of arrest. He claims he was saved only by the intervention of Stalin who 'looked deeply into the whole thing and then the charges against me were demolished'.[26] We must not forget that Stalin refused to 'look deeply' into the majority of cases of illegal repression and that many of Sholokhov's friends, regional administrators and writers, ended up in prison. It hardly needs stating that this atmosphere was not conducive to literary creativity.

After several extremely cordial meetings with Stalin Sholokhov himself evidently arrived at a point where he need have no further fear of repression. Early in 1939 he was elected a delegate of the Eighteenth Party Congress. In a speech at this congress on behalf of the writing fraternity this 'great humanist' spoke as follows.

What is the present position of literature? Like every other section of our lives Soviet literature by getting rid of its enemies has emerged the

---

* In 1930 25,000 experienced industrial workers with outstanding production records were selected from about 60,000 volunteers to work as organisers on farms during the period of mass collectivisation. They became known as 'the twenty-five-thousanders'. (*Translator's note.*)

healthier and stronger...We have got rid of spies from Fascist secret services, enemies of every shape and kind, but they were all scum, not really people or writers in the true sense of the word. They were simply parasites sucking the blood of the living, healthy organism of our Soviet literature. It is clear that our literary medium can only have gained from our self-purging.[27]

In the post-war years Sholokhov remained silent for a long period. Six years passed (1946–51) without his issuing in print a single new work. This silence began to trouble his readers. For this reason, apparently, he said over the radio on 5 April 1952,

At the present time I am working on the second and final book of *Virgin Soil Upturned*. You will forgive me for not stating any completion dates. I have learned from bitter experience that it is not possible to finish a book by an exact date as long as you are working with an unremitting sense of responsibility.[28]

But somehow the work still did not go right. Six more years passed and in 1958 Sholokhov again announced that he was 'working flat out on the second book of *Virgin Soil Upturned*'. In October 1959, in an interview with a correspondent of *Komsomol'skaya Pravda*, he said 'I am working on the final chapters of *Virgin Soil Upturned*. One of them is right up my street. It is a chapter about devoted love, as pure as a mountain stream.'[29] Now, however, work on the novel was indeed coming to an end. Early in 1960 *Pravda* published some of the concluding chapters of *Virgin Soil Upturned* and in March of that year the second book of the novel was published in a separate edition.

Despite the many conventional laudatory notices and reviews, Sholokhov's new book disappointed his readers. The second book of *Virgin Soil Upturned* proved nowhere near as popular with the reading public as its predecessor had been. Even in some published critical articles it was possible to read that in this second book 'the narrative slows down', the heroes 'lack a sense of purpose' and 'they are shown in contemplation rather than in action'.[30] One might have expected Sholokhov, writing in 1960, that is four years after the Twentieth Party Congress, to have drawn a more faithful picture of the consequences of collectivisation on the Don. This he failed to do. The book contains no mention of the dramatic events which occurred in the Don villages between 1932 and 1934. Despite his declared intentions, Sholokhov has advanced the story no further than the early autumn of 1930. In an effort to part from his characters with all speed Sholokhov arranges for Davydov and Nagulnov to perish in an exchange of fire with White officers hiding in Ostrovnov's house.

Here again it seems desirable to compare *Virgin Soil Upturned* with *The Quiet Don*. The latter novel is more than an epic, it is a tragedy.

In Soviet literary scholarship attempts are constantly being made to distort the fundamental meaning of this tragedy. L. Yakimenko writes in his monograph: 'The tragedy of Grigori Melekhov is the tragedy of a man whose property-owning, class-conscious prejudices made it impossible for him to attain the truth about social life at the very moment of its greatest change.'[31] But then, V. Kirpotin had written virtually the same thing in 1947:

Anyone who seeks only his own egoistic happiness when undergoing a historical ordeal and for that reason goes so far as to commit crimes against the masses, against the people, stands in the way of general happiness and loses himself. This is the meaning of Grigori Melekhov's fate. This, above all, is the meaning of the whole novel.[32]

This opinion is, of course, wrong. I have already claimed that *The Quiet Don* presents to us the tragedy of the Cossacks' failure to understand the Revolution and the failure of the Revolution to understand them. One of my correspondents holds the opinion that the meaning of the tragedy in *The Quiet Don* goes deeper still. He writes that,

the greatness of *The Quiet Don* lies not in its depiction of the tragedy of a certain class of people but in something much broader, the tragedy of Man caught in the maelstrom of historical events. In general terms *The Quiet Don*, like all the great creations of the human spirit, uses the material of a given time and given classes in order to pose the profound and eternal problems of human existence.

There is nothing like this in *Virgin Soil Upturned*. Even the deaths of Davydov and Nagulnov cannot be construed as tragedies, they have no more than a random connection with the logic of the novel and occur merely as a result of the incompetence of the State Political Directorate (the GPU) in that area. The GPU officers have been unable to trace the White officers and render them harmless. When Nagulnov discovers the enemy hiding in Ostrovnov's house he decides, for some reason, along with Davydov and Razmetnov, to capture them independently, which results in his death and that of Davydov.

The second book of *Virgin Soil Upturned* does not end with the mass arrests among Soviet Party workers on the Don which occurred in real life but the mass arrests of members of the kulak and White Guard underground resistance at the end of 1930. Sholokhov's version holds that this underground movement was preparing a counter-revolutionary *coup* in the area of the Don and the Kuban. Judging by the falsified trials concerning the Peasant Workers' Party and the Industrial Party conducted in Moscow in 1930 one is at liberty to conclude that the alleged preparations for this Don–Kuban *coup* were no more than the fruit of the author's artistic imagination. The second book of *Virgin Soil Upturned* shows clearly that Sholokhov has lost the art of truthful writing and exhausted such literary capabilities as he had had earlier, merely as the author of the *Tales of the Don* and the first book of *Virgin Soil Upturned*. The *Quite Don* need not be mentioned; the second book of *Virgin Soil Upturned* contains not a single page worthy of the author of that epic novel.

Everything written by Mikhail Sholokhov on the theme of the Great Patriotic War now has a strange and pathetic air. Sholokhov was thirty-six and thus at the peak of his powers when war broke out. Like most of the leading writers he asked to be drafted for active service, motivated particularly by the fact that no writer who has not observed war can be expected to give a truthful depiction of it in his books. This proposition is a sound one, we must admit, though it does conflict with Sholokhov's own experience in writing *The Quiet Don*. His request was granted. He was given the rank of Regimental Commissar, and later Colonel, and became a war correspondent for *Pravda* and *Krasnaya Zvezda* in the Soviet Army. Although Stalin debarred Sholokhov from showing his face in the very front line and from active participation in the fighting (and an officer was specially assigned to check the writer's movements) Mikhail Sholokhov spent a lot of time immediately behind the front line, at the headquarters of active units, held frequent conversations with officers and men, visited hospitals and interrogated German prisoners-of-war through an interpreter. He also received an enormous supply of letters from the front and the rear and a great number of documents and other materials connected with the war passed through his hands. Despite all this, the first sketches and articles written by Sholokhov about the war strike one as weak, superficial and merely descriptive. During the war his readers were strongly impressed by only one of Sholokhov's sketches, *The Science of Hatred*, published in February 1942. This was one of the first stories of the day to describe the sufferings of Soviet officers and men captured by the Germans. The artistic merits of this story, however, are not such that we can accept it as a work of any significance. The language is poor and unexpressive, while the plot amounts to a mere recapitulation of an account told to the author by an escaped prisoner, Lieutenant Gerasimov.

After February 1942 Sholokhov remained silent for a long period. Time passed and no material over the signature of Sholokhov appeared in either the central press or the front-line newspapers. Sholokhov has admitted himself that some of the sketches which he wrote were returned to him by the military newspapers as below the not-too-demanding editorial standards of the day. He complained to his friends that he was no newspaperman and had neither the physical nor mental skills needed to write quickly on current topics; his style was unsuited to the demands of social and political journalism. He was, he announced, beginning to write a long novel about the war entitled *They Fought for Their Country*.[33] 'I consider it my duty, and the duty of every Russian writer, to follow in the burning-hot footsteps of my people in their titanic struggle against foreign domination and to create a work of art equal in historical significance to the struggle itself.'[34] In no sense, however, did Sholokhov achieve this self-imposed aim; he did not succeed in 'following in the burning-hot footsteps' of his people. Work on the new novel proceeded slowly and at a low ebb of inspiration. True, the year 1945 saw the publication of a little booklet containing a few chapters of *They Fought for Their Country*, but this work aroused little interest among the reading public because of the obvious weakness of the extracts published.

It must be said that in spite of Stalin's régime the Great Patriotic War proved to be a source of inspiration for many artists. In the years immediately following the war quite a number of splendid books on that subject were published in our country. I still consider Aleksandr Bek's *The Highway of Volokolamsk* to be the finest prose work on the war, whereas the finest work in poetry is Aleksandr Tvardovsky's *Vasiliy Tyorkin*. These books really were created by 'following in the burning-hot footsteps' of the people. Several other books appeared just after the war which are remarkable in many different respects and which have survived the passage of time, works by P. Vershigora, V. Nekrasov, E. Kazakevich and V. Grossman. In the years that followed, stories and novels about the war brought deserved success to V. Bykov, G. Baklanov, K. Simonov, Yu. Bondarev and one or two other writers. All this time Sholokhov remained silent.

It was 1956 before a new story by Sholokhov on the theme of the war appeared. This was *The Fate of a Man*, a story, like *The Science of Hatred*, largely devoted to the hard lot of Soviet prisoners-of-war. However, Sholokhov renders the tragedy of the Soviet prisoners very one-sidedly. The story does contain Fascists jeering at them but the tragedy was more terrible and went deeper than this. Why were millions of Soviet officers and men taken prisoner? Why were the prisoners declared traitors by Stalin and doomed to death by starvation since they were denied the assistance of the Red Cross? Why did most of the survivors of the German prison camps end up in Stalin's own concentration camps? Not only does the writer fail to answer these questions, he does not even raise them or hint at them, although the story was written and published after the Twentieth Party Congress.

Unrestrained praise for this story started up immediately after its publication. It was even proposed as a joint-contender for the Lenin Prize. The artistic merits of the tale were, however, wildly exaggerated and they have continued to be overstated. It has recently been called, for instance, a 'masterpiece' of Soviet literature 'unsurpassed in strength'. The same writer goes on to say, 'Henceforth an opulent chronicle of the Great Patriotic War is going to flow out from *The Fate of a Man*.'[35] There are, of course, no grounds at all for such estimates which are put forward by way of disguising the extreme poverty of Mikhail Sholokhov's post-war work.

All the most popular Soviet writers are known to have received and still do receive every day dozens of letters including confessions and descriptions of dramatic human destinies. In 1965 Ilya Ehrenburg showed me some such letters, each of which could have formed the basis of a story or a novella. During the war and in the immediate post-war years these letters were mostly concerned with the accounts of ordeals undergone by Soviet men and women at the front and at the rear. Following the Twentieth Party Congress writers' postbags included many letters from rehabilitated people, people who had somehow survived the horrors of Stalin's labour camps. We are informed by M. Adriasov that Sholokhov also receives hundreds of letters and manuscripts daily.[36] It is reasonable to assume that *The Fate of a Man* might have been written on the basis of one such confessional letter given literary treatment. From the date of the story (1956) it is equally reasonable to assume, however, that the hero of the story, Sokolov, must have served time not only in a German prison camp but in a Soviet labour camp as well. In other words the fate of this man was much more bitter than Sholokhov leads us to believe. It is otherwise hard to understand why Sholokhov waited until 1956 to publish a story written 'in the first spring after the war', that is in 1946. This is only one of the minor mysteries in Sholokhov's literary biography.

The few chapters of *They Fought for Their Country* which were published in *Pravda* and then reissued in booklet form aroused little interest among the reading public. In the flood of post-war prose most readers soon forgot about those apparently draft stories. The published chapters essentially contained descriptions of one or two wartime incidents occurring during the retreat of the Red Army contingents in 1942 across the steppe-land of the Don towards Stalingrad. They did not deal with the defence of Stalingrad or Soviet offensives against the west, even though Sholokhov had stated repeatedly in interviews about his 'plans for writing' that his intention was to present a broad picture of the whole war. The pictures of war in *They Fought for Their Country* cannot in any way compare with the pictures of the 1914–18 war so skilfully portrayed in *The Quiet Don*. Sholokhov's new novel contained not a single memorable character; none of the heroes has entered into our literature or our consciousness.

Sholokhov's literary sterility in the first decade following the war began to disturb his supporters more and more, especially in view of the approaching second congress of Soviet writers. In his usual way Sholokhov started rumours (which his friends had the newspapers pick up and pass on) that *They Fought for Their Country* was finished and about to be published. This was, of course, mere bluff. The year 1954 saw the publication in *Leningradskiy Al'manakh* of the *first*, introductory chapter, ten pages of text, from which we learn that in 1940, a year before the war, a serious rift occurred between the hero of the novel, Strelstov, and his wife, though we are told nothing of the reasons behind it and nothing about the situation of the country generally or particularly on the Don. We are privy to a few chance exchanges between Streltsov and the manager of a machinery and tractor station; we are shown also a few landscapes of the Don region. This publication aroused no interest among Soviet writers and, to put it plainly, went unnoticed.

Years passed, *fourteen years*, and then in the summer of 1968 glad tidings began to circulate in the writing circles of Moscow and the Don: Mikhail Sholokhov had at last finished Part 1 of his novel and the journal *Oktyabr'* was about to begin publication of the new work. Without a single line of text appearing, some journals and even central newspapers began to issue glowing notices of Sholokhov's new work. On 4 October 1968, for instance, *Izvestiya* published a long piece by A. Kalinin, *Journey to Veshensk*. The author tells of the trepidation with which he travelled down to Veshensk at the author's invitation to read the new chapters of the novel. Receiving them from the hands of the author himself he started to read and could not put them down for four-and-a-half hours. Kalinin informs the readers that his expectations were not disappointed and he was proud to have become acquainted with an outstanding new work. He goes on,

There was no doubt even before this that the front-line chapters from *They Fought for Their Country* already published were the beginning of an epic canvas depicting the war. Now, however, having read these pre-war chapters my confidence remains unshaken and I shall go so far as to state that this is the only way in which the novel could have started, with these chapters. Without them the reader would not have the opportunity of re-creating for himself the powerful fascination of the life we were living at that time and the whole alternation of delight and suffering which is essential information for an understanding of our early defeats and the sources of our subsequent victories. You can really speak of authentic Socialist Realism in the most intimate sense when the author's pen conceals nothing, makes everything stand out in relief, brings everything to hot-blooded, passionate life, including what was hardest to bear in the pre-war life of the people...The truth is not covered over; neither is the artist's heart which is laid bare before the public. It is a truth that conceals nothing but ennobles the cause of its party by its very extreme frankness.

At the end of his piece, which is couched throughout in similar terms of pathetic fulsomeness, Kalinin exclaims,

Reader, I envy you. All that delight and all that enjoyment lies ahead of you. Your eyes have yet to gaze upon the unfolding in all its power of Sholokhov's canvas which devotes itself to the eve of the outbreak of war when the ominous storm-clouds in the skies above our mother country were just beginning to be illumined with the first sinister flashes of lightning.[37]

Nevertheless, for some reason the publication of the opening chapters of Sholokhov's novel was held up. They did not appear until the spring of 1969, when *Pravda* published them.[38] They extended to three printer's pages. The chapters published were so artistically weak that they disappointed both those who had been expecting something from Sholokhov and even those who had not, for his new work was worse than anyone could have predicted. But for the title and the name of the author one would have imagined *Pravda* to be publishing chapters from the work of a tiro, and a none-too-talented one at that. The writer who had ostensibly managed to produce an extraordinarily expressive, pulsating picture of the Don in the pre-war period 1912–14 (even though he was too young to have anything more than a hazy recollection of it) could not manage now to depict at all satisfactorily the Don in the pre-war period 1940–1, even though he had lived there all his life. The novel also lacks the 'truth that conceals nothing' referred to by Kalinin. We do read about Nikolay Streltsov's elder brother, Aleksandr, coming home on leave. He is a high-ranking military leader in the Red Army who has spent several years in prison and was only rehabilitated just before war broke out. Nikolay and the manager of the machinery and tractor station are not simply expecting a visitor, they are expecting him to tell them the reasons behind the terrible repressions which had burst upon the whole country, to let them know 'what the top brass are thinking and how they live'. But Aleksandr, though he does mention in passing the illegal mass repressions, the interrogations under torture and the appalling conditions in the labour camps, suddenly says, 'You can't hide all that. It did happen. *And I'm not going to hurt you again, unnecessarily, my little brother, I'm going to spare you.*' The manager never does manage to meet Aleksandr and have a chat with him. Yet he had looked forward to it so much! And so had Aleksandr, who says to Nikolay, 'I will ask you one thing. Invite that friend of yours, Ivan Stepanovich, over to see us. We must have a chat. He has some naive ideas about real life.' But Sholokhov does not bring these two characters together for a conversation; Aleksandr is summoned urgently to Moscow by Marshal Zhukov. We do also hear Aleksandr, the evening before, voicing something of a grudge against Stalin, though he lays most of the blame for the repression of honest Soviet citizens upon all kinds of slanders and the organs of the NKVD. Here, too, he stops short and says, 'Everything's complicated, Kolya, very complicated. Let's call it a day just now...This poison has to be sipped in small portions or it'll cause some harm. We've got a whole week ahead of us; there'll be plenty of time to talk about it.' Early next morning, however, Aleksandr departs, leaving behind a mystified brother, station manager and reading public.

Sholokhov's distortions and over-simplifications extend to more than the pre-war repressions. At one point he attempts through the words of one hero to justify the repression, for the most trivial forms of pilfering, to which the peasants were subjected in the early and mid-1930s, at the heights of the famine. An old shepherd tells Aleksandr and Nikolay that in 1933 his daughter-in-law was sentenced to ten years' imprisonment just because 'in that year of famine she pinched four kilos of wheat from the threshing-floor. What was she supposed to do, let herself and the kids die of hunger?', whereupon the recently rehabilitated Aleksandr replies gruffly, 'You know I wasn't put away for thieving. You're confusing things, making comparisons like that. A heaven-sent gift can't be compared with a sucking-pig...At that time if they hadn't locked up people who stole four kilos of grain, everybody would have gone around pinching four hundred kilos a head, wouldn't they, dad?' It seems not to have occurred to the two brothers that the famine-striken peasant woman with her starving children was not after 'community' grain; she had grown that corn herself, sown the seed, tended the crop and reaped the harvest. She could not rid herself of the impression that it was *her* corn and it was being taken away from her starving children. Surely it is not beyond Sholokhov's comprehension that, without attempting to vindicate theft, we must nevertheless acknowledge the monstrous injustice of the sentence given to that starving woman. She had, after all, the right to receive not just 4 kilograms of the corn which she had grown but the 400 kilograms a head referred to by Aleksandr. Puzzling questions like these assail the reader in virtually every chapter of Sholokhov's latest novel.

Even during the war the western press began to speculate about which Russian writer would be able to create an epic work on the most recent Patriotic War. Western literary experts agreed almost to a man that the most probable author of such an epic was Mikhail Sholokhov. But Sholokhov has not lived up to their expectations and even the most enthusiastic of his apologists devote no more than a page or two to his unfinished war novel while they scratch about in search of quotations exemplifying the 'literary mastery of this writer'.

More than once in post-war years Sholokhov has been condemned for his artistic unproductiveness. The speech at the Twentieth Party Congress by B. Gafurov and the letter from an old communist, A. Gindin, published shortly afterwards in *Pravda*, come quickly to mind. In reply to his critics Sholokhov exclaimed like a true demagogue, 'Working quickly produces blind offspring.' But after reading the opening of *They Fought for Their Country*, the birth-pangs of which were so protracted, one prominent Soviet writer observed that 'working slowly and taking too long can also produce blind offspring'.

Earlier, in 1939, Sholokhov had spoken himself at the Eighteenth Party Congress. He said on that occasion,

In the future we writers hope to outstrip some branches of production in the quantity and quality of what we produce but there is one branch that we do not aim to outstrip – the defence industry – firstly because it can't be outstripped anyway, and secondly because it is such a good and absolutely essential branch so that it somehow wouldn't be right to outstrip it...If the enemy attacks our country we Soviet writers shall lay down our pens and take up other arms. Serving in the Red Army beneath its glorious red banners we shall smash the enemy as no-one has ever smashed him before and I make so bold as to assure you, comrade delegates, that we shall not throw away our map-cases – this is a Japanese gesture which does not suit us (*applause*). We shall collect the enemy's map-cases (*laughter*) because in our literary economy the contents of those cases will be useful in the future (*laughter*). We shall rout the foe and then write books about how we smashed him *à la* Voroshilov. These books will serve our people and remain for the edification of any aggressors who happen not to have been smashed to pieces (*applause*).[39]

Although at headquarters Sholokhov was probably given, among other trophies, several German map-cases, he cannot have found any map-case with contents sufficient to help him write a great new novel.

Something must now be said about Mikhail Sholokhov's many speeches and addresses on current affairs. These take up a whole volume of his collected works and they have also been issued as a separate edition.[40] Reading them is a thankless task, and not by any means only because in his public utterances Sholokhov normally sounds dogmatic and reactionary. After all, many great writers of the past have clung on to hopelessly outmoded opinions. What strikes one in these addresses is the poverty of language and thought and also the free-and-easy tone which so often borders on vulgar philistinism. Here is an example of Sholokhov speaking from the platform at the Twenty-Second Party Congress:

We hold nothing more sacred than the bonds of party comradeship. We love our children and our wives as well but, in the words of Taras Bulba, 'they're not the same as brothers' (*laughter*). And don't let them complain about it, these children and wives of ours. It can't be helped, they'll just have to get used to it, and that's that. Wait a minute, though, I've run into a bit of trouble...It's as plain as a pikestaff that our wives will be the first to complain that the bonds of party comradeship are more sacred than the bonds tying us to them. I seem to have been a bit hasty, in fact I've made a bad mistake mentioning the wives like that without thinking. Taras didn't say anything about them! (*laughter*). Now I shall obviously have to be the first man to accept blows from my family. But I do not shrink from it, believing as I do in your high degree of sympathy, my dear married brothers and comrades (*laughter and applause*). Encouraged by that I am ready to face the harshest ordeals which lie ahead of me by my own fireside. Only don't forget to put a good word in for me, that's all I need! (*laughter and applause*)[41]

It is somehow hard to believe that the author of this vulgar blathering is the author of *The Quiet Don.*

At a ceremony during which he received the Lenin Prize Sholokhov proclaimed,

For me receiving the Lenin Prize may be considered a stage passed[??]. I should like to think that next year this place will be occupied by a young writer...I dare say I shall never get another Lenin Prize but it does not follow that I shall give up one of the highest places in literature without a struggle...I'm in favour of young people taking over from us, but let them sweat a bit to get to the same level as us. Next year I shall be present sitting here watching the prize go to a young author who has deserved to get it. It wouldn't be a bad idea if this became a tradition in literature, the symbolic handing over of the unextinguishable torch of socialist art.[42]

When he received the Nobel Prize, deservedly as the author of *The Quiet Don,* Sholokhov gave an address which was similarly colourless and devoid of thought-content. Yet he must surely have taken a good deal of time and trouble over the preparations for such important public utterances.

Here are a few more quotations from addresses made by Mikhail Sholokhov which call for no comment.

From a speech at the Third All-Union Congress of Young Writers

I should like to hope for your sakes that you will not become 'has-beens' in literature. We all know that category of long-unmarried woman referred to as 'old maids'. May creative maturity soon come upon you ...And one more wish for you in this connection: don't stay in literature until old age still wearing children's short trousers! Unfortunately this does happen still in our country.[43]

From a speech at a Provincial Party Conference

Through the efforts of the Provincial Party organisation and all workers on the Don our province has achieved not a little success in agriculture and has received the Order of Lenin. Let us dream of the not too distant day when it will receive the Order of Lenin for horticulture and wine-growing.[44]

From an essay entitled 'A Word about My Country'

Nowadays the most rapacious American imperialism has swelled up loathsome and spider-like ever since the Second World War. It is threatened by an inexorably approaching crisis and the awakening of the merciless fury of the deceived working masses of America. In order to distract attention from the position within the country and to find a way out of the deadlock they, the American imperialists, seek their salvation in war...In the eyes of the American people the lying hounds of the American imperialists are trying to portray us as defenceless and weak, in other words easy meat for the war-mongering Marlboroughs of the 'American Legion'.[45]

From a speech at a memorial meeting following the death of Gorky

Gorky was a passionate lover of man, the warrior for a bright future for mankind and with all the power of his ardent heart he loathed exploiters, shopkeepers and the petty bourgeoisie nodding in the quiet backwaters of provincial Russia...Gorky's works taught the Russian proletariat how to fight the Tsarist government...In Tsarist times the most talented representatives of the people were perishing, too weak to break through to the sources of knowledge. The old régime suffocated the finest manifestations of the people's talents. Now in our Soviet country all the necessary conditions have been created for young people to attain all heights of culture.[46]

From an article in Izvestiya on the occasion of A. Serafimovich's seventy-fifth birthday

I'm very fond of the old chap. He is a true artist, a great man, whose works are closely familiar to us. Serafimovich belongs to that generation of writers from whom we youngsters received our training...His *Iron Flood* has remained in the ranks of the finest works in Soviet Literature ...I can still recall the arrival of Serafimovich in Veshensk. He stayed with me for a few days. No matter how cold the water in the Don he never omitted to go for a bathe. Always impeccably clean-shaven and fresh from his bath, he impressed me with his untiring inexaustible cheerfulness. He is so exceedingly young at heart![47]

From a speech at the Eighteenth Party Congress

So, when the people tell a writer that he is not writing much or he is writing badly what can that writer say in self-justification? His face takes on a rather bored look and he babbles indistinctly about working better in the future (*laughter*). Sometimes it all comes right, but not always. At other times he would like to write better but it doesn't work out that way, he hasn't got enough powder (*laughter*). As they say, he was a writer but he's run out of steam.[48]

From an article entitled ' You can have culture on a collective farm '

Year by year the cultural level of the working masses of our country is growing [*sic.*, Tr.]. But in the general growth the collective farm-worker lags behind the industrial labourer. We are all to blame for this since we do not pay much attention to questions of culture on our collective farms...Questions of culture are assigned minute amounts of time and resources by those in authority...Building a bath-house or a lavatory is not the beginning and the end of work for culture and relaxation. This is not a bad time for us to bring the question up, just when the collective farms are totting up their accounts for the year.[49]

From an article on the soft landing of the automatic space-station ' Luna 9 ' on the surface of the moon (February 1966)

I have just heard over the radio about the latest triumph of our scientists, the soft landing on the moon, and my heart contracted tenderly. Well done, our lads! But the delight goes further than that: we've left the Americans behind again! After all, now and then you have to go up to those swanks in power on the other side of the ocean who haven't yet learned to keep their feet off the table, put them nicely out for the count and say softly, 'Don't keep on about your opportunities, don't think you're the only ones with the know-how...Better people than you have been re-educated by life and brought to their knees.' Thoughts about the Americans are by the way, but still it does make you feel marvellous![50]

From a speech at the Second Congress of Soviet Writers

The expression 'leading' applied to a man is in itself a good expression as long as he really is leading someone. But it sometimes happens that a writer was once leading and is now not leading any longer but standing still. And standing still not just for a month or year but for ten years or so, or more than that, let's say like yours truly and his like. You will understand, comrades, it is not always nice to have to say something like that to yourself, but you must. This is self-criticism.[51]

From a speech to the Twenty-Third Party Congress (about Sinyavsky and Daniel)

I am ashamed not of those who have slandered our country and sullied what is purest among us. They are amoral men. I am ashamed of those who attempted, and still attempt to defend them, whatever the motivation (*applause*). And doubly ashamed of those who offer their services and ask permission to go bail for convicted renegades (*stormy applause*). All that we have won for ourselves has been achieved at too great a cost and our Soviet power is too dear to us for us to allow people to get away with slandering and besmirching it (*stormy applause*). There are those who take refuge behind words about humaneness and moan about the severity of the sentence. I see here delegates from the party organisations of our own Red Army. How would they react if traitors turned up in one of their units? They know, our soldiers, they know very well what humaneness is – it certainly doesn't mean slobbering over people! (*stormy applause*).

And something else occurs to me. If only these lackeys with their dirty consciences had found themselves back in those memorable 1920s when people were tried and sentenced not with the help of clearly defined articles of the Criminal Code but 'under the direction of a revolutionary's sense of law and order' (*applause*). Oh dear me, these werewolves would have got a different sort of punishment then! (*applause*). And yet, I tell you, they go on about the severity of the sentence![52]

An earlier speech made by Sholokhov at the Second All-Union Congress of Writers was revolting in every way. In the Collected Works the text of the speech appears, of course, in an edited version but even so, this address is surprisingly free-and-easy and primitivist in tone. For all that, this was Sholokhov's first address to the Writers' Congress. (He did attend the First Congress in 1934; he did not make a speech but sat there nevertheless with the air of a 'literary general'.) Anyone is free to acquaint himself now with the published stenographic record of the Second Congress. Sholokhov's speech on the seventh day aroused such violent indignation in everyone present that next day one of the most venerable writers in the USSR, Fyodor Gladkov, mounted the platform for a second time in order to say:

My dear comrades! Although it is hard for me to step up on to this platform I nevertheless consider it my duty as a matter of conscience and in the interests of the Party to force myself to speak out against the unparty-like spirit and, if I may say so, the wispy sparseness of Comrade Sholokhov's speech (*applause*). A writer like Sholokhov, a man of such enormous authority, ought never to detract from his own merits. Criticism is possible and necessary, but criticism in principle has nothing in common with jeering mockery and the farcical, carping attitude of Zoilus (*applause*). The two or three true ideas expressed by Comrade Sholokhov in the form of feeble wit were followed by quite improper attacks upon certain individuals which sounded very much like gossip-mongering and the settling of personal accounts (*applause*).[53]

In a reply to Sholokhov, whose speech had cut across all the humanitarian traditions of Russia's great literature, the writer Lydia Chukovsky wrote an *Open Letter to Sholokhov* in which she predicted that Russian literature itself would punish him in the cruellest way for any writer, through artistic sterility. She was at least twenty-five years too late in making that prediction, for Sholokhov had long ceased making any contribution to Russian literature. Long ago readers had stopped expecting anything from him, this man whose seventieth-birthday celebrations are being prepared, even now as I write, with more pomp and ceremony than for the anniversary of any other classic of Russian literature. Let us state this in simple arithmetical terms. In the 7- or 8-year period from 1925 ot 1932 this writer published (as he aged from 20 to 27) not only 3 books of *The Quiet Don* but also the first book of *Virgin Soil Upturned.* Together with the *Tales of the Don* the overall amount of literary work published in this period extended to almost 100 printer's pages. In the course of the next 8 years Sholokhov published the fourth book of *The Quiet Don* (approximately 20 printer's pages). Thus in the 17 or 18 pre-war years of literary activity roughly 120 printer's pages of literary work appeared *under the name of Mikhail Sholokhov.* During the next 35 years (1941–75) Sholokhov issued around 40 printer's pages of literary work of poor quality. In this period his productions, quantitatively and qualitatively speaking, fall well behind those created by dozens of other writers, front-rank and second-rate.

It is indisputable that *The Quiet Don* is one of the masterpieces of world literature. But the literary biography of Mikhail Sholokhov is so inconsistent and full of problems that researchers and experts in literature are going to continue asking one another, 'Was it really Sholokhov who wrote *The Quiet Don?*'

7

WHAT LIES BEHIND THE RENEWED DISCUSSION OF THE AUTHORSHIP OF 'THE QUIET DON'?

The renewed discussion of the authorship of *The Quiet Don* which was set in train by Alexander Solzhenitsyn with the publication of 'D's' unfinished work had a clear connection with the seventieth-birthday celebrations being prepared for Mikhail Sholokhov in May 1975. These preparations evoked a lively discussion of 'D's' book in the foreign press (national and émigré) and also in the Soviet press, though in disguised form. However, the foreign press in general received 'D's' hypothesis with great scepticism and even within anti-Soviet émigré literature, which has little sympathy for Sholokhov, numerous articles criticised it and sought to defend Sholokhov's authorship.

In *The Mainstream of 'The Quiet Don'* the critic 'D' expresses his conviction that this great novel had both an author and a co-author. He attempts to show also that the co-author made a number of omissions from the novel and in many instances strove to distort the author's original design. He asks:

Could the author himself have readjusted his design in such a way that his new ideas did not interlock with the earlier ones and then have stuck stubbornly to his earlier artistic scheme, combining sections which conformed to it with sections which did not? Is this not the mechanically contrived combination and therefore a pointer to the interference not of the author but of some other person acting against his will? An affirmative answer to the latter question will give us the right to consider the co-author a criminal who distorted the author's creation and to proceed to an investigation less like critical analysis than detective work.[1]

Another literary figure whom we shall name only as Sh-v makes the following comment on *The Mainstream of 'The Quiet Don'*:

The question is unavoidable: which is better, to leave another person's draft manuscripts in obscurity, doomed to destruction, or to give them new life in the contaminated form of someone else's novel? No-one questions the fact that *The Quiet Don*, far from being a feeble potpourri, is a work of substantial unity and talent. My own view is that Sholokhov did in fact make use of Kryukov's manuscripts, but that he was sufficiently inspired by them to write large sections of the novel himself.

Despite my dislike of Sholokhov's extra-literary conduct over decades, I cannot deny his talent as a writer. Even when working on someone else's manuscript he must still have been endowed with courage, skill and a compositional sense not attainable by just anyone. Another way of looking at this is to claim that Sholokhov saved Kryukov's manuscript from total destruction. The existence of *The Quiet Don*, or the non-existence of the manuscript – can there be any comparison between these possibilities? I believe it to be irrefutable that if Sholokhov had not made use of the manuscripts which came his way Kryukov's embryonic novel would never have seen the light of day. *The Quiet Don* exists now in a single version which cannot be broken down and reassembled.

Yet another literary figure, T-v, is even more specific when he writes:

In a sense the saving of those books of *The Quiet Don* which had already been written and the presentation of them to the world was a real achievement by Sholokhov. He took a deadly risk. Without changing the name (Kryukov being a White Cossack public figure) the book could never have appeared – and the addition of characters like Abramson, Pogudko and Bunchuk was equally necessary.

Personally I cannot agree completely with any of these assessments. An examination of Mikhail Sholokhov's involvement in *The Quiet Don* cannot now, I submit, be conducted in judicial terms, using words like 'crime', and so on. On the other hand, should the plagiarism be confirmed, it would be unacceptable to construe Sholokhov's activities as 'a real achievement'. All the problems relating to the analysis and study of the creation of *The Quiet Don* must be examined in the context of literary research.

The various forms of social upheaval and transformation occurring in our country in the twentieth century have created a number of problems and situations which would be unthinkable under other conditions. For example, one of the best known Soviet scholars, 'B', early on in his academic career wrote a series of brilliant works on literature. Fearing arrest and probable death – not without good reason – 'B' asked a friend of his, 'K', whom he considered better placed, to publish certain completed manuscripts under 'K's' name. 'K' promptly did so, but in the late 1930s he was arrested and he died, while 'B' survived and returned from a long period of exile to produce a whole new series of absorbing and original scholarly works on literature. He does not now think it is possible for him to establish his authorship of those earlier works which came out in the thirties under his dead friend's name. There are, of course, other instances of manuscripts, inventions and other works created by people who suffered arrest and death being attributed to their former colleagues, though without the preliminary of a friendly agreement. Although these manuscripts, inventions and works were saved from destruction by these means alone, the immorality of the people who assumed the authorial rights of others is plain to see, especially since in many cases the names of the real authors have still not been established.

A few years ago the journal *Russkaya Literatura* published an article by A. I. Matsay, 'The Don Cossack M. Moshkarov and his literary works' in which the author gives a detailed analysis of Moshkarov's play *Red Cossack* and attempts to show that this work, which Sholokhov came to know in the early 1920s, played some part in providing the inspiration for *The Quiet Don.* 'It would, of course, be a fruitless task', says Matsay,

to scrutinise the works of the great artist in search of a few exactly coinciding moments in Moshkarov's play. In Sholokhov's stories and especially in his novels, everything is incomparably more complex and profound, as well as brighter and richer. Nevertheless it is possible to catch certain properties common to Sholokhov's works and the play *Red Cossack.*[2]

This claim by Matsay is completely without foundation. In the context of the current controversy over the authorship of *The Quiet Don,* Matsay's article may be considered nothing more or less than an attempt to lay a false trail for researchers. *Red Cossack,* an extremely weak piece of artistic work, was published in the village of Veshensk in 1920. The whole five-act drama fitted into thirteen small-format pages. Matsay's exposition and analysis of the content take up more space than the play itself. The plot goes as follows. A young Cossack, Vasiliy Grekov, falls in love with a working-girl Mariya Semyonova and, following a conversation with her and her brother, goes over to the side of the working class. (The action takes place in Petrograd before the February Revolution.) At the end of Act I Mariya soliloquises thus: 'My poor Vasya! His heroic Cossack blood is seething with a desire for revenge against those who have been deceiving him. He now realises they wanted to turn him into an executioner, the slaughterer of workers and peasants, and perhaps I, who love him so dearly, am to be his first victim.'[3] Vasiliy Grekov invites Mariya back to the barracks, but an officer refuses to admit her and strikes her across the face. Whereupon Grekov leaps upon the officer and throttles him with his bare hands, exclaiming as he does so, 'Die, you arrogant aristocrat!' The author's stage-directions inform us that, 'Mariya stands there calmly, watching Grekov with pride, pleased with his heroic action.' Then Grekov and his comrades go off to storm the prison and release the prisoners. Next he returns to his parents on the Don but they, disturbed by the breaking of Cossack traditions and oaths, demand that the village authorities try their son, whom they immediately hand over. Vasiliy is sentenced to death and shot before his father's eyes. This play has, of course, nothing whatever in common with *The Quiet Don*, although it is possible that it was performed in that small dramatic society which Sholokhov joined in 1920 at the age of fifteen.

I have already mentioned the many revisions and editorial changes to which *The Quiet Don* has been subjected since its first appearance in journal form. I had in mind the excision of certain epithets and similes expressing an attitude to events which seemed strange for a Young Communist. But the text of the novel has been subjected to other alterations. Many scenes, portraits and dialogues disappeared from the novel after being criticised for their low level of literary achievement, lack of correspondence with the general style, linguistic solecisms and the like. It is natural for every author to make all sorts of corrections to the original version of his work published in a journal and even to the first editions in book form. All the same the nature of the corrections made to *The Quiet Don* gives rise to a number of questions. In the first place, all these corrections take the form of cuts. Since 1928 the author has not added a single scene, dialogue or landscape. He has merely excised the extremely poor pages, those with no literary merit, and all of these cuts occur in chapters dealing with the Bolsheviks Bunchuk, Shtokman, Anna Pogudko and Kotlaryov. Here, for instance, is the original portrait of Anna Pogudko:

A touching harmony dwelt in her every feature, her every movement. Before him stood a young girl as unpretentious as a fairy story, with hairpins between her teeth, which were as white as pure silver, her taut eyebrows trembling. She seemed as if she would melt away at any moment like a sound in the pinewoods at dawn.[4]

The same Anna says to the convalescing Bunchuk:

'Won't life be beautiful under socialism? No wars, no poverty, no oppression, no national boundaries, nothing! How people have littered and dirtied the earth...' She rushed to Bunchuk and sought his hand. 'Oh, tell me. Is it not sweet to die for all that? Tell me, is it not? What can one believe in if not that? What can one live for?...It seems to me that if I should die in battle...' Here she pressed Bunchuk's hand to her breast so that he could hear the muffled beating of her heart and, gazing up at him with her darkened, profoundly serious eyes, she whispered, '...and if my death is not instantaneous, then the last thing that I shall be aware of is a solemn, stirring and lovely anthem of the future.'[5]

When death comes to Anna Pogudko the journal *Oktyabr'* described the scene as follows:

'Anna! My dear one!' Bunchuk straightened up, turned sharply and walked back with an unnatural stiffness, his arms rigid and pressed tight against his ribs. Like a blind man he bumped the gate open with his chest, gave a dull cry and, impelled onwards by some unearthly summons, he crawled forward on all fours, accelerating as he went, his face all but touching the ground. Words with no clear meaning issued from his foaming lips. He crawled along the fence-bottom like a half-killed beast, tensed up but moving sharply, watched expectantly all the way from inside the barn by the three surviving Red Guards. They could only exchange glances in silence, amazed at such a revolting, naked manifestation of human suffering.[6]

The following sentences were omitted from the scene of Shtokman's arrest.

Shtokman was sitting there in his undershirt, unfastened at the neck, with his back to the door cutting a crooked pattern out of plywood with a fretsaw. He glanced up at the investigator and the officials trooping in behind him and then pressed the fretsaw with his palm, at the same time sucking in his lower lip and biting at it.[7]

The following paragraph was omitted from the descriptions of Ivan Alekseyevich Kotlaryov.

As he shaped him Osip Davidovich Shtokman would reflect from time to time, 'Ivan Alekseyevich, all this rubbishy, nationalistic dross will melt away from you, it will peel off and you will be – oh yes you will – a little piece of good human steel, a tiny grain contributing to the massive general stock of the Party. The dross will burn off and melt away. Smelting invariably burns away all that is superfluous.' Thus he reflected, and he was not mistaken. Ivan Alekseyevich was boiled pure in his own reflections...He made a Bolshevik good and true, hard-forged and sound in his hatred of the old ways.[8]

The first chapter of the second book was cut almost by a half. This is the occasion when Bunchuk makes an unexpected attempt to expound to the officers of his unit the Bolshevik attitude to the war. The cut fell also upon a long quotation (running to a page and a half) from an article by Lenin, although a second, much shorter quotation survived. These words by Bunchuk were omitted:

Workers have no fatherland. There is profound truth in these words of Marx. We have no fatherland, we never had one! You live by patriotism. This accursed ground has given you food and drink while we grew up with weeds and wormwood on waste land...No blossoming at the same time for you and us.[9]

The following officers' comments on Lenin's article were also omitted:

Merkulov

He had a great talent for persuasion. Damn it, there's a lot of food for thought in this.

Listnitsky

That article is a pathetic attempt by a man ejected by his own country to influence the course of history.[10]

Sholokhov also omitted from the second book a paragraph describing Bunchuk's emotional reaction to his first meeting with Anna Pogudko, a reaction the like of which Bunchuk has experienced before, it would seem, only at the moment of attack during a battle or at a meeting after hearing a speech by Lenin.

Examples like these could be multiplied. It seems strange that these pages of such low artistic quality should stand side by side with other chapters and pages displaying what would appear to be impeccable artistic taste and skill on the part of the author of *The Quiet Don*. In the present version of *The Quiet Don*, in those sections and chapters ascribed by 'D' to the co-author, it is all too easy to discover quite a lot of strangely illiterate phrases. What, for example, is the value of these words in the portrait of Kerensky? 'The fleshiness gradually draining from his puffy cheeks, flexing his calves in their skin-tight leggings like Napoleon, he now addressed a routine session of the government on the subject of "complete political stabilisation"'.[11]

In the very latest editions of *The Quiet Don* in book-form a number of cuts have been made which seem to me to detract from the merit of the sections thus edited. We have seen that the author of the novel considers nature through the eyes of a Cossack farmer. In the chapters which deal with the War and the Civil War on the Don the author also watches with the eyes of a Cossack soldier. Pictures of nature's eternal loveliness are not contrasted in this novel with the ugliness of what is happening on the earth. The reverse is true; nature as it were participates in the fighting, which enables the author to emphasise all the more strongly the revulsion aroused in him by the violence of war. We read, 'The lifeless sun gave a widow's smile'; 'The Great Bear sprawls to one side of the Milky Way like an overturned cart with a shaft sticking up at an angle'; 'Grigori thrust forward into the forest which stuck out behind the trenches like a grey stubble on a black skull'; 'struck by the haft, the stork flooded red before dying and from a distance looked like a terribly lacerated tree'; 'the eastward-looking side seemed to be bleeding'; 'the moon was bandaged in cloud'; 'the wind ruthlessly tore off the moon its ragged bandage of dark clouds'; 'high above that spot the yellow moon collapsed, hacked down and wounded'; 'the moonlight streamed down like festering yellow pus', and so on. Most of these metaphors and similes have been excluded from the latest editions of *The Quiet Don*, and in books about Sholokhov this is mentioned as an example of his constant attention to the language of the novel and the removal of superfluous naturalistic detail from his description of nature.

One series of omissions from the first edition has a political explanation. Certain phrases and dialogues were excised which were *absolutely* incompatible with the philosphical outlook of the young Sholokhov. We have already noted that the October Revolution in Petrograd is frequently referred to in Vol. 1 of the first editions as 'the upheaval in Petrograd'. Excluded from the opening pages of the third book are Pyotr Melekhov's words to Grigori, 'It's true what the song says: Lenin, Trotsky, Dudakov set this foolish fighting off.' As well as the word 'black', omitted from the distorted smile of Podtelkov, elsewhere words describing his 'corpse-like' fixed stare have been cut out. Ever since 1945 all references to the ideas of the Bolsheviks as 'pernicious poison' have been removed from the characters' mouths. At the end of the second book, from the description of the stormy meeting in Tatarsk Sholokhov has dropped the words, 'the Chairman of the revolutionary committee began fidgeting on his chair like a wolf caught up in a trap'. Also at the end of the second book, in the references to the approach of the Red troops, the author has removed these two sentences: 'Bleak days were moving down upon the Don; awful times were upon them' and 'The Bolshevik noose was closing in, tightening round his throat.' This sentence concerning the Red Army units has disappeared: 'They were one-third topped up by Chinese, Latvians and other foreign types.'

A. Kosterin makes the following observation.

I cannot acknowledge Sholokhov as a Soviet classic, I deny him the right to a Nobel Prize and a place in the gallery of 'the immortals'. For this reason. Sholokhov as a writer is a typical Cossack from the Don. But for some reason we have a remarkably short memory for some historical facts and phenomena. Before the Revolution Russia was a state constructed upon class. Of all classes the most loyal were the nobility, the clergy and the Cossacks. These were the three whales which supported the Romanov dynasty. Anyone who has lived among the workers and remembers 1905 will not quickly forget the meaning of a Cossack whip. That is how the Cossack has been raised over hundreds of years; he may have callouses on his hands and holes in his trousers but he has never considered himself a peasant, a muzhik. 'I am a Cossack' is his claim, always and everywhere. We who worked in Cossack provinces at the start of the Revolution had a hard time drumming into the Cossacks' heads the fact that there was no difference between a Cossack and a peasant, that Cossack kulaks or Cossack muzhiks were all tarred with the same brush, and that a poor Cossack has everything in common with a poor or middle Russian peasant...Sholokhov has not brought out this contra-distinction between the Cossacks and the general mass of the Russian peasantry and workers. *The Quiet Don* is an artistic canvas depicting the tragedy of the Cossacks. It is very unevenly drawn. The first part is impressive and moving, but the following parts are much weaker. Sholokhov has obviously had trouble in 'spinning out' his novel and clearly did not believe in what he was writing.[12]

This same idea is spelt out even more clearly in Kosterin's *Open Letter to M. A. Sholokhov* where he says:

Art endures only through the truth which it brings to the people. Your works are untrue. The Russian working class, the intelligentsia and the other nationalities which make up the Russian Empire know very well what the Cossack caste is, and how much it upheld the monarch and nourished counter-revolution. In Baku and the province of Saratov I learned how eagerly Cossack whips, swords and bullets worked at the execution of unarmed workers and peasants. The terrible and ominous shadow of 'The Cossack Vendée' hung over the young Soviet republic throughout the three years of Civil War. But in *The Quiet Don* you attempt to rehabilitate the Cossack class by describing it as though it were the ordinary Russian peasantry. This, in a matter of basic principle, is your great untruth.[13]

With great respect to A. Kosterin, I must say that his view of the Cossacks is profoundly mistaken. The charges which he levels against *The Quiet Don* are an echo of those unforgivable errors and crimes of 1918 and 1919 committed by the Bolsheviks in Cossack regions which were themselves responsible for pushing the Cossacks into the counter-revolutionary camp and converting the Cossack provinces into a 'Russian Vendée'. The mistaken, prejudiced Bolshevik approach to the Cossacks which culminated in the fearful excesses of 'Decossacking' was to drag out the war at least for a further year and become the cause of dreadful sacrifices and privations affecting the whole country.[14] The Cossack class cannot possibly be set alongside the nobility and the clergy. Cossack privileges did not extend to the essentials; each Cossack family had to work hard to earn a living and the means of arming the men for military service. Thus the Cossack problem in Russia was without doubt the old familiar problem of the peasantry, but in a complicated variation.

The hostility which existed between Cossacks and 'outsiders' is by no means avoided in *The Quiet Don* as Kosterin suggests. This question is, on the contrary, one of the main themes of the novel and it is explored in the novel with exceptional profundity. This is emphasised quite correctly by 'D', who writes that hostility to 'outsiders', to any non-Cossacks, is, so to speak, rammed into the first two books of the novel through typical Cossack characters of both generations, the one which took part in the Russo-German war and the older generation which still topped Don Cossack village society. The spirit of freedom and the *pride* of a Cossack are depicted in the opening chapters of the novel in their rather wild and clannish form. This *pride* is seemingly caricatured in various manifestations of Cossack boastfulness and intolerance. Many powerful pages of this chronicle are devoted to the Cossack's conception, amusing and sometimes monstrous, of his superiority over the *muzhiks* and all *outsiders*...In the very first book we read of the slaughter carried out by the Cossacks at the mill. The Cossacks hurl themselves upon the outsiders, *Ukrainians* and *Crimeans*, battering them and murdering them savagely...But not only the adventurist or scandalous incidents and characters are depicted as prerequisites for the coming conflict; the first prerequisite of all is that spirit of independence which is shown to belong to the hero and his ancestors, to the simple-hearted Khristonya and the stubborn Podtelkov, even to a Cossack like Korshunov senior, old Grishaka...In the author's 'series of ideas'...we are constantly coming across pictures and characters which certainly do not speak of servile *inertness* or unconditional service of the Tsar but suggest the tragic inconsistencies of that service and the role of keepers of law and order.

The main hero and heroes of the novel, who represent the mass of the Cossacks, are somewhat uncivilised and uncultivated (the author not being inclined to turn them into idyllic shepherds) but this people is above all one that cherishes freedom and possesses a great sense of sociability, citizenship; these are the Cossack landowners and brave soldiers...The second book of the novel shows with some force how mistaken were the hopes placed in the Cossacks as loyal guardians of the Russian throne. The Cossacks did find something wildly attractive in the corporal punishment they were ordered to carry out by the Russian police (note how the Cossack Chubatyy is attracted to cruelty) but not for the reason assumed by the authorities who believed in the Cossacks as loyal subjects of the Russian throne. Neither was there any *inert* obedience in this. Their *inertness*, if that is the right word, consisted in a fierce hatred displayed over centuries towards anyone who had ever encroached upon their freedom (in the remote past) and then upon the lands won by shedding the blood of free Cossack people. Hence their intolerance of all *outsiders*. Even the workers quelled in 1905 were, for the Cossacks who put them down, simply *muzhik outsiders*. The Tsarist police had merely to make subtle use of the wild instincts of the Don Cossacks. 'I smell muzhik blood! Grrr! Here comes a Don Cossack!' yelled a Cossack, the worse for drink, mustering for mobilisation in 1914. But a sober man thinks what a drunken man says. In his incoherent way this man had expressed what lay hidden away in the heart of every Cossack. 'Let'em have it!' he howled, 'We'll give'em another dose. I was there when we put 'em down in 1905. Great fun!' 'There's going to be war. We'll have to go and put people down again.' 'Let them try! Let them pay volunteers. The police ought to do that. It's shameful work for us' (*Tikhiy Don*, Book I, Part 3, Chapter IV). The expressions 'Great fun!' and 'Let them try...it's shameful work' coming together like simultaneous recollections of a terrible evil, the killing of defenceless people, point to that tangled psychological knot which is not easily undone but which the author of *The Quiet Don* had tackled, deliberately including in his prologue the savage treatment of an outsider, the wife of Prokofiy Melekhov and then, after unfolding before the reader the cruel picture of carnage at the mill, proceeding to the violence of the Don revolt.

Such is the treatment in the novel of the bodyguard theme, the illusory Cossack loyalty to the throne, a painful subject for a Don Cossack patriot (and the author of *The Quiet Don* was certainly one of these). If we turn to actual historical facts we find confirmation not of the Shtokman version but of the author's...Cossack solidarity and the Cossack sense of honour to which the hero of the novel remains so true proved when it came to the crunch [during the Revolution] to be far stronger than loyalty to the monarchy.

For all their privileges the Cossacks did not stand out from the other front-line forces in their readiness to prolong the war...As to their political orientation, the February Revolution had already brought out the Cossacks' characteristic indifference to the destiny of the Russian Empire...The author proceeds with his chronicle on the basis of a rather diffuse concept of autonomy for the Don, one which he has not yet fully worked out for himself and which is to be ratified in the sphere of the Russian Revolution and the violent overthrow of despotism.[15]

This long extract from 'D's' book has been quoted partly in refutation of Kosterin's mistaken ideas about the Cossacks; but there is more to it than that. Despite one or two inaccuracies 'D' shows quite convincingly in the chapters 'Among Themselves' and 'Outsiders' that the theme of the relationship between Cossacks and outsiders is the principal theme, or one of the principal themes, of *The Quiet Don*. The author clearly had little sympathy for outsiders like Shtokman, or General Fitz-khalaurov or Lieutenant Colonel Georgidze. It is their interference which is capable of destroying, and does destroy, the familiar Don Cossack way of life beloved by the author. This is the main preoccupation of Alexander Solzhenitsyn in questioning Sholokhov's authorship. In his preface to 'D's' book he writes,

Ever since its first appearance in 1928 *The Quiet Don* has built up a long chain of problems which remain unresolved to this day. Before the eyes of the reading public there had occurred an event unprecedented in the history of world literature. A twenty-three-year-old novice had created a work out of material far beyond his experience of life and level of education (up to the fourth form). A young grain-requisitioner, afterwards an unskilled labourer and clerk to the management committee of a *Krasnaya Presnya* housing block, had published a work which could only have been born of a long association with the many different sections of pre-Revolutionary Don Cossack society and which showed particularly acute insight into the way of life and the psychology of the people living there. Himself an 'outsider' in terms of his ancestry and the circumstances of his life, this young author nevertheless directed his novel emotionally against the alien 'outsiders' who were destroying the beloved way of life of the Don at its very roots, although he was never to reiterate this message in anything he said later in real life. He remains to this day true to the psychology of a grain-requisitioner and a 'special duties' officer.[16]

The questions and misgivings expressed by 'D' and Solzhenitsyn are fully justified, given the inordinate distinction between the ideology of *The Quiet Don* and the publicly voiced opinions of Mikhail Sholokhov. The attitude to outsiders intrinsic in the whole system of characterisation in *The Quiet Don* has, of course, greater affinity with the philosophical outlook of a Cossack populist like Fyodor Kryukov than with that of a Young Communist like Mikhail Sholokhov who actually belonged to the outsiders. Although it does him no credit, Kryukov's dislike of the outsiders is clearly sensed in many of his public statements in 1917. A good example may be seen in his description of the first Cossack assembly on the Don which is contained in an essay entitled *New Things*. The essay has this to say about the problem of the outsiders:

You might say there never has been such anxiety as there is nowadays concerning the position of Cossacks and non-Cossacks, indigenous peasants and those who have recently arrived. Down on the Don they are living in clover (the non-Cossacks); that's how the Cossacks see it. They have been fruitful and multiplied, they have filled the broad Don Cossack steppe and settled in the towns and industrial areas. They have started trading in vodka, buying up the sheep and bullocks, the fish and the grain, making caps and boots, tinning samovars and going out with the haymakers...And while the Cossacks have been away serving on the borders of the realm this 'alloy' has grown so much that now there are fewer Cossacks on the Don than 'Russkies'. And they are all after plots of land; not just the privately owned land, most of which has already gone over to the peasants, but land belonging to the Cossacks, with their houses standing on it...There is good reason to squawk with anxiety and shake your fist...I think this is the reason why this old chap standing on my left is fidgeting with anger in his seat and sighing like that. It enrages his Cossack heart.[17]

A remarkable distance separates the speculation of several Sholokhov scholars about the ideological content of *The Quiet Don* from the actual ideological orientation of the novel. For example, I. Yermakov has written as follows:

Social progress on the Don has always been slowed down specifically by the principle of class-structure and authoritarianism which has rendered the way of living peculiarly repetitive, old-fashioned, antediluvian and inimical to forward movement...The mediaeval aspects of life there stand out just as sharply as their 'rustic idiom'. The underdevelopment of social mobility, the poverty of self-awareness, the suppression of personality, the triumph of the deadening power of routine, habit and tradition – all of this is what circumscribes the life there as depicted in *The Quiet Don*. This is what constituted the social and psychological prerequisite for a Vendée in the south...But the Cossacks, because they adhered to outmoded principles, *had to perish however frightful their end might be*. If they were to walk towards a new, inevitable destiny this could only be at the price of a *complete break* with the past. This tragedy is epitomised in Grigori Melekhov. Ivan Alekseyevich once warned Grigori, 'Don't stand in our way. You'll get trampled underfoot.' And the Revolution, in point of fact, did trample underfoot all that hindered its progress.[18]

This kind of interpretation of *The Quiet Don* is so remote from the actual artistic tone of the novel that there is no need to enter into an argument with Yermakov. It is enought to recall the novel itself. Without mentioning the inhumanity of Yermakov's speculation about the necessary demise of the Cossacks we might consider briefly the absurd and blasphemous proposition at which he finally arrives.

The fabric of the whole novel is permeated with a profound historical optimism. It is a genuine revolutionary epic which not only describes the destruction of a closely circumscribed world but depicts also the birth of normality and humanity in the minds and the consciousness of people leaving the realm of blind necessity for the realm of freedom.[19]

The 'realm of freedom' which we see in the pages of *The Quiet Don* is not a very attractive place.

The figure of Grigori Melekhov creates special difficulties for Soviet literary criticism. It would be possible to cite a large number of extremely varied and mutually exclusive evaluations of this character. L. Yakimenko, for instance, wrote that 'The fate of Grigori Melekhov does not correspond historically to the fate of the majority of middle Cossacks.'[20] And in his article 'The Creation of Characters' N. Chukovsky wrote, 'Two gigantic characters stand at the fountain-head of Soviet Literature, Chapayev and Grigori Melekhov. Two characters written with Shakespearean power, written to last. Two soldiers, two lives spent in continual battles, two warriors so different in every way.'[21] What is strange is that Sholokhov himself in public pronouncements about his novel has, at different times, given quite opposite interpretations of the character of Grigori Melekhov, thus leaving the critics nonplussed. In 1935 he said 'Melekhov's fate is distinctly his own. I have made no attempt to make him the incarnation of the middle Cossacks.'[22] Twenty years later his claim was different: 'In my opinion Grigori is a special symbol of the middle Cossacks.'[23]

Recently there has been an all too noticeable tendency when considering Sholokhov's work to overpraise his early stories. The long study in *Izvestiya* by Anatoliy Kalinin, 'From *Tales of The Don* to *The Quiet Don*' is a case in point.[24] Here the very title betrays the author's intention, which is an attempt to show that the *Tales* were a pre-history of *The Quiet Don*, in other words that his work on these stories gave Sholokhov a flying start towards the novel which he was to create over the next few years. The *Tales* are a very modest achievement in literary terms, yet Kalinin's sketch dispenses with a critical analysis in order to praise them to the skies. Kalinin claims that these tales are 'a precious scattering of small (but only in size) masterpieces of our literature'. They are 'saturated with the thought and feeling of irresistible originality' (?), they contain 'not words but molten lead and teardrops'. They are not literature at all, but 'the very hottest, quivering, bleeding slices of life'. Kalinin exclaims, 'How can it be called literature when everything there is so alive? Everything, yes, everything! Blood pulses, eyes sparkle, language lives...Oh, how Sholokhov loves his native region, how extraordinarily talented he is, how fearlessly honest, serious-minded and ironical! Everything seems to splash out from under his pen so visible and tangible.'

I have already spoken of the virtues of the *Tales of the Don*, which were a considerable achievement for their eighteen- or nineteen-year-old author. It is equally indisputable, however, that these tales are far from being literary masterpieces and that Sholokhov himself realised this at an early stage. The author's literary inexperience, his inadequate vocabulary, his imitativeness, his oversimplified attitude towards the many complex problems and inconsistencies of life on the Don will strike any reader of these tales. There is simply no comparison between them and *The Quiet Don* in language, style, depth of character-portrayal, thematic interest or the author's attitude towards the Cossacks. Here, for instance, is the way in which the young Sholokhov characterises the farm-labourer Fyodor during his winter studies on Komsomol courses:

In the evenings Fyodor would go to the club with Yegor. Fyodor would listen intently to the new ideas and words which he had never heard before, soaking up with his thirsty, eager mind all that he heard during those long week-end political readings and discussions with experts on agriculture on subjects as urgently close to his heart as farming...And yet it was one thing to grip the rough handles of a plough...but quite another to hold anything as fragile and unnecessary as a pencil. First his fingers started trembling and his forearm went numb, then it wasn't long before that deliberately awkward pencil broke. His hard hands were quite used to the former job, but his father had never thought when he had been training Fyodor that he would one day take up book-learning, so he had raised him with a farmer's hands, big broad bones, clumsy and hairy but strong as cast-iron. All the same Fyodor gradually imbibed the deep wisdom of the written word. One way or another, a bit wonkily like a broken-down sledge bumping over pot-holes, he learned to talk about 'class' and 'the Party' and what different tasks the Bolsheviks and Mensheviks had set themselves...

In December, a day or so before the general meeting, Rybnikov said to Fyodor, 'I'll tell you what, apply for membership. We'll accept you, get it confirmed by the District Committee and by the spring you can be a party worker. We've got a campaign going just now to attract as many young farm-workers as we can into the union. Our cell used to be asleep because it had a kulak's son as secretary and a lot of the members who were useless layabouts – they fell apart like carrion in the sunshine...We had a purge only a month before you came and now we've got to get down to some hard work. Our job is to raise the Dubovsk cell in the eyes of the people. Our Young Communists used to know nothing but how to guzzle home-made vodka and stick their hands down the girls' blouses when we had get-togethers. They've had to chuck all that. Now let's get down to some work and we'll let the whole Don region know about it!'

'But do you think I'll fit in all right? I'm not up to much with books...'

'Cut that out! Anything you don't know you can mug up this winter. Some of us are not all that, er...The Committee's been a bit stuck up; no books, no advice on how to carry on, only instructions...' Rybnikov's words about attracting young farm-labourers into the union sank deep into Fyodor's mind like a wheat-grain in the rich black soil. Recalling his life with Zakhar Denisovich he burned with a desire to start work. He scribbled out an application that night...'I wish to join and be a worker so as to learn it all and get all the young farm-workers to join the Young Communists because the Young Communists are better for the farm-workers than their own flesh and blood.'

Rybnikov frowned when he read it. 'It's all right. You've gone on a bit...but...oh, all right then, it'll have to do!'[25]

This story, *The Farm-labourers*, from which we have quoted a single page has, of course, nothing in common with the first parts of *The Quiet Don*, even though we shall encounter, among the thousand heroes of the epic, a Yegor, a Fyodor and a Zakhar. We shall also come across a 'cast-iron' fist belonging to a kulak, and phrases like 'plough', 'get-together', 'home-made vodka', 'chuck all that', 'wheat-grain', 'broken-down sledge' and so on.[26] Yet Kalinin builds his argument on just such primitive parallels between the *Tales of the Don* and *The Quiet Don*. In order to demonstrate that the latter is a sort of prolongation of the former, Kalinin writes that Sholokhov's stories include 'a Stepan, a Darya, three Grigoris, a mention somewhere of an Aksinya, and even a Red Guard by the name of Koshevoy. Both works mention "the steppe", "a she-wolf", "a black crow", "white swans", "a little bustard" etc.' Although Anatoliy Kalinin makes no mention of *The Mainstream of 'The Quiet Don'*, his study clearly takes issue with this book, its author 'D', and Solzhenitsyn. None of the discoveries made by Kalinin do anything to refute the hypothesis and the conclusions arrived at by 'D', for the obvious reason that the latter makes no attempt to prove that Sholokhov had no connection at all with *The Quiet Don*. The reverse is true; 'D' attempts to show that Sholokhov, the co-author, inserted into *The Quiet Don* occasional sentences, whole chapters and even quite new episodes, including heroes who had not appeared before in the epic. It is 'D's' opinion that in Books 3 and 4 of *The Quiet Don* this co-author wrote more than a third of the text and virtually the whole of the eighth and last section, which is where we read of the exploits of Fomin and his gang of whom we have heard mention on more than one occasion in the *Tales of the Don*. Thus it is that 'D' does not find anything strange in discovering in *The Quiet Don* many words and stylistic devices reminiscent of the *Tales*.

One of my correspondents writes with reference to 'D's' book,

The more I think about 'D's' book, at the same time rereading *The Quiet Don*, the more convinced I become that 'D' is wrong in claiming that everything introduced by the co-author is bad. Apart from one or two uneven passages *The Quiet Don* is a remarkably well-proportioned work with its own unity, and if Sholokhov did work on it after an original author, at least he did not spoil it. 'D's' conclusion that virtually all the sections where Bolsheviks are depicted sympathetically betray the hand of the co-author is without foundation. The sympathies of the author are not apportioned to the representatives of one side or another; at every point he feels for those who are suffering and castigates those who torture others. It seems to me, moreover, that this line holds good to the end of the novel. It is not parties who come in for censure or praise; human savagery and butchery is censured, mercy is praised and sympathy is extended to all victims. This recalls the position of Korolenko in Poltava. As the region kept changing hands he used to hide White officers from the Reds and Red officers from the Whites. And Kryukov, as we know, was very close to Korolenko. I cannot bring myself to agree with 'D' that the third, and especially the fourth, books are less tidily put together. Of course, the biggest mystery of all concerns the high artistic quality of those scenes which bring us beyond the winter of 1920, that is beyond the time of Kryukov's death. We must state directly that this is a mystery that needs solving, and not just by coming out as 'D' does with simplistic assertions that it is all badly written!

Another correspondent, B-v, writes more directly and more caustically on the same subject:

It is hard to imagine that the unknown author (Kryukov?) worked on the creation of his grandiose epic in the very furnace of the Civil War, describing events which had occurred a month or so earlier, and describing them not as a chronicler but as a novelist with a fairly clear idea of his heroes' origins, destinies and motivation. Such instantaneous conversion of a storm-tossed, ever-changing reality into epic prose is no less of a miracle than the authorship of the all-too-young Sholokhov. But the main point concerns the *ending* of the novel which is its *artistic apogee* bringing together in concentrated form the whole tragedy of its historical and philosophical meaning, the tragedy of a people (and by no means only the Cossacks) in the throes of revolution, the tragedy – and the exaltation – of the human personality in the catastrophic history of our century. Kryukov could not have written the eighth and final section not only because he died earlier than the events described in it, but also because it etches in a far broader historical range of experience – that of the period 1930–32 and the year 1937, thus enabling the author to sum up in artistic terms the *whole* great historical drama which has been played out in our country. Looked at from this angle the concept of the 'co-author' as defended by the critic 'D' is a non-starter. If we must probe in this direction greater probability attaches to the theory that Sholokhov came across certain *materials* which he concealed and later used without acknowledging his sources (diaries, notebooks, perhaps, plans, sketches and whole chapters of some literary, historical or documentary piece belonging to Kryukov or someone else). The scope and significance of these materials could well have been substantial and although the authorship of Sholokhov would still be unassailable, the unethical nature of the step taken would in no small measure explain his subsequent disastrous moral collapse... Kryukov's style, judging by the one or two stories it has been possible to read, has *nothing in common* with the style of *The Quiet Don* (and 'the style is the man'). It is hard to believe that a writer well set in his ways should suddenly have started to speak a quite new language.

By no means all of B-v's assertions seem to me convincing. I have already recorded my view that the eighth and last part of the novel is in artistic terms an extremely significant achievement on the part of Sholokhov. On the other hand, I cannot see in the novel any general summary of the historical experience of 1930–2 and 1937–8. The tragedy of 1937–8 was not reflected in any of Sholokhov's works, and the historical drama of 1930–3 is presented to us in *Virgin Soil Upturned* in a most distorted and oversimplified form, certainly not that of a drama or a tragedy. It would also be an exaggeration to consider the eighth part of *The Quiet Don* its finest section in literary terms. Thus Sholokhov's creation of that concluding section does not seem to me in any way miraculous, especially since it took him ten years or so to write the fourth book of the novel, that is almost three times as long as it took to write the first three books.

After reading most of Kryukov's stories I should not like to claim that this writer's style has *nothing in common* with that of *The Quiet Don*; even though there are clearly substantial differences between the two. However, a quite different literary assignment (writing not a story or an essay but an epic novel) can give birth to a new style of literary narrative. V. Molozhavenko informs us (probably repeating the words of Kryukov's relatives) that Kryukov began to write a long novel about the Cossacks before the war. Thus there was enough time for him to have completed the first book of the novel. Most readers notice the strikingly fragmentary nature of the second book of *The Quiet Don* even though Kryukov (if one accepts the theory of his authorship) had about three years in which to create it (1917–18). As to the third book and the seventh part of the fourth book, here, according to 'D', the co-author had no more than a set of unconnected sketches, plans, portraits, chronicled events and perhaps a few short chapters, which were collated to form a consecutive text by 'some literate person'. What seems to me wrong in 'D's' proposal is that this 'literate person' was A. Serafimovich rather than Sholokhov. I can see little likelihood in Solzhenitsyn's suggestion that it was not Kryukov but some other writer who created the basic part of *The Quiet Don*, that perhaps 'once upon a time there lived another Don Cossack literary genius who never appeared before the public but remained quite unknown, who blossomed out during the Civil War and died soon after it'.[27] Certainly, during the last forty or fifty years quite a lot of authors have been writing numerous works, including those which they consider to be of first importance, 'for their desks' rather than for publication, often without showing them to their closest friends. Everyone knows that Solzhenitsyn himself was fully formed as a writer before November 1962 when his first story *One Day in the Life of Ivan Denisovich* was published. But before 1917 there was no reason for a writer as undoubtedly important as the author of *The Quiet Don* to hide his works away.

8

SHOLOKHOV'S BIRTHDAY CELEBRATIONS AND AFTERWARDS: OBSERVATIONS AND POINTS FOR DISCUSSION

At the end of May 1975 our country celebrated the seventieth birthday of Mikhail Sholokhov. Although the festivities began as early as the first half of 1974 the main celebrations occurred in the latter half of May and the May editions of our literary and socio-literary journals were those which contained most of the anniversary articles and other material devoted to Sholokhov. In the summer of 1974 an Anniversary Commission had been set up to arrange and control the various forms of celebration. Its members included not only the leaders of the Writers' Union but also the Secretary of the Central Committee of the Communist Party, now Minister of Culture, P. Demichev, the Secretary of the Central Committee of the Komsomol (Young Communists), V. Tyazhelnikov, the head of Soviet Army Political Administration, A. Yepishev and many other high-ranking statesmen and public figures. The schedule of anniversary celebrations worked out by this commission was so extensive that we can safely say that no other Russian or Soviet writer has ever been officially honoured on this scale within his own lifetime.

True, not all the scheduled celebrations took place. The grand festival planned to take place in Veshensk was cancelled through the author's illness. Festive gatherings in many other large cities were cancelled too. The anniversary evening in Moscow was held in the Bolshoi Theatre, not in The Kremlin Palace of Congresses, and it was rather short. After an introduction by N. S. Tikhonov and a short address by the Administrative Secretary of the Writers' Union, G. Markov, only one or two other speeches were made. The leaders of the Writers' Unions of the various Republics did not speak and all the foreign writers in attendance were represented by a single speech by J. Iwankiewicz, chairman of the leading organisation of Polish writers. The Sholokhov anniversary was hardly mentioned in the communist press outside Russia and no invitations were issued to acknowledged front-rank writers in the west, not even those who had in recent years maintained an allegiance to the political left.

Nevertheless the anniversary was, as they say, widely celebrated. All the universities and institutes of higher education held symposia devoted to Sholokhov's work. In Moscow University alone 153 papers were read and the numbers of such papers throughout the country doubtless ran into many thousands, although these lectures and innumerable articles amounted in the main to a repetition of what had been heard many times over about Sholokhov and his work. No new ideas were advanced by the Sholokhov school in 1975 and not even any new biographical details were made known. For this reason, perhaps, the bookshops displayed nothing more than an occasional new booklet on Sholokhov if we discount A. Khvatov's *Down the Mainstream of the Age* (Moscow, 1975) as being a slightly extended edition of the same author's *The Artistic World of Sholokhov*. All the same, amid the great torrent of anniversary literature on Sholokhov there appeared quite an amount of factual or documentary material and opinion, seemingly included by accident or else through the short-sightedness of authors and editors, some of which calls for closer scrutiny and analysis within our present terms of reference. We must now proceed, therefore, to an examination of one or two publications concerning Sholokhov which have appeared in print for the most part during the last year and also of other controversial material and pronouncements.

In the autumn of 1974, following publication of 'D's' book *The Mainstream of 'The Quiet Don'*, a decision was taken to refute the 'libellous fabrications' of Alexander Solzhenitsyn and the anonymous author of the Paris edition. To this end several long articles were composed and the author of one of them, L. Yakimenko, was actually given a fortnight's leave to complete this 'urgent' assignment. Not one of them was published. It was decided not to indulge in overt argument with the 'libellers'. Whatever may have been said behind the scenes in favour of these tactics no doubt there was one overriding consideration: given the general mistrust by the intelligentsia of the truthfulness and objectivity of the Soviet press, any overt argument with Solzhenitsyn and 'D' about the authorship of *The Quiet Don* could only be counter-productive.

Nevertheless, many of the articles published in connection with Sholokhov's seventieth birthday included hidden arguments directed against Solzhenitsyn and 'D' and the first edition of this present book which was announced in the foreign press in February 1975. The very title of a long article by A. Kalinin in *Izvestiya* was overtly polemical. It was *The Time of 'The Quiet Don'*.*

An article by the English writer C. P. Snow, '*The Quiet Don*, a Great

* In Russian *Vremya 'Tikhogo Dona'*, an obvious pun on the title of 'D's' book *Stremya 'Tikhogo Dona'*. (*Translator's note.*)

Novel', published in *Literaturnaya Gazeta* on 21 May 1975, is of particular significance in this respect. In vindication of Sholokhov's surprising literary sterility over the last thirty-five years Snow makes a quite unexpected comparison between him and Charles Dickens, one of the most productive of all English writers.

We must not forget that Sholokhov became world-famous within a few months of the first part of the novel being published. This is an unusual, but not unprecedented, event. Several similar instances have occurred in the west, perhaps the most famous one being that of Dickens. When he began publishing instalments of *The Pickwick Papers* he was twenty-four, younger, that is, than Sholokhov in 1930, and in the space of a few weeks he attained in England the stature of a national figure... This, however, is a mixed blessing. To earn in your early twenties every reward that literature is capable of bestowing is enough to turn anyone's head. This is what happened with Dickens, even though he was a man of great self-control. As English sportsmen put it, 'When you get to the top there's only one way – down.'

Acknowledging that 'Sholokhov's productivity dropped' after *The Quiet Don* Snow exclaims,

Again there are many examples similar to this, particularly among writers who displayed extraordinary gifts when still young. Throughout the final decade of his life Dickens published comparatively little even though he died at the early age of fifty-eight. After *Anna Karenina* Tolstoy wrote only one more novel, and not a very good one at that. We know very little about the processes of high-quality artistic creativity except that they vary a lot from writer to writer.

This discourse by Snow is superficial and unconvincing in the extreme. Certainly *The Pickwick Papers* brought Dickens great and early fame. This novel, however, was far from being an epic comparable to *The Quiet Don*. It was only after a long series of brilliant novels over the ensuing years (*Oliver Twist, Nicholas Nickleby, Martin Chuzzlewit* etc.) that Charles Dickens, then aged thirty-six, wrote his principal epic work, *Dombey and Son*. Even after that Dickens went on to further novels, *David Copperfield, Hard Times, Great Expectations* and others, which have become classics of English and world literature. It is thus absurd to compare the literary biographies of Dickens, whose activity as a writer did certainly decline somewhat after the age of fifty, and Mikhail Sholokhov. Even more weird is Snow's comment on Tolstoy. This novelist created his two main epic novels *War and Peace* and *Anna Karenina* between 1863 and 1877, that is between the ages of thirty-five and fifty. Even after *Anna Karenina*, to mention literary works alone, Tolstoy produced masterpieces like *The Death of Ivan Ilyich, The Power of Darkness, The Kreutzer Sonata, The Fruits of Enlightenment, Father Sergius* and many others. At the age of seventy Tolstoy wrote a novel, *Resurrection*, while the novella entitled *Hadji*

Murat, one of the most impressive works in Russian and world literature, was written when he was seventy-five. Fully aware of this, *Literaturnaya Gazeta* went ahead and printed Snow's fiction concerning Tolstoy's 'artistic sterility' after *Anna Karenina*!

It is hardly necessary to point out that in the anniversary articles Sholokhov's books, and *The Quiet Don* in particular, are praised beyond measure. For instance, in an appreciation of the first book of *The Quiet Don* A. Kalinin wrote, 'No-one before or since has proved capable of anything even remotely approaching the mighty artistry of these descriptions of pre-Revolutionary life on the Don, the period of the First World War and the age when the new social structure was confirmed in the battles of the Civil War.'[1] 'On an unprecedentedly high level', asserts Yu. Andreyev,

Sholokhov has discovered a new continent for world literature, the inner world of the ordinary, so-called rank-and-file Russian, a man of the masses, a man of the overwhelming majority of people, and he has depicted the infinite complexity and profundity of his spiritual make-up. Even on the scale of the history of the culture of the entire world a revelation such as this is epoch-making; what can we say of the scale of our century alone![2]

L. Yershov states that, 'Sholokhov is a great optimist and humanist, even though the twentieth century has known no other tragic artist of similar power. Neither has it in the arsenal any epic canvas [*sic*, Tr.] comparable with Sholokhov's epic in scope, profundity and mighty strength.'[3] V. Baranov rightly asserts that,

The Quiet Don belongs to the number of those works in world literature which are like mighty mountain-peaks towering above the age that created them. *The Iliad, Hamlet, Faust, War and Peace...The Quiet Don* has earned the right to join their ranks, the right to be considered a worthy representative of the storm-tossed twentieth century standing on the main highways of the artistic development of mankind.[4]

The same Baranov, however, comments later that *The Quiet Don* was created though the author did not live in a literary environment; Serafimovich received the first books of the novel fully completed, and arranged for them to be published without any corrections or revision. 'This novel', he states,

was born outside any literary milieu...How can we think of such a milieu when the young author, living at that time in Karginsk, shut himself away for the night in a half-underground room rented from the blacksmith next door, with only the omnipresent village leaders squinting through the clouded glass and making out a figure bent over the table submerged in great clouds of rough tobacco smoke?[5]

Clearly the explanation of a phenomenon like this can only come from the realms of the supernatural, a point which is made with particular insistence by another writer, G. Konovalov, who says, 'It is surely beyond anyone to explain why the genius of Sholokhov ever appeared. Anyway, does it have to be explained? Explanations are for ordinary phenomena. This genius was created by nature for enigma and solution – and that is what it contains. A mystery and the search for a solution – this is its uniqueness.'[6] Elsewhere the same Konovalov writes, 'Scientists can explain where worlds came from, but the mystery of artistic genius they cannot explain. This is a mystery beyond our comprehension.'[7] All this seems somehow remote from the philosophical outlook based upon dialectical materialism employed by V. Petelin in his attempt to explain *The Quiet Don*.

One general tendency observable in the anniversary articles was a striving to establish some kind of proximity between the events of *The Quiet Don* and the events of Sholokhov's own biography. In earlier years both Sholokhov and some of his friends had attempted to demonstrate that everything occurring at the mill in the first book of *The Quiet Don* was written from Sholokhov's memories of the mill once managed by his father. There was only one slip: at the end of the second book he killed off Valet and even has a little chapel raised for him, and then suddenly one day a hero bearing the same name appeared before the writer offended because he was still alive and they had written him off as dead. (Valet was apparently not offended by Sholokhov's having turned him into an extremely unsympathetic character.) Sholokhov claimed he had modelled Kopylov, the chief of staff in an insurgent division, on a teacher at the local village school who had once had charge of little Misha. A Father Vissarion also turned up unexpectedly in the course of the anniversary months. In a notice entitled 'With Sholokhov in Veshensk' a correspondent of the journal *V Mire Knig* reports the following claim made by Sholokhov:

'I was a great reader from childhood on. I could always find a way to run away with the lads and also to sit down with a book, hidden away from human eyes. At such moments no-one saw me or heard me or looked for me. It was no good calling for me.' Here Sholokhov smiled to himself, evidently calling up a distant memory. 'In those days when I was a lad in Karginsk there was a well-educated parson living in the village – Father Vissarion. He lived alone and had a sumptuous library of books on the history and ethnography of the Don region. He read a great deal himself but never lent any of his books to anyone. I can't think how it was I came to win his confidence but he did start to let me approach his tall bookcases. Every time he lent me a book Father Vissarion would say, 'Always remember that heaven on earth is to be found in a good book and a clear conscience!' And although I have always been, and remain, a convinced atheist I still recall his lessons with a feeling of gratitude. Father Vissarion had the reputation of being a talented parson, but he was above his clerical calling.[8]

Well, it is quite possible that everything occurred exactly like that. Except that it was hardly from a sense of gratitude that Sholokhov gave the name Vissarion to the parson from Tatarsk. Let us recall his portrait: 'Father Vissarion was a widower, now living with his Ukrainian house-keeper. He had a funny way of speaking – the legacy of syphilis – but he was easy to get along with.'[9]

A further tendency which also emerged from the anniversary articles was an attempt to show the closest possible relationship in style and content between *The Quiet Don* and the *Tales of the Don*. Sholokhov had previously objected to this; now he has been persuaded to change his point of view, thus providing assistance for Sholokhov scholars in their work of research and investigation. On 23 May 1975 *Literaturnaya Rossiya* published a television interview in which Sholokhov said, amongst other things:

There was the theme in front of me, a theme for stories and essays. It was a very tragic age. It asked to be written about, it was all so terribly interesting that it demanded irresistibly to be set down. That is how the *Tales of the Don* came to be written. Now *The Quiet Don* was different. You might say it grew out of *The Tales of the Don*.

During this interview Sholokhov made what was probably the first reference to one of his memoir sources for *The Quiet Don* when he said:

The way that an adolescent looks at things is the most searching look of all. It sees everything, notices everything, gets around everywhere. It was easy for me as far as factual material was concerned. The difficulties came later when it became necessary to know and write about the history of the Civil War. Then one had to sit there in the archives studying memoir material. And not just ours, but émigré memoirs as well and Denikin's *Essays on the Russian Troubles*.[10]

It is important to note that anyone who had read these *Essays* by Denikin realises how little could have been extracted from them to help with a description of the Civil War actually on the Don.

Although for the most part the anniversary articles and reports contributed nothing new to Sholokhov scholarship the deluge of material did include a number of interesting pieces of research. One thinks particularly of an article by S. Semanov, '*The Quiet Don*: literature and history', published in the fifth number of *Moskva* in 1975. In this article, as in some others by the same author (e.g. *Molodaya Gvardiya*, No. 5), Semanov argues persuasively that the knowledge displayed by the author of *The*

Quiet Don in all things concerning the Cossacks and their way of life was encyclopaedic and exceedingly accurate. Looking into certain ostensibly fictional incidents in the vast epic, Semanov uses pre-Revolutionary and military archive material to show that many of them contain no fiction at all, but are actually drawings taken from real life. Semanov concludes:

Everything narrated in *The Quiet Don* is to the greatest possible extent genuine. Genuine in the most exalted, that is the most accurate sense of the word. Everything described in the novel 'happened that way' and that's all there is to it. Events large and small. Incidentally in a true work of art it is not at all easy to distinguish exactly between 'large' and 'small'. The historical reality of *The Quiet Don* is comprehensive to an unparalleled extent. We are quite justified in claiming that if *The Quiet Don* were the only thing remaining from the Civil War it would be sufficient in itself to give posterity a complete picture of that era.[11]

In this instance, of course, Semanov clearly overstates his case. In order to achieve a complete picture of the Civil War even an enormously significant novel like *The Quiet Don* is scarcely sufficient. All the same, the examples of the historical authenticity of virtually all incidents large and small in *The Quiet Don*, only a small number of which are cited by Semanov in his articles, are most impressive. One such example concerns the Lieutenant Izvarin, an intellectual in favour of Cossack self-rule whose opinions have some influence upon Grigori. Until now, he has always been considered a fictional hero. Semanov produces documentary evidence to show that among the members of the Don Cossack Military Assembly in 1918 appears one, Lieutenant Boris Yefimovich Izvarin (exactly the same name that appears in the novel). Under Krasnov, Izvarin's star rose and he quickly attained the rank of Lieutenant Colonel. Izvarin was indeed a supporter of Cossack self-rule and he published occasional articles in pro-Krasnov newspapers.[12] Semanov shows that the novel is entirely accurate not only in its geographical and topographical minutiae but even in the distances between settlements which the Cossacks or their units had to traverse. The well-known abundance of geographical details in *The Quiet Don* relating to descriptions of the First World War and the Civil War have been checked against *contemporary* maps and Semanov has found no inaccuracies at all. He writes with a sense of surprise:

Mikhail Sholokhov went about the creation of his novel as if holding before himself a detailed geographical map of Russia, a map which changed now and then into a topographical plan. One thinks of all the details unique to Novocherkassk or Rostov, Petrograd or Novorossiysk. And when it comes to the Upper Don region, the main setting for the action of the novel, every last geographical point down to tiny villages and country lanes, everything corresponds to the reality of that time.[13]

In January 1914, judging from the circumstances, Grigori Melekhov, a recent recruit, was assigned to the 12th Don Cossack Regiment. Grigori's company commander, Lieutenant Polkovnikov, is mentioned in passing. Semanov has established from the archives that early in 1914 there really was a Lieutenant Polkovnikov serving as a commander in the 12th Don Cossack Regiment, the same Polkovnikov who in 1917, with the rank of Colonel, was appointed Commanding Officer of the Petrograd military district by the Provisional Government. This degree of accuracy extends to all the other details of the location and co-ordination of Cossack units during the war, as well as to all the incidents connected with Red Army units dispatched to put down the Veshensk Uprising and also to the activities of the insurgent units and their disposition on different days during the conflict.

How did the author achieve such accuracy in every last detail? The most satisfactory explanation would seem to be that he undertook a vast amount of preparatory work, visiting the front and the Cossack units and noting down *for future use* the names of the various detachments, their officers, the minutiae unique to each area, and so on. In such an event it would be extremely risky to rely on memory alone, especially the popular memory, as it is sometimes called. Sholokhov, it must be remembered, interviewed surviving battle veterans twelve or thirteen years after the events described. We also know that even when interviewing Cossacks Sholokhov never took notes and even left his 'writer's' notebook at home. In an interview with the writer M. Neznamov in 1940 Sholokhov admitted, 'Essentially I have no notebook in the literal sense of the word... I do make notes, but only very rarely. One jots down the occasional successful image or simile and everything else somehow stays in one's head.'[14] Confirmation of this came recently from a friend of Sholokhov's, Pyotr Lugovoy, who stated that,

In the spring of 1931 when the sowing of the early wheat was in full swing Sholokhov and I went round the local collective farms. As we met people and discussed the progress of the sowing, the likelihood of the plan being fulfilled and the amount of livestock on the farms, Sholokhov never made a note. His memory was what he used as an extraordinary kind of 'notebook'. He committed everything to memory, the numerous facts that we came across in the teams of workers, the surnames, first names and patronymics of dozens of people whom he had never met before, their faces, their general appearance, their clothing, even down to the colours of the scarves worn by the young girl farm-workers. I was amazed at this ability to commit to memory with such infallible accuracy so many facts, people, numbers, names, faces and small details – yes, and then the ability to re-create them on paper.[15]

People with phenomenal powers of memory are sometimes to be

found in the writing fraternity, although usually even they tend not to scorn primary note-taking. It is possible that Sholokhov is one of the most gifted of such people. If so, however, it is strange that he is not too good at recalling many of the most vital details of his own biography, since he has frequently given conflicting information about various periods of his life – for instance, the time spent in Moscow during his childhood (two years or three), the size of his novel *Life on the Don*, the precursor of *The Quiet Don* (described at various times as between four and twelve printer's pages in length), and the evacuation of his archives which he witnessed himself but which he has described with many serious inaccuracies of detail.

We have already seen that Sholokhov created *The Quiet Don* without the advantage of living in a literary environment. He never informed any of his friends of his original plans for the novel or showed them his first drafts of incident and dialogue, his draft chapters and sections, and he never felt the urge to discuss the possible future destiny of his heroes with anyone. From the remote village of Veshensk Sholokhov brought to Moscow a fully completed work in typescript prepared none too expertly on the village machine. The first book of *The Quiet Don*, for instance, had been typed out in one unbroken text which made life extremely difficult for the editors who had to read it.

If we discount the content of *The Quiet Don* there is nothing extraordinary about this fact alone. In the literary history of all countries you will probably be able to find an example of an unknown young (or not so young) author arriving in the capital with a work created without the benefit of a literary environment which then became enormously successful, even achieving the status of a world classic. We learn from Alexander Solzhenitsyn's recently published biography *The Calf Butted the Oak* that this writer created his first works away from any literary environment. Solzhenitsyn carefully hid everything away as he wrote it and quite naturally destroyed his very earliest sketches, drafts and plans, relying upon his memory to retain a good deal of material. However, once it became possible for him to work in a more normal way Solzhenitsyn started to turn out new novels, novellas and stories one after the other and these won him a Nobel Prize in 1970. Whereas Sholokhov has never managed to produce anything to equal the creative power of the first books of *The Quiet Don*.

These circumstances inevitably give rise to serious doubts about the authorship of *The Quiet Don*. A major contribution towards the dispelling of such doubts could be made by a scrutiny of the writer's archives, his preparatory materials, extracts from his files, his plans, draft versions and the like. Here we encounter an insurmountable obstacle: Sholokhov has, it seems, no archive material at all relating to the 1920s and 1930s. Where has it all gone?

The simplest of all answers to this question has been attempted by Anatoliy Kalinin, who observed in his article, 'From the *Tales of the Don* to *The Quiet Don*':

At no time in the past or more recently has Sholokhov paid serious attention to what is now of no value. He had never shown the slightest concern for the preservation of his manuscripts and he has treated his draft versions with the kind of scorn which only a writer who can count on eternity may permit himself. Geniuses have never been notable for having the foresight of graphomaniacs.[16]

This position is patently absurd. Both Tolstoy and Balzac, for example, diligently preserved the outline schemes and first drafts of their works, though not many people would describe them as graphomaniacs. It is hard to imagine how Pushkin scholarship would fare without the availability for study of Pushkin's innumerable draft poems, long and short. In any case Kalinin seems to forget that many of Sholokhov's friends have answered this question quite differently. V. Zakrutin claimed recently that there used to be drafts but they were unfortunately destroyed during the war.

Unfortunately the manuscripts of this celebrated epic have perished. But if only the researchers had had at their disposal those heaps of pages covered with Sholokhov's neat handwriting, the numerous variant versions, plans, copy after copy with all those multitudinous corrections – they would have been more than amazed at the sheer industry and the punishing, self-imposed demands of this artist.[17]

When the first scholars began to arrive in Veshensk with the aim of learning the history behind the origin of the first books of *The Quiet Don*, Sholokhov himself invariably told them that all his papers relating to the period before 1940 had been destroyed during the war. His most frequent explanation was that they had gone up in smoke when his farm had burned down or had been filched by the villagers before the evacuation. This version was clearly in Solzhenitsyn's mind when he wrote, in his preface to *The Mainstream of 'The Quiet Don'*,

And another thing: the rough drafts and manuscripts of this novel have not survived in any archives or been produced or shown to anyone (other than Anatoliy Sofonov, far too partial a witness). In 1942 when the front was approaching the village of Veshensk Sholokhov, as the leading figure in the district, could have obtained transport for the evacuation of his precious archives ahead of the regional party-committee itself. Through a strange sort of indifference this was not done. And we are now told that the whole of the archive material was destroyed in the bombardment.[18]

In this instance Solzhenitsyn's information is none too accurate. The evacuation of Veshensk was proceeding quite smoothly and in July 1942 Sholokhov himself arrived to assist with the evacuation of his family and his archives. I shall not rest my case on the testimony of an officer involved in the evacuation of the village who (while asking for his anonymity to be preserved) told me that army headquarters assigned twelve Studebaker lorries for this purpose and that orders were issued for them to pay particular attention to the evacuation of the local institutions and to the archives and the family of Mikhail Sholokhov. Let us restrict ourselves to nothing more than published materials. In 1958 I. Lezhnyov, in his book *The Way of Sholokhov*, testifies as follows:

The evacuation of the Sholokhov family was being carried out on July 13 during a daylight air-raid by the Germans. The car was loaded and waiting. Inside sat the writer's wife and children but his mother Anastasya Danilovna seemed to be dawdling. He got out and ran into the yard to fetch her, calling out, 'Get your things together. Come on!' She replied, 'Go on, you make a start. I'll just finish getting ready.' The car drove off. Mikhail Sholokhov went back to fetch his mother but was told that she had been killed. A bomb had exploded a few feet away from her. The house had been hit by several bombs and was completely burnt out. One army unit passing through the village expressed concern for the writer's library. The commanding officer, a lover of literature, made a lorry available and had it loaded with Sholokhov's archives, files containing manuscripts, boxes of letters and part of his library. The whole lot was sent to Stalingrad and handed over for the safe-keeping to the city library which shortly afterwards was totally destroyed in a furious bombardment.[19]

More or less the same version is put forward by A. Khvatov, except that he does not mention the destruction of the archives in Stalingrad. Khvatov recounts that Sholokhov arrived in person to evacuate his family and save his archives.

Carts were moving through the village day and night. Artillery vehicles were passing through, lorries went by and infantrymen marched along with their tired rhythmic tread...everyone was retreating to pastures new. Enemy aircraft kept up a ceaseless bombardment of the village. A lorry drove up to Sholokhov's house where everyone was busy mustering. Only Anastasya Danilovna, the writer's mother, lagged behind. She found it hard to say goodbye to the family house. An enemy aircraft flew past and dropped a bomb, scoring a direct hit on Sholokhov's house. His mother was killed and the house went up in flames. Passing soldiers helped load up part of the library and the archives of the writer. Last respects were paid to the dead woman.[20]

Khvatov goes on to give the account of I. P. Gromoslavsky, Sholokhov's brother-in-law, who told how the Sholokhov family made their first stop in the town of Nikolayevsk on the Volga before going on to the village of Daryinsk in the Urals.

Several years after Khvatov's book another scholar, V. Petelin, in his book *Mikhail Sholokhov*, announced to his readers a completely new version of what happened to the Sholokhov archives. He wrote that,

Sholokhov himself had lost a lot of colleagues and friends from the district. At the front he was informed of his son's serious illness but could do nothing to help him. His house and library were destroyed by enemy bombs. The story goes that his seventy-year-old mother died in that very bombardment as she rushed out to save her son's archives which had been packed up in special boxes. Only a meagre portion of Sholokhov's archives has been preserved and the fate of the rest is unknown.[21]

Petelin has it that during the defence of Veshensk the whole of Sholokhov's yard was littered with papers from his archives. These papers were being picked up all the time by men and women Cossack evacuees who crammed them into their brief-cases and bags. Soldiers used some of them to roll their own cigarettes. Petelin goes on to say that in November 1942 an officer by the name of I. I. Urkin, inspecting the Soviet Army positions on the left bank of the Don, confiscated from one soldier twenty pages of these precious Sholokhov manuscripts which had been used for rolling cigarettes. Acting on Urkin's report the unit commander ordered all the books and papers in Sholokhov's deserted house to be collected and handed into army headquarters for safekeeping. The village of Veshensk, it is worth remembering, was never occupied. This was a region in which German troops never managed to force a crossing of the Don. Thus military personnel and even local party workers and Soviet officials continued their normal functions. Given these conditions how was it possible for Sholokhov's pre-war archives to disappear in their entirety?

The number of different versions of the loss of Sholokhov's archives became so great that there arose a demand for someone to settle on a single one of them, thus giving it official ratification. The task was evidently entrusted to the Rostov writer, K. Priyma, who published in the journal *Inostrannaya Literatura* a long article entitled 'The Pride of Soviet and World Literature'. Mentioning briefly the work of the 1929 commission headed by A. Serafimovich, Priyma claimed, without citing his sources, that in 1929 Sholokhov handed over to the commission the original manuscripts of the *Tales of the Don* and even *Life on the Don*, along with the plans, sketches and all the available manuscripts of *The Quiet Don*, that is Book 1, Book 2 and three-quarters of Book 3. But the commission apparently kept no records and it was not long before Sholokhov took his manuscripts back to Veshensk. And what did happen to them twelve years later? This is Priyma's account:

In the autumn of 1941 he packed up in a zinc box the original manu-scripts of *The Quiet Don* and *Virgin Soil Upturned* (Book One and the rough copy of Book Two), his letters and telegrams from Stalin, his Stalin Prize Certificate and the unique foreign editions of his works, handed the whole lot, locked up, over to the Veshensk regional branch of the People's Commissariat for Internal Affairs (NKVD) for safe-keeping and then left for the front. In the summer of 1942 when the Germans achieved a breakthrough the box containing Sholokhov's arc-hives was lost in the chaos of evacuation. In the morning the members of a tank crew defending the village came across more than a hundred pages of Part Three and Part Four of *The Quiet Don* on the village street. These were collected up and returned to Mikhail Sholokhov after the war.[22]

Priyma goes on to say that in the summer of 1968 Sholokhov deposited these priceless pages safely in a Sholokhov archive set up in a Rostov museum of which Priyma himself had just been appointed director. Whereupon 2 pages were sent to the Royal Library of Sweden and all the rest, 134 pages in manuscript and 109 pages of typescript corrected by Sholokhov have been kept under lock and key in the State Bank. They are soon to be published with an appropriate scholarly commentary. All the principal Soviet newspapers announced in the summer of 1975 that K. Priyma had, at Sholokhov's bidding, solemnly transferred the materials described by him from the State Bank to the Leningrad Institute of Russian Literature (Pushkinsky Dom). We look forward to their publication in a scholarly edition.

It turns out, however, that Moscow also possesses some of the manus-cripts of *The Quiet Don*. The writer Mikhail Shevchenko said in some notes of his,

I have seen several pages of the manuscripts of *The Quiet Don* in the Literary Museum in Moscow. They are terribly difficult to read. I think Sholokhov would be hard put to make them out now. Every line is struck through and crossed out. Corrections up and down the page, between the lines and in the margins. It's simply awful to read – hard labour![23]

These remarks came from the realms of pure fiction, as was made clear by a lady who works in the Literary Museum, D. Aleksandrova. In an article entitled 'One or Two Pages from a Writer's Archives' she coun-tered with this pronouncement:

Sholokhov's private archives were destroyed during the Great Patriotic War. The State Literary Museum in Moscow is in possession of the only documentary and literary materials surviving from Sholokhov's pre-war work. The prize holding consists of five pages from the fair copy of *The Quiet Don*. The handwriting is all but calligraphic and there is not a single correction on any of these pages. This original manuscript has been given a place of honour in the exhibition now opening in the galleries on Leninsky Prospekt.[24]

I went recently to the Literary Museum in Moscow where I was able to check that in this case Aleksandrova, not Shevchenko, is in the right. The museum holds two pages of typescript from the third book of *The Quiet Don*, in which the author has corrected only the typist's errors, and the totally uncorrected five pages of fair copy referred to. Incidentally, during the hour which I spent in the galleries of the Literary Museum I was the only visitor there.

Thus it is clear that all the information announced in our press about the fate of Mikhail Sholokhov's literary archives in no way dispels the doubts surrounding his authorship.

In the light of all that is known about *The Quiet Don* the position occupied by Aleksandr Serafimovich is most peculiar. A veteran Russian writer from the same region as Sholokhov and a personal friend of Kryukov's, Serafimovich was the first notable writer to draw attention to Sholokhov's talent and he wrote an encouraging preface to the *Tales of the Don*. In this he advised Sholokhov not to hurry and to take more care over the artistic finish of his works. Nevertheless within eighteen months of the publication of the *Tales* the editorial office of *Oktyabr'* received the massive manuscript of Book 1 of *The Quiet Don*. Serafimovich, ignoring objections from all the editorial staff and without making a single correction or requiring the slightest revision, insisted that the office print *The Quiet Don* in the exact form in which it had been received. This was a rare event in journalistic practice at that time. It was also Serafimovich who then brushed aside all criticism from RAPP quarters and published a glowing tribute in a review in *Pravda*. He showed undiminished energy in his support of the publication of Book 2 and then Book 3, which ran into greater trouble. In an article entitled 'Mentor equals Friend', devoted to the friendship between Serafimovich and Sholokhov V. Osipov has produced some hitherto unpublished comments on *The Quiet Don* made by Serafimovich. This is one of them. 'No writer has ever given such vivid pictures of Cossack life.... and not just in one province. The writer has managed to make this depiction of Cossack life profound and wide-ranging. A magnificent, vast canvas.'[25] Yet Serafimovich knew full well that Sholokhov was too young to have produced such a mature piece of work and that he was not even a Cossack by extraction. Can he have had no doubts about Sholokhov's authorship? Questions like that cannot be answered today. Alexander Solzhenitsyn writes in his preface to 'D's' book,

Evidently the real story behind this book was known to Aleksandr Serafimovich, a Don Cossack writer who was by then getting on in years. But he was passionately fond of the Don and was primarily interested in clearing the way for a brilliant novel based on that region. Any mention of a certain 'White Guard' author could only have prevented publication. Overcoming all opposition from the editors of *Oktyabr'* Serafimovich insisted upon publication of the novel and his glowing review in *Pravda* (April 19, 1928) cleared the way for it.[26]

This hypothesis suggested by Solzhenitsyn seems to me highly plausible.

Despite the excessively respectful tone adopted by many critics of *The Quiet Don*, their praises contain an element of truth and are for the most part well merited. This certainly cannot be said of the wild encomia addressed during the anniversary celebrations to Sholokhov's work on the Second World War. In his article on Sholokhov's wartime prose I. Kozlov, for example, writes that the unfinished novel *They Fought for Their Country* and all the wartime essays of 1941–2 may be placed '*in the front rank* of our wartime prose works, while *The Fate of a Man* has become a Soviet classic'.[27] Another writer, G. Konovalov, claims that *They Fought for Their Country* 'for all its inchoate condition is the best book on the war'.[28]

I shall not now concern myself with refuting this quite unmerited praise; my views on Sholokhov's wartime work are made plain in an earlier chapter. It is, however, worth mentioning that even among the anniversary articles some extremely critical comments were made with reference to *They Fought for Their Country*. True, the authors nevertheless attempted to make excuses for Sholokhov. M. Shevchenko, for instance, seeks to show that an epic novel of the war was beyond the powers of even Mikhail Sholokhov. Here is his reasoning.

A lad of twenty began the writing of *The Quiet Don*...The novel was written according to that loftiest of principles – write as if you were writing your last book: give yourself wholly to the novel. The novel makes sense of critical events in the history of Russia in its own unique way. Sholokhov has his own personal manner of setting down the 'eternal issues', enlistment, a man's first taste of action, killing an enemy for the first time, the birth of hatred for the enemy, the birth of love for his native soil, for a woman, for children, parting from his mother and his sweetheart, the retreat, the losses, the death of friends, his own sons, his own death in battle. Then came another 'wartime' novel and with it the necessity to give a philosophical interpretation of all that was new in this war, all that distinguished it from other wars. Again there would also be 'eternal issues' to be dealt with in this novel. Turgenev said that talent is detail. How could the repetition of detail be avoided? How could a new freshness be infused into the impressions recorded? And all of this was subject to the special demands made on Sholokhov. What other people could be forgiven he could not.[29]

The artificiality of this explanation of Sholokhov's failures during and after the war years stares one in the face. It is well known that 1975 saw the appearance on our screens of a film based on Sholokhov's novel *They Fought for Their Country*. The author had previously objected strenuously to his unfinished novel being turned into a film, just as he had objected to stage versions such as *Regiment on the Move*. His comment was, 'Theatres thinking of making stage versions of my novel *They Fought for Their Country* are in my opinion being too hasty. It is very difficult to create a complete and unified drama out of an unfinished work.'[30] Nevertheless in 1974, we are told by S. Bondarchuk, Sholokhov himself suggested that his novel should be made into a film. What are we to say about this film? It is not, of course, a distinguished work of the cinema; neither can it be described as a bad or unsuccessful film. Every film-goer can see clearly, however, that any relative success enjoyed by *They Fought for Their Country* is due not in the slightest degree to the novel, but to a fine director, a splendid cameraman, a superb cast and above all to the screenplay of that remarkable writer, actor and director, V. Shukshin, whom we lost during the shooting of the film.

When 'D's' book and Alexander Solzhenitsyn's pronouncements on Sholokhov's authorship came in for discussion in the foreign press, doubts were expressed about the truthfulness of the charges made. It is a fact that Fyodor Kryukov's son was among the Cossacks who emigrated to the west and he never made any claims against Sholokhov. No such claims were made anywhere in émigré Cossack literature. This is, of course, an extremely delicate question. Kryukov never married and had no son of his own. He had an adopted son, but we have no idea of the extent to which this man was privy to the literary plans of his adoptive father. Furthermore, like all Cossacks who ended up as émigrés, he lacked any documents or conclusive evidence to support a possible claim. Circumstances had worked out in such a way that everyone with any connection with Kryukov's archives remained in Russia.

The 1965 Nobel Prize for Literature was awarded to Sholokhov not for all his work but specifically for *The Quiet Don*, a fact which was stressed in the verdict of the Swedish Academy of Sciences. The Nobel Prize citation said: 'The 1965 Nobel Prize for Literature is awarded to Mikhail Sholokhov in recognition of the artistic power and honesty shown by him in his Don Cossack epic about certain historical stages in the life of the Russian people.'[31] Announcing to the press the official verdict of the Swedish Academy, the Chairman of the Nobel Committee, Anders Österling, said, 'Sholokhov's *The Quiet Don* is in all respects a mighty work fully deserving of the reward now being paid to it late in the day but, fortunately, not too late.'[32] The Secretary of the Nobel Committee, the writer Karl Ragnar Gierow, gave his opinion in an article published on 16 October 1965 in the newspaper *Svenska Dagbladet*:

The Quiet Don is one of the best loved books of the Russian people. It is a national epic about the birth of a new state. *The Quiet Don* is an enormous triumph of Sholokhov's creativity, the triumph of the truth which he infuses into his works. This truth flows out far beyond the frontiers of his own country. The man who wrote the greatest historical novel in Russian literature since *War and Peace* takes his place today among the classics of world literature.[33]

Every Russian winner of the Nobel Prize has been treated unkindly by fate. The first of our compatriots to win the Nobel Prize was Ivan Bunin, who had emigrated to France following the Revolution. The second was Boris Pasternak who was subjected after the award to torment and persecution sufficient to make him officially renounce the Prize and the citation. A later winner, Alexander Solzhenitsyn, has been forcibly expelled from his country, in which all his principal works have yet to be published. Finally, Mikhail Sholokhov has had to spend all his life defending himself against charges of plagiarism.

NOTES

Chapter 1. The novel 'The Quiet Don'

1 P. V. Paliyevsky, *Puti realizma* (Moscow, 1974), pp. 197–8, 209–10. (Paliyevsky is not quite accurate. The first volume of the novel was ready when Sholokhov was still only twenty-two. We know that Sholokhov was born in May 1905 and in the autumn of 1927 he brought the completed manuscript of the first volume to Moscow. Paliyevsky also exaggerates the epoch-making significance of the turning point in literature which *The Quiet Don* created, although we are, of course, dealing with a work of universal significance. Naturally the war, and even more the Revolution, threw up so many new seams of life, created so many new situations and brought forth so many new personalities that there can be no question here of a mere 'development of material' already created by Tolstoy and Chekhov. This was just the sort of age liable to create the right conditions for the appearance of great new names both in literature and in all other areas of social life.)

2 L. Yakimenko, *Tvorchestvo Sholokhova* (Moscow, 1970), p. 68.

3 I. Lezhnyov, *Put' Sholokhova* (Moscow, 1958), pp. 104–5. These questions arise also, of course, for the reader of the second volume of *The Quiet Don* where remarkably accurate pictures of the war in the autumn of 1916 are given in minute detail.

4 F. A. Abramov and V. V. Gura, *Sholokhov: Seminariy* (Moscow, 1962), p. 43.

5 *Ibid.*, p. 70 (opinion of the critic V. Shcherbina).

6 *Ibid.*, p. 67.

7 *Ibid.*

8 *Tikhiy Don* (Moscow, 1957), Books 1 and 2, p. 10. All subsequent references to *Tikhiy Don* apply to this edition.

9 'The people had gone on in front and Grigori stayed behind vacillating...It turned out that he did not have the strength to break free from the snares of class prejudice cultivated by Tsarism for centuries in the Cossacks. Grigori was essentially capable of becoming a Soviet man but the inescapable contradictions and bonds which held him proved too complex for him. Such is the tragic meaning of the character of Grigori' (Yu. Lukin, *Mikhail Sholokhov* (Moscow, 1952, rev. ed. 1962), p. 57).

'In depicting the character of Grigori the writer rose to generalisations of a universal historical significance. Either for the people or against the people, history knows no other way; this is Sholokhov's claim throughout his epic work. The tragic sum total of Melekhov's life shows how fatal it is for a man to be cut off from the people' (*Bol'shaya Sovetskaya Entsiklopediya*, Vol. 48, pp. 138–9).

10 The theme of civil war in the Don, Kuban and other Cossack regions is encountered in many authors. In the books of D. Petrov-Biryuk, especially in his trilogy, *Legend of the Cossacks*, there is some depiction of the brutality of the White Cossacks but not of the Red Guards or the Red Cossacks. In Nikolay Sukhov's novel, *Cossack Girl*, the Civil War in the Khopersk district of the Don is depicted just as one-sidedly. We come across more faithful pictures of the Civil War in the pages of books like A. Serafimovich's *Iron Flood*, A. Vesyoly's *Russia Washed in Blood* and A. Perventsev's *Kochubey*. In his *Red Cavalry* I. Babel also writes about the many bestialities and the lack of discipline of the Red Army, which was the source of his clash with Budyonny. But in this book as in several others it is generally a question of spontaneous lynch-law carried out by rank-and-file Cossacks, soldiers and sailors together with their odious officers. Thus *The Quiet Don* differs from all other books on the Civil War by reason of its *degree of truthfulness*.

11 *Tikhiy Don*, Books 1 and 2, pp. 638–40. In the first version of the novel which was published in the journal *Oktyabr'* in 1928 there is an even more detailed account of how Podtelkov went beserk, hacking at the dead body of Chernetsov as it lay on the ground.

12 *Ibid.*, p. 688.

13 *Ibid.*, pp. 694–5. The Cossack alarm or call to mobilisation, is called a *spolokh*. All Cossacks were armed; they had war horses and could mobilise at an hour's notice, especially since Cossack companies and regiments were organised along territorial lines. Even under Tsarism the Cossacks enjoyed considerable liberties and no ruling power could endure in their regions by means of violence alone.

14 *Tsentral'nyy Partiynyy Arkhiv*, fond 17, opis' 4, delo 21, list 216.

15 *Tikhiy Don*, Books 3 and 4, pp. 166–8.

16 *Ibid.*, p. 234.

17 *Ibid.*, pp. 234, 239. It is not widely known that the task entrusted to Malkin, the evacuation of the male population of the villages into the middle of Russia was actually part of the 'Decossacking' policy which continued to be pursued by party organs on the Don even after the annulment of the Central Committee's January directive. Cossacks aged between eighteen and fifty-five were subjected to evacuation and placed in concentration camps because of the risk that they might join the uprising. These punitive measures, however, led only to a widening of the areas involved in the uprising and to increased bitterness on both sides.

18 *Ibid.*, p. 763.

Chapter 2. If ' The Quiet Don' had appeared anonymously. . .
The author's distinguishing features

1 See Yu. Masonov, *V mire psevdonimov, anonimov i literaturnykh pod-delok* (Moscow, 1963), pp. 65–7. In his introduction to Masonov's book Prof. P. N. Berkov defines plagiarism as the borrowing of another person's material, firstly, when this is done without acknowledge-ment of the source and, secondly, when the material borrowed con-stitutes quantitatively the larger part of the new work (*ibid.*, p. 28).

2 R. Khigerovich, *Put' pisatelya* (Moscow, 1956), pp. 299–301.

3 According to the evidence of this critic and editor, Sholokhov never *himself* corrected his galleys or page-proofs which he received for a short period either in Moscow or by post in Veshensk. He did not use the galleys to change epithets or similes, did not insert new scenes, landscape descriptions, etc. In the surviving page-proofs of the late 1920s and early 1930s there are various editorial emendations but there are no corrections made by Sholokhov himself. This was a source of surprise for the editors, who were used to receiving from their authors page-proofs covered all over with corrections. But by no means every writer follows the example of Balzac who sometimes went through a dozen or more sets of proofs and whose corrections drove his type-setters to distraction. It is well known that Alexandre Dumas *père* never corrected his manuscripts. Georges Simenon is another writer who never bothers to correct the proofs of his novels.

4 After reading *The Quiet Don* Stalin wrote to F. Kon, 'In his novel *The Quiet Don* the outstanding writer of our time, comrade Sholo-khov, has committed a number of the crudest errors and actually presents incorrect information concerning Syrtsov, Podtelkov, Krivoshlykov and others, but does it therefore follow that *The Quiet Don* is a useless piece of literature which deserves to be suppressed?' (*Sochineniya* (Moscow, 1946–9), Vol. 12, p. 112).

5 I. S. Shkapa was Gorky's assistant until 1935. He spent the next twenty years in prisons and labour camps, but he survived and was rehabilitated. He was the author of a book, *Sem' let s Gor'kim* (Moscow, 1964), which included only some of Shkapa's reminiscences of Gorky, his surroundings and the people he met.
   Many memoirists testify to the extreme reserve, taciturnity, even timidity, of Sholokhov. 'When I first saw Mikhail Sholokhov', writes Stepan Shchipachev, for instance,
      'he had already achieved national fame. I recall that far-off day when it fell to me to listen to some new chapters of *The Quiet Don* amid a small group of writers...A lot has slipped away from my memory but I can still see clearly that tall well-proportioned youth. The resounding, perhaps unexpected, fame had not turned his head. He stood there looking as if this fame and *the universally acclaimed first part of the celebrated novel had very little to do with him*' (*Novy Mir* (1975), No. 4, 253 (author's italics)).

6 *Vestnik literatury* (1920), No. 6, 18, 15. The writer of the obituary was A. Gornfel'd.

7 'Ob odnom nezasluzhenno zabytom imeni', *Molot* (13 August 1965).

According to M. A. Solntsevaya, whose evidence I wrote down several years ago, in one of the camps in the north she met the well-known Mordvinian–Russian poet D. Morskoy. Morskoy began to be published in 1920 and then completed his course at the Bryusov Institute for Advanced Literary and Artistic Studies. He was later arrested and spent more than ten years in captivity. He told Solntsevaya that at the beginning of the 1920s once when he was staying with Demyan Bednyy an emaciated, poorly-dressed woman came to see Bednyy and said she was F. Kryukov's sister. She told him of her brother's death and showed him a small box containing some papers which had been handed over to her in a Kuban hospital together with other papers which had belonged to the deceased writer. Demyan Bednyy gave Kryukov's sister some money and kept the box and papers. When D. Morskoy asked Bednyy about these papers a few weeks later, the latter replied that they had to do with the Cossacks and that he had handed the box over to A. Serafimovich. According to a different version, Kryukov's sister, on the contrary, demanded that Bednyy return to her the manuscripts which had been stolen or lost. The money had been paid to her so that she would not make a fuss. Only Kryukov's relatives, who still live in Leningrad and Rostov, can confirm whether there are grains of truth in all this evidence.

8 Podolsky is an obscure literary figure in Leningrad. It is known from reliable sources that the article was ordered from him by F. Shakhmagonov who was once Sholokhov's literary secretary. Shakhmagonov then had a lot of trouble getting it published.

9 According to one literary figure in the Far East the plot of *Far from Moscow* was borrowed by Azhayev from the author of an unsuccessful novella received by the editors of *Far East*. This, however, cannot be considered plagiarism, especially since it was done with the author's permission.

10 *Metodicheskiye i Metodologicheskiye Problemy Kontent-Analiza*, Tezisy, vyp. 1 i 2 (Moscow–Leningrad, 1973).

11 B. Rybakov, *Russkiye Letopistsy i Avtor 'Slova o polku Igoreve'* (Moscow, 1972), pp. 5–6.

12 *Ibid.*

13 *Ibid.*

14 M. Gorky, *Dve besedy* (Moscow, 1931), p. 30.

15 *Mikhail Sholokhov: Sbornik statey* (Moscow, 1931), p. 7.

16 K. Priyma '*Tikhiy Don*' *srazhayetsya* (Rostov, 1973) pp. 103, 193 *et al.*

17 *Slovo o Sholokhove* (Moscow, 1973), p. 97.

18 *Tikhiy Don*, Books 3 and 4, p. 505.

19 *Ibid.*, Books 1 and 2, p. 496.

20 *Ibid.*, p. 648.

21 *Ibid.*, Books 3 and 4, p. 322.

22 *Ibid.*, p. 249.

23 *Ibid.*, pp. 352–3.

24 'D', *Stremya 'Tikhogo Dona'* (Paris, 1974). This work will henceforth be referred to in notes simply as *Stremya*.
25 *Ibid.*, pp. 101–3.
26 D. Petrov-Biryuk, *Skazan'ye o Kazakakh* (Rostov, 1960).
27 *Ibid.*, p. 20.
28 *Stremya*, p. 35.
29 *Tikhiy Don*, Books 1 and 2, p. 61.
30 *Ibid.*, p. 643.
31 *Literaturnyy Kritik* (1940), Nos. 5–6, 213.
32 Yakimenko, *Tvorchestvo Sholokhova*, p. 453.
33 V. Litvinov, *Tragediya Grigoriya Melekhova* (Moscow, 1965), p. 95. Yakimenko, *Tvorchestvo Sholokhova*, p. 85.
34 *Sbornik: Mikhail Sholokhov* (Moscow, 1931), p. 40.
35 *Tikhiy Don*, Books 1 and 2, pp. 663–4.
36 *Ibid.*, Books 3 and 4, pp. 154–5.
37 *Ibid.*, pp. 67–70.
38 *Ibid.*, Books 1 and 2, pp. 28–9.
39 *Ibid.*, p. 33.
40 *Ibid.*, p. 661.
41 *Ibid.*, p. 41.
42 *Ibid.*, p. 86.
43 The journal *Segodnya i Zavtra* (East Germany, 1949), No. 3.
44 *Tikhiy Don*, Books 3 and 4, p. 144.
45 *Ibid.*, Books 1 and 2, pp. 459–60.
46 Rybakov, *Russkiye Letopistsy*, p. 398.
47 *Tikhiy Don*, Books 1 and 2, p. 488.
48 *Ibid.*, p. 463.
49 *Ibid.*, p. 466.
50 *Ibid.*, p. 463.
51 *Ibid.*, pp. 73–4.
52 *Ocherk po Politicheskoy Istorii Vsevelikogo Voyska Donskogo* (Novocherkassk, 1919), p. 8.
53 One recalls the colourful little scene in Chapter 38 of the sixth part of the novel, when Grigori asks a messenger from the Alexeyev village, a great big fellow, whether the people there are going to support the uprising which has just begun. 'Can't speak for everybody', the messenger replies, 'The farming Cossacks are all right, you can depend on them.' 'What about the others, the poor ones?' 'Hm! Idle swine...this kind of rule gives them a good life.'
54 *Tikhiy Don*, Books 1 and 2, p. 563.
55 *Ibid.*, p. 438.
56 *Ibid.*, p. 463.
57 *Ibid.*, Books 3 and 4, pp. 152–3.
58 *Ibid.*, pp. 147–9.
59 *Ibid.*, p. 158.
60 *Ibid.*, p. 159.
61 *Ibid.*, p. 172.
62 *Ibid.*, pp. 390–1.
63 Lukin, *Mikhail Sholokhov*, p. 41.

64 It is clear that class-conscious humanism can only be one concrete manifestation of the all-embracing humanism to which we refer. The two concepts cannot be opposed to each other without also justifying quite unjustifiable violence and atrocities. This, unfortunately, is just what did occur in the periods with which our story deals.

65 *Tikhiy Don*, Books 1 and 2, p. 323.

66 *Ibid.*, p. 601.

67 This scene has been subjected to all kinds of amendment in the various editions of the novel. In the 1953 edition the editor changed the scene completely. Chernetsov is made to seize the revolver and attempt to shoot Podtelkov who then cuts him down in self-defence. The 1956 edition restored the earlier version, omitting only the words describing the 'black' smile. Our quotation here is from the first version as published in the journal *Oktyabr'* (1928), No. 7, 160.

Chapter 3. If 'The Quiet Don' had appeared anonymously . . .
Mikhail Sholokhov as a possible author of the epic

1 M. Sholokhov, *Sochineniya*, Vol. 8 (Moscow, 1969), p. 431.

2 A. Shamaro, 'Marshrutami poiska', in the journal *V Mire Knig* (1975), No. 5, 86.

3 Abramov and Gura, *Sholokhov: Seminariy*, p. 165.

4 *Tikhiy Don*, introduction by L. Yakimenko, p. 4.

5 M. Sholokhov, *Rasskazy*, 'Narodnaya Biblioteka' (Moscow, 1969), pp. 17–18.

6 *Lazorevaya Step'* (Moscow, 1926).

7 *Mikhail Sholokhov: Sbornik statey*, pp. 144–5.

8 *Slovo o Sholokhove*, p. 70.

9 I. M. Kirilenko, *Stanovleniye sotsialisticheskogo realizma v tvorchestve Sholokhova* (Chardzhou, 1959), p. 10.

10 *Izvestiya* (14 December 1974).

11 Article under *Sholokhov* in the *Malaya Sovetskaya Entsiklopediya* (Moscow, 1931), Vol. 10, p. 87.

12 Yakimenko, *Tvorchestvo Sholokhova*, p. 52.

13 M. Sholokhov, *Sochineniya*, Vol. 1 (Moscow, 1956), pp. 167, 170–1. In this extract every edition perpetuates a serious error which displays the ignorance of the author and editor concerning Cossack administration. From May 1917 onwards no more atamans were appointed, i.e. determined by the government. Neither Kaledin nor Krasnov was appointed by anyone. They were elected by the Military Assembly.

14 *Tikhiy Don*, Books 1 and 2, pp. 644, 646.

15 Sholokhov, *Sochineniya*, Vol. 1, p. 209.

16 *Ibid.*, p. 323.

17 *Ibid.*, p. 173.

18 V. Goffenshefer, *Mikhail Sholokhov* (Moscow, 1940), p. 20.

19 K. Priyma, 'Sholokhov v Veshkakh', in the journal *Sovetskiy Kazakhstan* (1955), No. 5, 76. See also Yakimenko, *Tvorchestvo Sholokhova*, p. 31.

20 V. Petelin, *Gumanizm Sholokhova* (Moscow, 1965), p. 8.

21 *Ibid.*

NOTES TO PP. 67-81

22 *Slovo o Sholokhove*, p. 120.
23 *Ibid.*, p. 72.
24 'Problemy sotsial'nogo otbora', Manuscript (St. Petersburg), p. 264.
25 Letter from G. A-v (his italics throughout).
26 Yakimenko, *Tvorchestvo Sholokhova*, p. 51.
27 Lezhnyov, *Put' Sholokhova*, p. 87.
28 *Ibid.*, p. 106.
29 *Tikhiy Don*, Books 1 and 2, p. 385.
30 *Na Pod'yome* (1930), No. 6, 172.
31 *Uchenyye Zapiski Gor'kovskogo Pedagogicheskogo Instituta*, XIV (1950), 5.
32 *Mikhail Sholokhov: sbornik* (Moscow, 1931), pp. 25-6.
33 *Na Pod'yome* (1930), No. 12, 130.
34 N. Ostrovsky, *Sochineniya* (Moscow, 1968), Vol. 3, pp. 349-50.
35 *Na Pod'yome* (1930), No. 6, 223-4.
36 Sholokhov, *Sochineniya*, Vol. 1, p. 322.
37 *Tikhiy Don*, Books 3 and 4, p. 40. In the first editions, even in editions published in the 1940s, the phrase 'storm-tossed days' read 'heroic days'. The reference to Chernetsov in the above quotation is a clear indication that at an earlier stage the novel included somewhere a description of Chernetsov denouncing and shaming the White officers who were unwilling to serve either in the Volunteer Army or with the Kaledin partisans. At the beginning of 1918 there were about 16,000 officers in Rostov and Novocherkassk, of whom about 200 offered themselves to the Volunteer Army and a few hundred became Kaledin partisans. All the rest waited to see how things would turn out. Notices were put up in Rostov saying 'Join Lt. Chernetsov's Units' but there was little response to the call. Here we see indubitable confirmation of the fact that Sholokhov cut out of *The Quiet Don* certain chapters which were originally included. The same incidents are described from an entirely different standpoint by D. Petrov-Biryuk in his trilogy, *Legend of the Cossacks (Skazan'ye o Kazakakh)*, pp. 350-400.

Chapter 4. If 'The Quiet Don' had appeared anonymously...
Fyodor Kryukov as a possible author

1 V. Gura, *Zhizn' i Tvorchestvo Sholokhova* (Moscow, 1960). p. 21.
2 A. S. Serafimovich, *Materialy Mezhvuzovskoy Konferentsii* (Volgograd, 1963).
3 A. Serafimovich was the dedicatee of Kryukov's story *Marking Time* (pictures of Cossack mobilisation). This story, incidentally, is the only one by Kryukov to have been published after the Revolution. It appeared in 1926 in *1905-y God v Russkoy Khudozhestvennoy Literature*.
4 Serafimovich, *Materialy*, pp. 148-9.
5 *Kratkaya Literaturnaya Entsiklopediya* (Moscow, 1966), Vol. 3, pp. 858-9.
6 In 1966 the journal *Russkaya Literatura* appeared four times a year, so that the fourth edition was the last one for that year. This edition went to press late and actually appeared in 1967. Proskurin's article (and only that article) contained a footnote: 'Editorial acceptance:

January 1966'. My experience of editorial and publishing practice suggests that it was the Proskurin article that gave rise to serious editorial objections and held up publication.

7 (Moscow, 1969), p. 408.
8 (Moscow, 1973), p. 344.
9 *Sbornik Vospominaniy o Rylenkove* (Moscow, 1973).
10 *Russkiye Zapiski* (1916), No. 3, the sketch 'Pervyye Vybory', 164.
11 F. D. Kryukov, *Kazatskiye Motivy* (St Petersburg, 1907), p. 174.
12 *Ibid.*, p. 168.
13 *Ibid.*, p. 175.
14 Stenographic Records of the State Duma, Session 1, Meeting No. 26, 13 June 1906.
15 Kryukov, *Kazatskiye Motivy*, p. 137.
16 There is one article in my files in which Kryukov's adopted son is called Pyotr and another in which he is called Pavlusha (diminutive of Pavel). It is known that he emigrated in 1920 along with many other Cossacks and died abroad.
17 *Zyab'*, Biblioteka 'Znaniye', Book 27 (Moscow, 1910), p. 10.
18 *Ibid.*, p. 11.
19 A. Gornfel'd, *Knigi i Lyudi* (1908), 115–16.
20 *Severnyye Zapiski* (August–September 1914), 249–50.
21 The collection *Rodnoy Kray* (*K 25–letiyu literaturnoy deyatel'nosti F. D. Kryukova*) (Ust-Medveditsk, 1918), p. 6.
22 *Ibid.*, p. 7.
23 *Russkaya Literatura* (1966), No. 4, 180.
24 *Ibid.*, p. 179.
25 V. I. Lenin, *Polnoye Sobraniye Sochineniy*, 5th ed. (55 vols., Moscow, 1958–65), Vol. 22, pp. 363–9.
26 *Ibid.*, p. 365.
27 *Ibid.*, p. 366.
28 *Ibid.*
29 *Russkoye Bogatstvo* (1912), No. 12, 174–5. It is significant that this sharply critical sketch of Kryukov's, like many other equally sharp and equally critical sketches written by him and like-minded people on virtually every aspect of government policy, was published openly in the pages of *Russkoye Bogatstvo* despite the censorship. Lenin describes this journal as 'the principal, most reliable organ of the people' (*Poln. Sob. Soch.*, Vol. 22, p. 364). I cannot say whether Sholokhov ever read *Russkoye Bogatstvo* but the merchant Mokhov who claimed to be a liberal and gathered the local intelligentsia around himself was a regular reader of it. 'Sergey Platonovich lay on the cool leather couch flicking through the June number of *Russkoye Bogatstvo*. On the floor lay a yellow ivory knife... Sergey Platonovich loved reading.' (*Tikhiy Don*, Books 1 and 2, pp. 127–8).
30 Lenin, *Poln. Sob. Soch.*, Vol. 22, pp. 363, 368.
31 The sketch *Close to the War* in *Russkiye Zapiski* (1915), No. 3, 219.
32 *Russkiye Zapiski* (1917), Nos. 4–5, 308.
33 *Ibid.*, p. 301.
34 *Ibid.*, Nos. 6–7, p. 197.

35 *Ibid.*, Nos. 4–5, pp. 298–9.
36 In 1918 Mironov was commander of the 23rd Division of the Red Army and then commander of a main attack force of two divisions. In 1919 he commanded the Don Cossack Corps and the 2nd Cavalry. In 1921 he was arrested following a defamatory denunciation and shot in the Butyrki Prison. He was rehabilitated in 1960. (See the book by R. A. Medvedev and S. P. Starikov, *The Life and Death of Filipp Mironov,* (*Zhizn' i Gibel' Filippa Mironova*, 1973), New York, in press).
37 *Donskaya Volna* 1918), No. 23, 5–6.
38 An article by G. R., 'Belaya Pechat' na yuge Rossii v 1918–20' in *Byloye* (1925), No. 6 (34), 207–8.
39 *Rodnoy Kray.*
40 *Donskiye Vedomosti* (14 April 1919). After the withdrawal of the Germans from the Don and the retirement of General Krasnov, Kryukov gave his support to the new Don Cossack Ataman A. Bogayevsky. He also resumed his activity in the Don Cossack press and his editorial work for *Donskiye Vedomosti.*
41 *Donskiye Vedomosti* (24 May 1919). Not in style but in content this uprising corresponds to the thoughts swirling through Grigori Mele-khov's head as he runs from cover to join the insurgents:
'The path of the Cossacks had crossed with that of the landless peasants of Russia... Fight to the death! Seize from them the heavy Don earth awash with Cossack blood. Drive them out over the borders like the Tatars. Shake Moscow! Fasten her with a shameful peace! This is a narrow path; there is no passing. Someone has to be cast aside' *Tikhiy Don*, Books 3 and 4, p. 182).
42 *Donskiye Vedomosti* (25 September 1919).
43 *Utra Yuga* (25 February 1920). S. Svatikov, was a well-known public figure of the time.
44 *Sever Dona* (November 1918).
45 *Molot* (13 August 1965).
46 *Ibid.*
47 Gornfel'd, *Knigi i Lyudi* (1908), 115. The critic adds, however, and with great significance, 'Kryukov has no heroes but he does have one hero: THE QUIET DON.'
48 *Tikhiy Don*, Book 1, Chapter 16.
49 Biblioteka 'Znaniye', Book 27, p. 42.
50 *Ibid.*, pp. 46–7.
51 *Kazatskiye Motivy*, p. 11.
52 *Ibid.*, p. 92.
53 *Ibid.*, p. 199.
54 *Ibid.*, p. 220.
55 *Russkoye Bogatstvo* (1912), No. 1, 164.
56 *Ibid.*, No. 12, 3.
57 *Ibid.*, p. 12.
58 *Ibid.*, p. 8.
59 F. Kryukov, *Rasskazy* (1914), 179.
60 *Russkiye Zapiski* (1916), No. 2, 163.
61 *Tovarishchestvo 'Znaniye'* (1919), No. 27, 3.

62 Kryukov, *Rasskazy* (1914), 67.
63 *Tikhiy Don*, Books 1 and 2, p. 28.
64 *Ibid.*, p. 29.
65 *Ibid.*, p. 44.
66 *Russkoye Bogatstvo* (1912), No. 4, 17.
67 *Tikhiy Don*, Books 1 and 2, pp. 256–7.
68 *Ibid.*, p. 354.
69 Kryukov, *Rasskazy* (1914), pp. 170–1.
70 *Tikhiy Don*, Books 3 and 4, p. 135.
71 *Rodimyy Kray: sbornik k 25-letiyu literaturnoy deyatel'nosti F. D. Kryukova* (Ust-Medveditsk, 1918), p. 30.
72 *Tikhiy Don*, Books 3 and 4, pp. 56–7.

Chapter 5. 'D's' book 'The Mainstream of "The Quiet Don"'

1 'D'., *Stremya*, p. 12.
2 *Ibid.*, pp. 15–18.
3 K. P. Spasskaya, 'Iz nablyudeniy za leksikoy proizvedeniy M. A. Sholokhova', *Russkiy yazyk v shkole* (1947), No. 6.
4 *Ibid.*
5 *Ibid.*
6 Yakimenko, *Tvorchestvo Sholokhova*, p. 460.
7 *Tikhiy Don*, Books 1 and 2, p. 153.
8 *Ibid.*, p. 393.
9 *Ibid.*, p. 648.
10 *Ibid.*, p. 211.
11 Yakimenko, *Tvorchestvo Sholokhova*, pp. 331–2.
12 *Tikhiy Don*, Books 3 and 4, pp. 277–8.
13 Yakimenko, *Tvorchestvo Sholokhova*, p. 335.
14 *Tikhiy Don*, Books 3 and 4, pp. 457, 463–4.
15 *Ibid.*, p. 141.
16 *Ibid.*, p. 162.
17 *Ibid.*, pp. 273–4.
18 *Ibid.*, pp. 179–81.
19 *Ibid.*, pp. 268–9.
20 *Tikhiy Don*, Books 1 and 2, pp. 166–7.
21 *Ibid.*, p. 142.
22 *Ibid.*, p. 199.
23 *Ibid.*, pp. 702–3.
24 *Tikhiy Don*, Books 3 and 4, p. 35.
25 *Ibid.*, p. 178.
26 *Tikhiy Don*, Books 1 and 2, p. 629.
27 *Na literaturnom postu* (1928), Nos. 21–2, 141.
28 *Mikhail Sholokhov: Sbornik statey*, pp. 11–13.
29 *Ibid.*, p. 47.
30 *Literaturnaya Gazeta* (6 May 1940), 3.
31 *Znamya* (1954), No. 4, 166.
32 Gura and Abramov, *Sholokhov: Seminariy*, pp. 128–9.
33 *Stremya*, p. 49.

34 *Ibid.*, p. 48.
35 *Tikhiy Don, Books 1 and 2, p. 759.*
36 *Ibid.*, Books 3 and 4, p. 712.
37 *Ibid.*, p. 690.
38 *Ibid.*, p. 696.
39 *Stremya*, p. 114.
40 *Tikhiy Don*, Books 3 and 4, p. 251.
41 *Ibid.*, p. 746.
42 *Ibid.*, pp. 680–1.
43 *Stremya*, pp, 146–7.
44 *Tikhiy Don*, Books 3 and 4, p. 851.
45 *Bol'shevistskaya Smena* (24 May 1940).
46 *Stremya*, p. 16.
47 *Russkoye Bogatstvo* (1907), No. 4; Kryukov's article 'O Kazakakh', p. 40.
48 *Ibid.*, pp. 41–2.
49 *Stremya*, p. 9.
50 *Tekstologiya Proizvedeniy Sovetskoy Literatury*, No. 4 (1967); see the article by L. N. Smirnova.
51 *Ibid.*
52 *Stremya*, p. 172.
53 *Ibid.*, p. 173.
54 *Tikhiy Don*, Books 3 and 4, p. 7.
55 *Stremya*, p. 138.
56 *Tsentral'nyy Gosudarstvennyy Arkhiv Oktyabr'skoy Revolyutsii*, fond 1258, opis' 1, delo 246, list 9.
57 *Stremya*, pp. 95–6.
58 *Ibid.*, p. 109.
59 *Ibid.*, pp. 41–2.
60 Article by V. Gura in *Uchenyye Zapiski Vologodskogo Pedagogicheskogo Instituta*, Vol. XVIII (1956).
61 A. Frenkel, *Orly Revolyutsii* (Rostov, 1920), pp. 21–3.
62 *Tikhiy Don*, Books 1 and 2, pp. 730–8.
63 Frenkel, *Orly Revolyutsii* pp. 28–32. The only strange thing is that the name of the Cossack Mikhail Lukin has disappeared from the death-sentence text with the result that the number sentenced is reduced from seventy-six to seventy-five.
64 *Institut Russkoy Literatury*, fond 9, opis' 3, yedinitsa khraneniya 11, list 1.
65 *Ibid.*, list 18.
66 *Stremya*, p. 10.
67 *Novy Mir* (1975), No. 4, p. 253.

Chapter 6. Further problems in Sholokhov's literary biography

1 We refer in this instance to the first three books of *The Quiet Don*.
2 Sholokhov, *Sochineniya*, Vol. 8, p. 276. The belief that geniuses may be cultivated with the aid of increased fees is not without interest.
3 *Sovetskiy Kazakhstan* (1955), No. 5, 81–2.

4 *Russkaya Mysl'* (Paris, 16 January 1975), No. 3034, 7.

5 In private conversation, when doubts are expressed as to the author-ship of *The Quiet Don* Sholokhov scholars normally exclaim, 'Yes, but Sholokhov also created *Virgin Soil Upturned*, which is just as significant as *The Quiet Don!*'

6 *Podnyataya Tselina* (Moscow, 1960), p. 85.

7 *Ibid.*, pp. 107-8.

8 *Ibid.*, p. 127.

9 *Ibid.*, pp. 195-6. There is a striking and evidently not accidental similarity between the vocabulary of Marina Poyarkova and that of the 'suddenly fluent' Natalya Melekhova.

10 His actual words were,
    'I did not, of course, have to walk about all over the place collecting the facts. There was no need for me to collect material; there it was under my nose. I did not collect it, I just scraped it together in a heap. Live on a collective farm for a month or so and the people line up before you' (A. Khvatov, *Khudozhestvennyy Mir Sholokhova* (Moscow, 1970, p. 33.)

11 *Podnyataya Tselina*, p. 10.

12 *Ibid.*, p. 53.

13 *Ibid.*

14 A. Khvatov, *Na Strezhne Veka* (Moscow, 1975), p. 169.

15 The great void which exists between literary scholarship and Sholo-khov's actual characters is noticeable in the various assessments of Nagulnov. A. Dubrovin wrote that Nagulnov was a man 'dis-tinguished by his enormous spiritual sensitivity and solicitude'. V. Chalmayev described him as a hero 'bearing within him the delight of inspired historical creativity, conveying through the credo by which he lived all the opulent content of socialist humanism' (*Novy Mir* (1974), No. 12, 249). For Chalmayev, though, this 'Nagulnovian' interpretation of humanism is no accident. Chalmayev in his poetry called for the rehabilitation of Stalin and dreamt of the time when men would 'one day raise up such a building...as would house our Generalissimo and his great marshals' (*Molodaya Gvardiya* (1969), No. 12, 212). Chalmayev's unpublished poetry makes all this much more explicit.

16 *Podnyataya Tselina*, p. 606.

17 *Literaturnaya Gazeta* (26 June 1940), 4.

18 *Podnyataya Tselina*, p. 267.

19 *Ibid.*, p. 286. Ignoring these scenes completely, the critic V. Litvinov is able to write nowadays, '*Virgin Soil Upturned* is a book about the mighty power of the life of the people, one in which the life of the people is glorified by its success in destroying before our very eyes yet another libertarian pretence incompatible with the real march of history' (*Novy Mir* (1974), No. 12, 248).

20 *Ibid.*, p. 37.

21 *Vechernyaya Moskva* (March 1933).

22 *Literaturnaya Gazeta* (6 February 1934).

23 *Komsomol'skaya Pravda* (22 June 1934).

24 *Krasnaya Gazeta* (22 January 1938).
25 *Pravda* (1 January 1939).
26 K. Priyma, '*Tikhiy Don*' *srazhayetsya*, p. 431.
27 Eighteenth Party Congress, *Stenograficheskiy otchet* (Moscow, 1939).
28 Gura and Abramov, *Sholokhov: seminariy; biokhronika.*
29 *Komsomol'skaya Pravda* (18 October 1959).
30 In the months leading up to Sholokhov's anniversary the tone of this criticism naturally changed. In an article by V. Litvinov in *Novy Mir* (1974), No. 12, 247, we were able to read the following:
'Sholokhov scholars are unanimous in saying that the second book of the novel, as compared with the first is particularly enriched by "the poetry of feeling", that the social content in it frequently finds expression in the moral and aesthetic content and the portrayal of the past is corrected by looking down from the heights of the present. A special feature of this book is Sholokhov's own peculiarly penetrating treatment of real-life problems such as historical necessity or the principles of the future development of popular sovereignty in our country and the nature of political work among people. It is an oration on the subject of the moral standards which have formed in the womb of the working people, their innate talents and their social initiative...Even Davydov owes much to the second book for the enrichment of his character. The further one reads into the novel the more one notices the growing strength of both the lyrical and the philosophical principles and this growing strength is substantially dependent on the characters appearing for the first time, Arkhanov, Nesterenko, Varyukha... I should like to lay particular emphasis on the unity of the two volumes. The reader of today who takes up this famous book is not dealing with something "two-tiered" but with a unified artistic narrative which develops within the wholeness of its conception and plot, its destinies and characters. We have before us a book written from the first line to the last wholly by the hand of Sholokhov.'
31 *Tvorchestvo Sholokhova*, p. 182.
32 *Sovetskaya Literatura: Sbornik* (Moscow, 1947), p. 119.
33 The question of the loss of Sholokhov's archives in 1942 is examined in the concluding chapter.
34 Khvatov, *Khudozhestvennyy Mir Sholokhova*, p. 302.
35 *Izvestiya* (14 December 1974).
36 M. Adriasov, *Syn Tikhogo Dona* (Moscow, 1969).
37 *Izvestiya* (4 October 1968).
38 *Pravda* (12–15 March 1969).
39 Eighteenth Communist Party Conference, *Stenograficheskiy otchet*, p. 476.
40 M. Sholokhov, *Po veleniyu dushi* (Moscow, 1970).
41 Twenty-Second Communist Party Conference; *Stenograficheskiy otchet* (Moscow, 1961), Vol. 2, p. 163.
42 M. Sholokhov, *Sochineniya* (Moscow, 1969), Vol. 8, pp. 353–4.
43 *Ibid.*, p. 300.

44 *Ibid.*, p. 341.
45 *Pravda* (23 January 1948).
46 *Sochineniya*, Vol. 8, p. 103.
47 *Ibid.*, p. 114.
48 *Ibid.*, p. 122.
49 *Ibid.*, pp. 100–1.
50 *Luna otkryvayetsya lyudyam*, Politizdat (Moscow, 1966), p. 171.
51 *Sochineniya*, Vol. 8, p. 285.
52 Twenty-Third Communist Party Conference; *Stenograficheskiy otchet* (Moscow, 1966), Vol. 1, pp. 357–8.
53 Second All-Union Congress of Soviet Writers; *Stenograficheskiy otchet*, (Moscow, 1956), p. 401. Incidentally in one study of Sholokhov's work we read, 'Mikhail Sholokhov spoke with passion and inspiration at the Second Congress of Writers (1954) about the need to militate vigorously in favour of raising the artistic quality in creative works and the role of criticism in the literary process' (P. G. Mineyev, *K voprosu ob izuchenii tvorchestva Sholokhova* (1965), p. 13).

Chapter 7. What lies behind the renewed discussion of 'The Quiet Don'?

1 *Stremya*, p. 30.
2 *Russkaya Literatura* (1970), No. 2, 148.
3 M. Moshkarov, *Krasnyy Kazak* (Veshensk, 1920), p. 5. Moshkarov also wrote a few plays for amateur groups. These were not published. He later abandoned literature and worked in the mid-1920s in the secretariat of M. Kalinin. In the 1930s he was an adviser in the Lenin Library. He was a special pensioner from 1940 until his death in 1961.
4 *Oktyabr'* (1928), No. 7, 130.
5 *Ibid.*, No. 8, p. 99.
6 *Ibid.*, Nos. 9–10, p. 155.
7 *Ibid.*, No. 3, p. 152.
8 *Ibid.*, No. 6, p. 115.
9 *Ibid.*, No. 5, p. 109.
10 *Ibid.*, No. 5, p. 111.
11 *Tikhiy Don*, Books 1 and 2, p. 551.
12 A. Kosterin, 'Zapiski v Lunnuyu Noch' (manuscript).
13 A. Kosterin, 'Otkrytoye Pis'mo M. A. Sholokhovu' (manuscript).
14 In the autumn of 1917, analysing the reasons for the failure of the Kornilov *coup*, Lenin wrote:
   'As to the Cossacks, here we have a section of the population made up of rich, middle and small-time landowners from one of the Russian outer regions who have retained an inordinate amount of mediaevalism in their lives, their economy and their daily affairs. Here the eye detects the socio-economic basis for a Russian Vendée. Yet what were the facts of the Kornilov–Kaledin movement? Even Kaledin, the 'beloved leader', *could not arouse* a mass movement. There is no objective factual material describing how

the various sections and economic groups of Cossack society stand in relation to democracy and Kornilovism. All we have are indications that a majority of the poor and middle Cossacks lean more towards democracy and only the officers and prosperous upper-class Cossacks are true supporters of Kornilov' (*Poln. Sob. Soch.*, Vol. 34, pp. 219–20).

These words by Lenin make it quite clear that at the very beginning there was no Cossack tendency towards counter-revolution and that, given correct policies, the possibility of a Russian Vendée need not have come about. Prominent Bolsheviks like V. Trifonov and V. Kovalev proposed a number of sensible measures designed to win over the Cossacks to the side of the October Revolution. But their proposals were not accepted and instead party policy in Cossack regions came to be dominated for a time by a most extreme and adventurist line based upon the unfounded charge that the Cossacks were counter-revolutionaries. This line was taken by Shtokman in *The Quiet Don* and in real life by the Don Office headed by S. Syrtsov.

15 *Stremya*, pp. 35–9.
16 *Ibid.*, pp. 5–6.
17 *Russkiye Zapiski* (1917), Nos. 2–3, 252.
18 *Uchenyye Zapiski Gor'kovskogo Pedagogicheskogo Instituta* XIV, (1950), 7, 12. (My italics. R. M.)
19 *Ibid.*, p. 11.
20 *Tvorchestvo Sholokhova*, p. 269.
21 *Znamya* (1956), No. 4, 171.
22 *Izvestiya* (10 March 1935).
23 *Sovetskaya Rossiya* (25 August 1957).
24 *Izvestiya* (14 and 16 December 1974).
25 *Sochineniya*, Vol. 1, pp. 263–4.
26 The extract quoted also recalls the general tone of *Virgin Soil Upturned.*
27 *Stremya*, p. 192.

Chapter 8. Sholokhov's birthday celebrations and afterwards: observations and points for discussion

1 *Izvestiya* (21 February 1975).
2 *Neva* (1975), No. 5, 189.
3 *Zvezda* (1975), No. 5, 162.
4 *Voprosy Literatury* (1975), No. 4, 34.
5 *Ibid.*, p. 35.
6 *Moskva* (1975), No. 4, 5.
7 *Don* (1975), No. 5, 144.
8 *V Mire Knig* (1975), No. 5, 14.
9 *Tikhiy Don*, Books 1 and 2, p. 129.
10 *Literaturnaya Rossiya* (23 May 1975), 13.
11 *Moskva* (1975), No. 5, 207.
12 *Ibid.*, p. 208.

13 *Loc. cit.*
14 *Bol'shevistskaya Smena* (24 May 1940).
15 *Literaturnaya Gazeta* (12 March 1975), 2.
16 *Izvestiya* (16 December 1974).
17 *Slovo o Sholokhove*, p. 223.
18 *Stremya*, p. 8.
19 Lezhnyov, *Put' Sholokhova*, p. 403.
20 Khvatov, *Khudozhestvennyy Mir Sholokhova*, p. 300.
21 V. Petelin, *Mikhail Sholokhov* (1974), pp. 264–7.
22 *Inostrannaya Literatura* (1975), No. 5, 204.
23 *Moskva* (1975), No. 4, 24.
24 *Vechernyaya Moskva* (24 May 1975).
25 *Smena* (1975), No. 10, 11.
26 *Stremya*, pp. 6–7.
27 *Voprosy Literatury* (1975), No. 5, 118.
28 *Moskva* (1975), No. 5, 8.
29 *Moskva* (1975), No. 4, 25.
30 Sholokhov, *Po Veleniyu Dushi*, p. 368.
31 Priyma, '*Tikhiy Don*' *srazhayetsya*, p. 343.
32 *Ibid.*, p. 338.
33 *Ibid.*, pp. 339–40.

INDEX

REFERENCES TO CHARACTERS IN 'THE QUIET DON'